Nobler in the Mind

Hamlet and Horatio in the Cemetery by Eugène Delacroix. Reproduction courtesy of Musée du Louvre.

Nobler in the Mind

The Stoic-Skeptic Dialectic
in English Renaissance Tragedy

Geoffrey Aggeler

DELAWARE

Newark: University of Delaware Press
London: Associated University Presses

Associated University Presses
440 Forsgate Drive
Cranbury, NJ 08512

Associated University Presses
16 Barter Street
London WC1A 2AH, England

Associated University Presses
P.O. Box 338, Port Credit
Mississauga, Ontario
Canada L5G 4L8

'NDEXED IN *ECLL*

Library of Congress Cataloging-in-Publication Data

Aggeler, Geoffrey, 1939–
    Nobler in the mind : the stoic-skeptic dialectic in English
Renaissance tragedy / Geoffrey Aggeler.
        p.   cm.
    Includes bibliographical references (p.   ) and index.
    ISBN 0-87413-661-X (alk. paper)
    1. English drama—Early modern and Elizabethan, 1500–1600—History
and criticism.   2. English drama—17th century—History and
criticism.   3. English drama (Tragedy)—History and criticism.
4. Skepticism in literature.   5. Philosophy in literature.
6. Stoics in literature.   7. Renaissance—England.   I. Title.
PR658.T7A35   1998
822'.309384—dc21
                                                        98-14035
                                                           CIP

To the memory of Professors Linda Van Norden and Elizabeth Homann, two gracious mentors at Davis who introduced me to Renaissance literature, and, as always, to Sondra.

Contents

Acknowledgments

I am indebted to the following persons and organizations for permitting me to reprint in revised form material that has appeared elsewhere: to Professor François Paré, for permitting me to base part of chapter 1 on an essay that appeared in *Renaissance and Reformation/ Renaissance et Réforme* (26); to the editors of the *Journal of English and Germanic Philology* for permitting me to base part of chapter 2 on an article that appeared in Vol. 86; to Professor R. W. Desai for permission to reprint part of an article that appeared in *Hamlet Studies* (9); and to the Swets Publishing Service, Amsterdam, for permitting me to reprint part of an article that appeared in *English Studies* (51).

I am especially grateful to my colleagues Michael Rudick, Mark Matheson, Brooke Hopkins, and Barry Weller, who read parts of the manuscript in progress, and to Stephen Orgel, Norman Rabkin, and Jonas Barish, who critiqued chapters that originally appeared as journal articles. I would also like to thank the University of Utah Research Committee and the College of Humanities Faculty Development Committee for several grants and leaves enabling me to work in the British Library and the Bodleian. Thanks as well to my son Brian for designing yet another stunning jacket. Mainly, I would like to thank my wife Sondra for her unflagging support and good humor during all the years this book was in preparation.

Nobler in the Mind

1

Reason's Spark and Skeptical Doubt

SENECAN SENSIBILITY

What's here! a stoic i' the stocks? The fool is turned philosopher.
—Ben Jonson, *Bartholomew Fair*

IT WAS AN OLD GIBE, BUT A SUREFIRE LAUGH, NONETHELESS, LIKENING THE adherents of unfeeling Stoic philosophy to lifeless blocks and implying that they were as senseless or stupid.[1] By the time *Bartholomew Fair* was first performed, in 1614, the figure of the Stoic sage had become a familiar dramatic stereotype. Deriving mainly from the essays of Seneca, rather than from his tragedies, this ideal of imperturbable tranquility and rational resignation had been embodied dramatically in the characters Feliche and Pandulpho in Marston's *Antonio* plays, Chapman's Clermont D'Ambois in *The Revenge of Bussy D'Ambois,* and Shakespeare's Brutus and Horatio among others. But the Stoic revival, which was largely responsible for the stereotype, was coming to an end, and an anti-Stoic reaction that would contribute eventually to the rise of sentimentalism had already begun.[2]

The Senecan stereotype is only one of the more obvious manifestations of how English Renaissance drama, tragedy especially, was influenced by the Stoic revival that began in England about the time Sackville and Norton wrote *Gorboduc.* Not coincidentally, this movement coincides with the rise of English Protestantism, and those who have discerned connections between Reformation theology and the drama may find additional support for their arguments with reference to the linkage of the revival with the progress of the Reformation.[3] I will be discussing this linkage and its influence on the drama at some length, but first it will be useful to review some recent contributions to the long critical debate concerning the relationship between Seneca's Stoic philosophy and his tragedies and the influence of both on Renaissance drama.[4]

13

Most critics have agreed with T. S. Eliot "that Roman stoicism is an important ingredient in Elizabethan drama."[5] Where there has been disagreement is with regard to its sources in the Senecan canon and how it manifests itself in the drama. Eliot remarked that "The influence of Seneca on Elizabethan drama has been exhaustively studied in its formal aspect . . . the penetration of Senecan sensibility would be much more difficult to trace."[6] He proposed "a Shakespeare under the influence of the stoicism of Seneca,"as he might have remembered it from reading Seneca's tragedies at school and encountered it in the work of his contemporaries, notably Kyd, but he believed it to be "quite unlikely that Shakespeare knew anything of that extraordinarily dull and uninteresting body of Seneca's prose which was translated by Lodge and printed in 1612." Disagreeing strongly, G. K. Hunter cautioned: "It is common, though it is dangerous, to forget that Seneca was much better known to the Elizabethans as a Stoic philosopher than as a dramatist; the De Beneficiis had by 1614 been translated three times (Haward, 1569; Golding, 1578; Lodge, 1614) when none of the tragedies had received more than a single translation."[7]

But if Thomas Newton's dedication to his 1581 edition in translation, Seneca His Tenne Tragedies, reflects a common view, the Elizabethans did not separate the moral philosopher from the tragedian. Answering the objections of "some squeymish Areopagites" that the phrases and sentences within the tragedies in praise of ambition, cruelty, incontinence and tyranny "cannot be digested without great daüger of infection," Newton assures Sir Thomas Heneage that nothing could be more foreign to the meaning of Seneca than the countenancing of vice:

> For it may not at any hād be thought and deemed the direct meaning of
> Seneca himselfe, whose whole wrytinges [penned with a peereless sublim-
> ity and loftinesse of Style,] are so farre from countenancing vice, that I
> doubt whether there bee any amonge all the Catalogue of Heathen wryt-
> ers, that with more grauity of Philosophicall sentences, more waightyness
> of sappy words, or greater authority of soūd matter beateth down sinne,
> loose lyfe, dissolute dealinge, and unbrydled sensuality: or that more sen-
> sibly, pithily, and bytingly layeth doune the guēdon of filthy lust, cloaked
> dissimulation and odious treachery: which is the dryft, whereunto he
> leueleth the whole yssue of ech one of his Tragedies.[8]

One must, of course, be aware of the didactic bias of the age and that most dedications emphasize the moral value of the literature they introduce, but Newton's dedication reveals perhaps something more than the mere fact that the tragedies were to be read as condemnations of the vices they presented. His defense of them against the objections of "squeymish Areopagites" suggests that the harmony of the tragedies with the Stoic moral philosophy of the essays and epistles was not readily apparent to some Elizabethan readers. Indeed, it has been anything but apparent to some readers in this century. As Norman T. Pratt observes, "Recognition of the Stoicism in the drama has been a long process."[9] The opinions of scholars have ranged from the view that the whole group of the tragedies should be read as a unit comprising a "Stoic treatise" that might be regarded as "a sort of glorified Essay on Man" to the view that the plays are devoid of philosophical meaning and even run counter to Stoic philosophy.[10]

One of the more astute and persuasive recent discussions of this question is contained in the opening chapters of Gordon Braden's *Renaissance Tragedy and the Senecan Tradition*. Braden argues that what the plays and the philosophy have in common is a "vision of human possibility." Acknowledging the stimulus of Eliot's essay, he elaborates "Eliot's central insight, that of an important nexus between Senecan dramatic style and the workings of Stoic philosophy."[11] In Braden's view "the rage that is the all-consuming subject of Senecan tragedy is the voice of a style of autarkic selfhood" that is "not altogether paradoxically mirrored" in Seneca's Stoic philosophy. Stoicism and the rage of the characters in the tragedies possessed by *furor* are two opposed manifestations of the same drives: "Stoic detachment is continuous and deeply involved with the most paralytic kind of anger."[12] This provocative insight is one that gains support if we consider how much the Stoic viewpoint of Seneca's essays has in common with the raging viewpoint of Juvenal's satires. The attitude of ironic detachment, the insistence on the futility of all human striving for "greatness" and the piety are the same, as are the revulsion and disgust with vice and folly. The point is relevant to a discussion of the Senecan heritage of Renaissance tragedy wherein, especially in the plays of Marston and Chapman, Stoic and satiric voices fuse.

Another recent landmark study is Thomas Rosenmeyer's *Senecan Drama and Stoic Cosmology*. Rosenmeyer's main focus is indicated by his title, but he also refers in passing to a number of English Renaissance tragedies that, like the work of Seneca himself, reveal a "'total imaginative assimilation of a basically Stoic cosmos and Stoic ethics.'"[13] In Rosenmeyer's view, the Stoic sage is "a figment of the utopian imagination":

> The ideal of the Stoic saint who stands off by himself or who harmonizes his being with the larger world is just that, an ideal, and a blind one at that, in the light of what Stoic science tells Stoic ethics. It is an ideal

conceivable only in terms of a partial understanding of what Stoic cosmology mandates.[14]

The Stoic cosmos informed by *sumpatheia* is unified and cohesive, but that which binds also threatens, because the interconnectedness of things leaves them vulnerable to "the uncontrollable and potentially invidious operation of the swarm of causes."[15] He argues that we should distinguish between "Stoic perfectionism" and "Stoic realism" and that Seneca's plays reveal him submitting "the more controversial, less settled movements of his thinking to the test of a confrontation with the realities of a familiar world."[16]

Much of what Rosenmeyer says about Seneca's tragedies could, as he realizes, be applied to English Renaissance plays, and my own discussion of the Stoic-Skeptic dialectic will, to some extent, parallel and further elaborate his arguments and those of Braden. The "familiar world" of Seneca, Imperial Rome, had much in common with Elizabethan England, as Elizabethan students of history recognized. As a recent editor of Bacon's *The History of King Henry VII* notes, their taste in Roman historians reflected an awareness of the resemblance of their own "closed" society to that of Rome under the emperors:

> The historian who proved most illuminating, in terms of his convertibility into the contemporary idiom, was Tacitus, the recorder of empire and the struggle against it, not Livy, the encomiast of republican virtue.[17]

In both worlds there was much to challenge Stoic idealism, including an abundance of ritualized violence that is reflected in the literature. Braden remarks how "The metaphor of the gladiatorial show filters through" the rhetoric of Seneca's plays.[18] This is not surprising, since "The place occupied by athletic games in Greek culture was taken in Rome by gladiatorial shows: ritualized competition cruder in its content but more bluntly real in its consequences."[19] Given the popularity of this form of entertainment, it is perhaps not surprising that the literature, well before Seneca, reveals a fascination with dismemberment. Rosenmeyer observes that "Roman literature, from Ennius on, delights in scenes where heads or limbs cut off continue to have a life of their own."[20]

In Elizabethan England the public execution was an immensely popular form of entertainment, especially when it involved convicted traitors, such as the Babington conspirators or seminary priests from the continent. The popularity of Fox's *Book of Martyrs* may, as one critic argues, attest "to the society's fascination with torture, couched though the fascination is in a text with an aggressively Protestant stake in the abasement it presents."[21] In discussing the sham death scenes in Marlowe's plays, the same critic points out how for an Elizabethan audience "reanimation was real enough on the scaffold when many a head, severed from its body, appeared to continue breathing and to scream at the crowd; when bodies, sometimes surviving the awkward use of noose or ax, seemed to rise from the dead and lift themselves from the block."[22] John Donne obviously assumes his readers' familiarity with such horrific phenomena as he begins his *Second Anniversarie:*

> Or as sometimes in a beheaded man,
> Though at those two Red seas, which freely ranne,
> One from the Trunke, another from the Head,
> His soule be sail'd, to her eternall bed,
> His eyes will twinckle, and his tongue will roll,
> As though he beckned, and cal'd backe his soule,
> He graspes his hands, and he pulls up his feet,
> And seemes to reach, and to step forth to meet
> His soule; when all these motions which we saw,
> Are but as Ice, which crackles at a thaw:

In discussing the "Senecan sensibility" that shaped the drama to suit the tastes of a Renaissance audience, one must take account of many factors, including its taste for violence and pain that coexisted harmoniously with its love of beauty in every form. The same cruel aestheticism that fascinated Browning in his studies of Renaissance Italy is abundantly evident in English Renaissance drama, as Anthony Burgess notes in his biography of Shakespeare:

> When we recoil from the brutality of Shakespeare's own plays, as early as *Titus Andronicus* and as late as *King Lear,* we have made the mistake of assuming that Will is one of us and that he has unaccountably lapsed into the cruelty of a period that is his only by accident. But it is only by accident that Will is "for all time"; he is essentially one of them—the pre-Freudian relishers of anything that could quicken the blood and fire the libido. And the brutality was, in a way incomprehensible to us, capable of being reconciled with the aesthetic instinct. Thus, the hangman who officiated at Tyburn had to be more than a butcher. It required huge skill to cut out the heart of the hanged victim and show it to him before his eyes closed. And the quartering of the still steaming corpse had to be effected with the swift economy of the true artist.[23]

In such a world, as the dramatists reveal repeatedly, Stoic idealism or perfectionism is bound to be challenged by realism and, as we shall see, skepticism, but it presents, nonetheless, an attractive refuge or retreat, and its appeal during the great age of the drama may be partly accounted for with reference to the close linkage of the Stoic revival with the rise of Protestantism. In the words of Philip A. Smith, "The great web of English Protestantism had been woven partly of Stoic threads. Hooker and Taylor, Milton, the Cambridge Platonists, Barrow, Tillotson, and many other Christian humanists adopted and exploited fully the basic Stoic concept of 'right reason,' the *recta ratio* which had long since been incorporated into Christian thought by early Fathers of the Church like Lactantius, Jerome and Tertullian."[24] And Rudolph Kirk has pointed out how the translation of Stoic works "seemed to accompany and follow the Reformation." Most of the English translators of the classical Stoic and continental Neostoic texts were Protestants, and virtually all translations of these texts were made either before or after the reign of Mary. "Apparently," Kirk suggests, "the mind of the Reformation found Stoic thought more congenial than did the Catholic mind of Mary's reign."[25]

"SPARKES OF HOLY THINGS": NEOSTOICISM AND THE PROTESTANT CONSCIENCE

It is a curious fact that in England, as on the continent, Stoicism seems to have been most attractive to Protestants with strong Calvinist leanings, to the extent that some later commentators have even seen Calvinism itself as "baptized Stoicism."[26] This is curious because Stoicism is commonly associated with an ideal of self-sufficiency, while Calvinist Christianity, in harmony with the Pauline-Augustinian tradition, stresses man's insufficiency without grace. At first glance there would seem to be little common ground other than a shared faith in a providentially ordered universe. Additional shared concerns and beliefs emerge as we examine such Calvinist Neostoic works as La Primaudaye's *The French Academie,* the works of Philippe de Mornay, and Joseph Hall's *Heaven Upon Earth.* These common concerns emerged much earlier, however, in the works of Calvin himself.

Calvin's first published book was his commentary on Seneca's *De Clementia,* a treatise addressed to the Emperor Nero that attempts to persuade him that mercy is the most becoming virtue a ruler can manifest in his dealings with his subjects. In it Nero is also asked to see that his role ideally is that of a servant of humanity. A ruler who understands this is not resentful when he must restrain himself: "'That,' you say, 'is servitude, not sovereignty.' What? are you not aware that the sovereignty is ours, the servitude yours?"[27] Since man is "a social creature, begotten for the common good," no virtue is more becoming than mercy. The necessity of practicing it is all the more manifest when one considers the corrupt and depraved condition of most of humanity and the sinfulness of even those who appear to be saintly:

> We have all sinned—some in serious, some in trivial things; some from deliberate intention, some by chance impulse, or because we were led away by the wickedness of others; some of us have not stood strongly enough by good resolutions, and have lost our innocence against our will and though still clinging to it; and not only have we done wrong, but we shall go on doing wrong to the very end of life. Even if there is any one who has so thoroughly cleansed his mind that nothing can any more confound him and betray him, yet it is by sinning that he has reached the sinless state.[28]

While he doesn't entirely support Professor Rosenmeyer's argument that the sage is an impossible ideal, Seneca admits that such individuals are extremely rare, and even they have experienced the corruption that affects all mankind. Commenting on this passage, Calvin calls attention to a related passage in *De Ira* in which Seneca enjoins us to "be more gentle one to another: we live as bad men, among bad men: there is only one thing which can afford us peace, and that is to agree to forgive one another."[29] Such passages enable us to see readily why it was believed during the middle ages that Seneca had carried on a correspondence with St. Paul.[30] While the term "fallen" is not used to describe the human condition, the myth of Eden being unknown to Seneca except perhaps in its Hesiodic analogue, his Stoic view of man is essentially the same as that of Paul. And while there is nothing resembling grace in the Stoic scheme of things, man's corrupted state is presented as, in the words of a recent translator, "the basis of a plea for mercy and kindness."[31] Calvin's citation of the passage from *De Ira* is perfectly relevant, emphasizing the necessity of forgiveness among men. All that is needed to baptize both passages as Christian utterances are some references to God's forgiveness through the Redemption.

Calvin did not, of course, agree with everything in *De Clementia*. Seneca distinguishes *clementia* from *misericordia*, pity, which he regards as a form of destructive passion. While it may appear to be like the clemency he is praising, even as cruelty may assume the guise of a praiseworthy strictness, it, like cruelty, ought to be avoided.

> We ought to avoid both pity and cruelty, closely related as they are to strictness and clemency, lest under the guise of clemency we lapse into pity.[32]

Commenting on this passage, Calvin explains that pity fails to qualify as a virtue, according to the Stoics, because it involves perturbation of the mind. He then goes on to express his strong disagreement with the Stoics on this point:

> Obviously we ought to be persuaded of the fact that pity is a virtue and that he who feels not pity cannot be a good man—whatever these idle sages may discuss in their shady nooks. To use Pliny's words: *I know not whether they are sages, but they certainly are not men. For it is man's nature to be affected by sorrow, to feel, yet to resist, and to accept comforting, not to go without it.* Rightly, therefore, the Athenians in ancient times consecrated an altar to Pity.[33]

And Calvin restates this view on pity later in his *Commentary on Genesis* (45.1) when he is discussing the compassion of Joseph, and also in his *Commentary on Romans*.[34] His harsh condemnation of the Stoics with regard to their view of pity is a little misleading, however, for he tends to agree with most of Seneca's arguments in *De Clementia,* and, like many of his followers both on the continent and in England, he seems to have found Stoicism generally congenial.

Most of the English translators of the continental Neostoics were Calvinist Protestants.[35] The importance of the works they translated in influencing English thought has not been widely recognized, perhaps because they have not been available in modern editions. One can only hope that an editor or editors will undertake the completion of the very worthwhile scholarly task begun by Rudolph Kirk with his editions of Neostoic texts and make these works available to students of the English Renaissance and Reformation.

An editor might well begin with some of the works of Philippe de Mornay, Seigneur du Plessis (1549–1623), a very prolific French Neostoic moralist, theologian, political leader, and diplomat. Commonly known as the "Huguenot Pope," he appears as the character Pleshé in Marlowe's *The Massacre at Paris.* Mornay was a friend of Sir Philip Sidney, who shared his zeal for the Protestant cause. Sidney stood godfather to Mornay's infant daughter, born during a visit to England in June 1578. He also translated into English part of Mornay's *De la vérité de la religion Chrestienne* (Antwerp, 1581), and at his request the translation was completed by Arthur Golding and was published in 1587.[36] Most of his other moral and theological writings were also translated into English within a few years of their original publication in French or Latin.[37] The works that are most clearly informed by a Neostoic viewpoint are the *Discourse of Life and Death, The True Knowledge of a Mans owne Selfe, The Trewnesse of* the Christian Religion, and Lord of Plessis His Teares. For the Death of His Sonne.

The Trewnesse of the Christian Religion consists largely of arguments from scriptural and classical authorities for the immortality of the soul. Among the latter, Mornay finds Plato, Socrates, and the Stoics to be the most helpful in supporting Christian beliefs. Aristotle's observations on the soul he sees as contradicting each other. He approves of most of Epictetus's "goodly sayings" concerning man as the "offspring" or "braunch of the Godhead," though he considers the description of man as "a diuine ympe or a spark of God" to be "somewhat unproper" (for what wordes can a man finde to fit the matter:)" (TCR, p. 2). But his principal Stoic authority is Seneca, whom he clearly regards as the wisest of the Stoics. He finds the ring of truth concerning the soul's immortality "in almost all of Seneca's writings" and quotes approvingly Seneca's statements that our souls "are a part of God's Spirit, and sparkes of holy things shining vpon the earth." In his view Seneca's beliefs concerning the soul were nearly Christian: "This may suffice to giue us knowledge of that great personage, in whom wee see that the more he grewe in age, the nerer he came still to the true birth. For in his latest bookes he treateth alwaies both more assuredly and more evidently thereof" (TCR, p. 268).

Mornay reposes a typically Stoic faith in right reason, and while he acknowledges that reason is not sufficient by itself to lead one to the truths of revelation, he, like Aquinas and Dante, believes that it can be trusted to prepare one to make a leap of faith:

> In answer to those who say that faith (that is, the Christian doctrine) ought not to be proued or declared by reason: And their reason is, because it consisteth in manie things which exceed the capacitie of man. . . . But we say that mans reason is able to lead vs to that point: namely, that we ought to belue euen beyond reason. I meane the things whereunto all the capacitie of man cannot attaine. . . . For surely all truth cannot be proued by reason, considering that many thinges exceede reason and nature. But yet cannot any vntruth preuayle by reason against truth: nor any truth bee vanquished by the judgement of reason. For vntruth is contrary to nature, nature helpeth reason, reason is seruant to truth: and one truth is not contrary to another, that is to say, to it selfe. For truth cannot be but truth, and Reason, reason. (TCR , The Preface to the Reader, ii.)

After the works of Mornay and the early pro-Stoic essays of Montaigne, perhaps the most influential continental Neostoic work translated into English was The French Academie of Pierre La Primaudaye. Like Mornay, La Primaudaye was a Huguenot, and there is in his great book the same curious fusion of Augustinian Protestant and Senecan sensibility. At times it is not a fusion but a division, a conflict in which Calvinist Christianity is pitted against Stoicism, but as with Mornay, the Calvinist element is always victorious. The "presumptuous" Stoic opinion that man can master all passion and achieve an understanding of God and nature through an exercise of natural virtue is vigorously attacked, even as Mornay attacks the "heathen" view of Fortune in his *Discourse of Life and Death.*

In a number of ways, however, *The French Academie* reveals why, with these reservations, Stoic philosophy was especially attractive to Protestants during the Reformation. Of particular interest in this connection is La Primaudaye's discussion of "what conscience is properly." In his discussion of conscience, La Primaudaye introduces the term *Synteresis,* and T.B.'s translation of 1594 contains the first occurrence of the word in English (*O.E.D.*).

He tells us that although the mind is troubled and darkened by error and ignorance, the effects of sin, "yet it coulde not so wholly blind it, but still there remayned in it some sparkes of that light of the knowledge of God, and of good and evil, which is naturally in men, and which is borne with them."[38] This "remnant" of light is called *Synteresis,* a Greek word signifying that which preserves the "remnant of the light and law of nature that remaineth in vs." It is innate and indestructible, "yea in the most wicked that can bee, an aduertisement or instruction which telleth him what is right and iust, and that there is a judgement of God." While some distinguish *Synteresis* from the conscience itself, others identify it with conscience. Philosophers who spoke of "Anticipations" had a sense of this faculty, to the extent that they were distinguishing the means whereby we apprehend rules not through instruction or experience but "haue drawn and received them from nature, whom God hath appoynted in this respect to be our mistres." (*FA,* pt. 2, p. 576).[39]

La Primaudaye's description of it as being "some sparkes of that light" that is innate in men indicates that he, like Mornay, Pierre Charron, and other Renaissance Neostoics, accepts the doctrine of the divine spark, a doctrine that has a classical Stoic basis. For the ancient Stoics, generally, God is identified with seminal reason, the *Logos spermatikos* out of which all things emanate and by which all things are formed. Sparks of divinity within individual men, *logoi spermatikoi,* "denote the generative powers as a part of the soul, and must be thought of as bearing the same relation to the individual soul as the generative powers of Nature do to the soul of nature."[40] According to Seneca, it is only because of this element of divinity within man that he is able to achieve Stoic perfection:

> A soul which is of superior stature and well governed, which deflates the imposing by passing it by and laughs at all our fears and prayers,is impelled by a celestial force. So great a thing cannot stand without a buttress of divinity. Its larger portion therefore abides at its source. Just as the rays of the sun do indeed warm the earth but remain at the source of their radiation, so a great and holy soul is lowered to earth to give us a nearer knowledge of the divine; but though it is in intercourse with us, it cleaves to its source; it is tied to it, it looks toward it, it seeks to rejoin it, and its concern with our affairs is superior and detached.[41]

A closely analogous concept of a divine spark evolved in the writings of the Christian mystics during the middle ages. They used St. Jerome's *synteresis* for the divine spark, which they described as the "apex of the soul," the "natural will toward God," or "the remnant of the sinless state before the fall." The term first occurs in St. Jerome's commentary on *Ezekiel*. After that it occurs in Aquinas and in the Christian mystics.[42] Among the schoolmen, generally, it was spelled "*Synderesis*." These writers present various views of its nature and functions as a moral agency within man.

During the Reformation, the concept of *synteresis* appears prominently in the writings of Protestant casuists, and their use of it suggests that they incorporated the Stoic concept of the divine spark along with the similar concept they inherited from the Christian mystics.[43] William Ames, among many others, discusses it at length in his *Conscience with the Power and Cases Thereof*. According to Ames and other casuists, *Synteresis*, in effect, dictates the major premise or proposition of the "practical syllogism." It is a natural habit "whereby the understanding of man is fitted to giue assent unto Naturall principles." The minor premise, or assumption, is called "*Syneidesis*," and the conclusion is the "*Krisis*," or "*Iudgement*."[44]

Like La Primaudaye, Ames asserts that *Synteresis* is innate and indestructible: "This *Synteresis* may for a time be hindered from acting, but cannot be utterly extinguished or lost. Hence it is that no man is so desperately wicked as to be void of all Conscience." Through God's goodness, *Synteresis* continued to preserve or conserve, as its name indicates, an awareness of the principles of moral actions in the mind of man "even after his fall."[45]

The appeal to the Protestant mind of the Stoic concept of the divine spark is readily understandable, and not surprisingly there was a tendency among Protestant Neostoics to identify *Synteresis* with the divine spark. John Marston, a Neostoic satirist and dramatist who eventually became an Anglican divine, does this in his early satires.[46] In one satire, he invokes *Synteresis*, which he spells in the Scholastic fashion, as a force that can raise man from the disgusting, sinful state into which he has fallen:

> Returne, returne, sacred *Synderesis*,
> Inspire our truncks, let not such mud as this
> Pollute vs still. Awake our lethargie,
> Raise vs from out our brain-sicke foolerie.
>
> (*The Scourge of Villainy*, VIII, ll. 211–14)[47]

Marston's satires generally are notorious for their bitterness and cynicism, and his implication that *Synteresis* has departed suggests that human behavior provides no evidence to the observer that there is such a thing within man. When we consider that the indestructability of *Synteresis* was a commonplace notion, the suggestion is bitter indeed, as is another reference to *Synteresis* elsewhere in *The Scourge of Villainy*:

> The poore soules better part so feeble is,
> So cold and dead is his *Synderesis*,
> *That shadowes by odde chaunce sometimes are got,*
> *But o the substance is respected not.*
>
> (*The Scourge of Villainy*, XI, ll. 235–38)

In his plays, especially *Antonio and Mellida I & II*, *Sophonisba*, and *The Malcontent* Marston juxtaposes classical Stoic, Skeptical, and Machiavellian views of the world. Significantly, conscience plays a major role in all these plays, especially *The Malcontent* wherein the activity of conscience turns an impending revenge tragedy into a comedy of forgiveness. In contrast to his bitter satires, these plays, in effect, assert the indestructibility of conscience. It is perhaps interesting to reflect that Marston's development from a "sharp-fanged satirist" into a playwright and finally an Anglican preacher has several elements in common with the career of his great rival satirist and fellow Neostoic, Joseph Hall.

The importance of the role of conscience in the thinking of Protestants in the late sixteenth and early seventeenth centuries can hardly be overstressed. Prior to this time, works of casuistry belonging to the encyclopaedic genre *Summa confessorum* or *Summa de casibus conscientiae* were written mainly for the use of Roman Catholic confessors, providing ready answers to virtually every conceivable problem of conscience.[48] Having discarded the institution of sacramental confession, along with the authoritarian, conscience-keeping role of the Roman Church, the Protestant reformers of the sixteenth century did not initially acknowledge a need for such encyclopaedic reference guides with their copious references to nonscriptural authorities. By the end of the century, however, there seems to have been a growing recognition of the need for guides other than the Bible itself to assist in the informing of the conscience.

In Protestant England, casuistry begins with William Perkins (1558–1602). Perkins asserted that Christians must have faith in the ability of the individual conscience to guide men aright, and he insisted that it must be heeded before any other authority. His teachings were grounded on St. Paul's, mainly the *Epistle to the Romans*. According to Paul, conscience operates in all men, even the Gentiles, for whom it will bear witness either for or against them (*Rom.* 2:13–16). It must be obeyed even if it is in error. *The Whole Treatise of the Cases of Conscience* by Perkins is prefaced with a verse from *Romans* that virtually contains the whole Protestant concept of duty to conscience: "*Whatsouer is not of Faith, is sinne*" (*Rom.* 14:23). Discussing this particular verse in *The Whole Treatise*, Perkins glosses it as follows: "Whatsoeuer man doth, whereof he is not certainely perswaded in iudgement and conscience out of God's words, that the thing may be done, *it is sin.*"[49] In *A Discourse of Conscience*, Perkins emphasizes the role of conscience as God's representative within man: "because conscience is of a diuine nature, and is a thing placed by God in the midst betweene him and man, as an arbitratour to give sentence & to pronounce either with man or against man vnto God."[50] In a later edition of the *Discourse*, he goes even further in emphasizing the divine nature of conscience, which

> is (as it were) a little God setting in the middle of mens hearts, arraigning them in this life as they shall be arraigned for their offences at the Tribunal seat of the euerliving God in the day of iudgement. Wherefore the temporarie iudgement that is given by the conscience is nothing els but a beginning, or a fore-runner of the last iudgement.[51]

The implications of this teaching were destined to have a profound effect on the whole course of English political history in the seventeenth century. Among the many issues over which the Puritans and the Stuart monarchs confronted each other was this very matter of the sovereignty of the individual conscience. It is now generally recognized that the conflicts that led to the outbreak of civil war in 1642 had their origins in movements and events of the late sixteenth century. Reading *A Discourse of Conscience* when it first appeared in

1596, one might have prophesied an eventual confrontation between those who shared the beliefs of the writer and supporters of absolutism, though obviously there were many other causes for the war, which are still being debated by historians.

Because conscience is God's representative within man, a little God within men's hearts, "God is the onely Lord of conscience."[52] With regard to any conflict between a commandment issued by a magistrate and the word of God speaking through the conscience, there is nothing to ponder: "God commandes one thing, & the magistrate commaunds the flat contrarie: in this case which of these two commaundments must be obeyed, Honour God, or Honour the Magistrate? the answer is, that the latter must giue place to the former, & the former alone in this case must be obeied."[53] While it is true that St. Paul tells us that obedience is due to a magistrate for conscience sake (Rom. 13:15) "that subiection is indeede to be performed to ciuill authoritie ordained by God, and obedience also to the Lawes of the Magistrate for fear of wrath, and for auoiding of punishment, but not for conscience of the saide authoritie or lawes properly or directly, but for conscience of Gods commandment, which appointeth both Magistracie, and the authoritie thereof."[54] This Pauline insistence on the sovereignty of conscience, coupled with a Pauline emphasis on the equality of men in their sinfulness before God, was to have no small influence on those responsible for England's progress toward democracy in the seventeenth century.[55]

Especially relevant to the present study is the fact that Paul's emphasis on the sovereignty of the individual conscience encouraged as well the growing emphasis upon introspection that characterizes sixteenth- and seventeenth-century Protestantism.[56] While there may be room for disagreement about whether or not Paul himself provides a model of the introspective conscience in his epistles, there is no denying that he encouraged the turning inward of the Christian conscience.[57] Braden relates this to the influence of Stoicism:

> Paul is already Stoic in his concern with control of the passions, particularly anger, which Christianity early establishes as an almost exclusively divine prerogative. "Beloved, never avenge yourselves, but leave it to the wrath of God." (Rom. 12:19, Revised Standard). As Christianity becomes Romanized, such injunctions gain powerful Stoic vibrations. So does a related emphasis on what Paul calls autarceia (Cor. 9:8, Phil. 4:11, Tim. 6:6), the province of an inmost self (ho esô anthrôpose; Rom. 7:22, Eph. 3:16) radically separate from the externals of its condition.[58]

Paul was obviously familiar with the commonplace Stoic conception of a self apart from and impervious to external direction, but he seems to question, especially in *Rom.* 7:22 , the Stoic belief that this self can remain unmoved by a lower self, i.e., passions and appetites. There is endless strife between the law of sin dwelling in his members and the law of his mind which delights in the law of God.

Protestant introspection was also strongly encouraged by contemporary Neostoic writings in which there is the recurrent classical Stoic theme that self-knowledge is an avenue to knowledge of the divine. Mornay's *The True Knowledge of a Mans owne Selfe* was written, as the translator explains, "for the reformation of a mightie Atheist," and La Primaudaye announces at the beginning of *The French Academie* that one of its informing themes is "that the perfect knowledge of ones selfe, which consisteth in the soule, is in such sort ioined with the knowledge of God, that the one without the other cannot be sincere and perfect." (*FA*, pt. 1, p. 11). This is inseperable from the other main theme, "that the dutie of a wise man is to seeke out the reasons of things, that in the ende he may find that diuine reason whereby they were made and having found it, may worship and serue it." These were the teachings of Socrates, and "Plato his disciple" added to these the concept of duty to one's fellow men as derivatiue from the other two imperatives: "That the perfect dutie of man is, first to knowe his owne nature: then to contemplate the diuine nature: and last of all to bestow his labor in those things, which may be most beneficiall to all men." (*FA*, pt. 1, p. 11).

La Primaudaye's linkage of self-knowledge, knowledge of the divine, and duty to one's fellows is typical of Protestant Neostoic writings.[59] Obviously one of the attractions of Stoicism for Protestants was its emphasis on active commitment on the part of the individual to the moral betterment of the community. The concept of moral stewardship, generally regarded as a Calvinist notion with scriptural roots, could find a great deal of support in the writings of the ancient Stoics, who generally shared the belief that while one should be primarily concerned with preserving one's own moral purpose through self-discipline, one should also strive to restore one's less disciplined fellows to a correct moral purpose as well and thus bring about an improvement of the community as a whole. The emphasis on discipline and a sense of responsibility for the moral welfare of the community that gave Stoicism virtually the status of a state religion in ancient Rome also recommended it to Calvin and his followers, and we can see this clearly in Joseph Hall's discussion of that most responsible of individuals in a community, the magistrate.

"Of the Good Magistrate" is one of the pieces in Hall's *Characters of Vertues and Vices,* a work that, as Kirk points out, delineates the four cardinal virtues of the ancient Stoics—Prudence, Fortitude, Justice, and Temperance—along with various Christian virtues, such as humility and fidelity, and their opposites. The essay is concerned mainly with the role of the good judge, but its injunctions may be readily extended to include the functions of a good prince as well. In delineating the character of this "faithfull Deputy of his Maker," Hall imparts concrete vital form to the abstract Stoic virtue of justice. We are made to visualize the good magistrate in action, hearing case after case, resting seldom, eating in haste, "all which he beares well, because he knowes himselfe made for a publike servant of Peace and Justice."[60]

Like Seneca, and unlike Calvin, Hall regards pity as a weakness, but only in a magistrate. Calvin, it should be pointed out, recognized that Seneca was talking about pity as it manifested itself in an excess of clemency, but his indignation at Seneca's description of it as a vice *per se* seems to have provoked him to refute what he regarded as an instance of simplistic Stoic moral psychology. Hall, who was certainly familiar with *De Clementia* and probably with Calvin's commentary on it, does not follow Seneca in asserting that pity itself is a weakness of the mind or "mental defect" (*vitium animi*). Rather he is saying that what is a virtue in private individuals is a vice in a magistrate, who should dispense justice as dispassionately as a god: "He is the Guard of good laws, the Refuge of innocency, the Comet of the guilty, the Paymaster of good deserts, the Champion of justice, the Patron of peace, the Tutor of the Church, the Father of his Country, &, as it were, another God vpon earth."[61]

A recent biographer of Hall is probably correct in his surmise that this memorable passage was written with King James in mind. Theological wisdom and success in peacekeeping were essential parts of the king's Solomonic self-image, and Hall seems to have incorporated this self-image into his "Character" of an ideal Stoic justicer with the intention of flattering the king, who would presumably recognize such an idealized image of himself.[62] But it is also not unlikely that Ben Jonson, if he knew the passage, had it in mind when he drew his own "Character" Justice Overdo in *Bartholomew Fair*. When Overdo is first placed in the stocks (IV.i), he embraces the opportunity to witness Stoically in adversity. Forgetting that he is still in the guise of a fool, he believes that his heroic longsuffering demeanor will arouse general admiration, "beget a kind of reverence toward me hereafter even from mine enemies."[63] And hearing mad Trouble-All express reverence for his warrant, "the warrant of warrants," he is consoled by the thought that "good fame" has followed him into misfortune. Surrounded by the chaotic activity of the Fair, he will maintain perfect tranquillity and "be the author of mine own rest."

In this scene and others involving Overdo, Jonson represents comically one of the central paradoxes of Stoicism. On the one hand, there is the injunction to withdraw from the external world into a detached inner self and maintain *apatheia*.[64] On the other, one is urged to perform virtuously like a good actor on a stage that is the world. In the words of Seneca, "Do whatever you do as if someone were watching."[65] The logic of Stoic withdrawal leads to solipsism, while the injunction to perform can lead to exhibitionism, and, as Overdo repeatedly demonstrates, a passion for self-dramatization. Overdo becomes so absorbed in the contemplation of his own virtue and his sense of the role he is playing that he cannot accurately observe what is taking place before his eyes, as when, for instance, he remains convinced that Edgeworth is a decent young man, and while he inveighs against tobacco, Edgeworth snatches Cokes's purse (II. vi).

But for all his self-absorption and exhibitionism, Overdo is capable of growth, and the first sign of progress is his recognition of the need for compassion. When he hears Bristle describing the madness of Trouble-All, wrought by his own severity in dismissing him from his place, he is assailed by guilt and, moved by pity, feels "bound to satisfy this poor man." As Bristle and Haggis go on conversing about his harshness as a justice, Overdo resolves to change:

> I will be more tender hereafter. I see compassion may become a justice, though it be a weakness, I confess, and nearer a vice than a virtue.
> (IV. i. 74–76)

Overdo's progress toward compassion and an acceptance of his own erring humanity that will, presumably, enable him to function effectively as a justice is a comic parallel with one of the main thematic developments common to several Shakespearean dramas, including *King Lear* and *The Merchant of Venice*. In the fallen world of Lear, where 'the strong lance of justice hurtless breaks' and magistrates are as corrupt as other men, if not moreso, Joseph Hall's passionless "Champion of justice" is an unattainable ideal, and the play, in effect, questions the desirability of striving to achieve it. Paradoxically, what enables Edgar to become a pitiless "Champion of justice" of which Seneca or Hall would approve when he deals with Edmund is the compassion or "good pity" he has acquired through painful experience.[66] And as Lear comes to realize, since the heavens are pitiless to man, divine compassion becomes a tangible reality only when it is exhibited by human beings, especially those whose authority is assumed to have a heavenly sanction. In *The Merchant of Venice* Shylock refuses to be compassionate, then suffers the effects of having the law applied to himself without compassion. Without compassion, the "mercy" Portia describes in her great speech, the court becomes as vindictive and amoral as Shylock in its imposition of what it believes is legal equity. For Shakespeare, as for Jonson, compassion and acceptance of one's flawed humanity are prerequisites to moral growth and activity and indispensable attributes in one who would impose "justice" on fellow creatures.

Little wonder that Joseph Hall, made perhaps of sterner stuff than Jonson or Shakespeare, was drawn to Seneca, whose *De Tranquillitate* he, in a sense, completes in *Heaven Upon Earth* by providing the vital components known only to Christians. Chief among these is grace, which would have made Seneca unrivaled as a moral philosopher had he been capable of receiving it: "If *Seneca* could have had grace to his wit, what wonders would he have done in this kinde? what Divine might not have yeelded him the chaire for precepts of Tranquillity without any disparagement?" As it was, he "wrote more divinely" on the subject than any other heathen philosopher, and if "Nature" were sufficient to guide men to tranquility, Seneca would be his master. But in fact neither Seneca nor any other heathen, for all their wisdom and their efforts, actually attained tranquility, and no wonder for "Not *Athens* must teach this lesson, but *Ierusalem*."[67]

Thus in typical Christian Neostoic fashion, Hall makes his orthodox position clear at the outset. But for all his orthdox insistence on the necessity of grace, one perceives, as in Charron's *De la Sagesse,* a nearly existentialist Stoic emphasis on the necessity of human striving against natural human weakness.[68] Sartre himself might have approved of some of Hall's injunctions against what he was to call *la mauvaise foi,* in spite of what he would also have regarded as a fatally contaminating admixture of Calvinist orthodoxy:

> The power of nature is a good plea for those that acknowledge nothing above nature. But for a Christian to excuse his intemperatenesse, by his naturall inclination, and to say, I am born cholerike, sullen amorous, is an Apologie worse than the fault. Wherefore serves Religion, but to subdue or governe nature: We are so much Christians, as wee can rule our selves, the rest is but forme and speculation.[69]

Indeed, tranquility itself is not, like grace, a free gift, but something that must be striven for. Hall emphasizes this in the concluding section of *Heaven upon Earth,* a passage which reveals that dynamic fusion of Stoic activism, Calvinist piety and tough-minded worldliness that went into the shaping of the English Puritan sensibility:

> Saiest thou then, this peace is good to have, but hard to get? It were a shameful neglect that hath no pretence. Is difficulty sufficient excuse to

hinder thee from the pursuit of riches, of preferment, of learning, of bodily pleasures? Art thou content to sit shrugging in a base cottage, ragged, famished, because house, clothes, and food will neither bee had without money, nor money without labour, nor labour without trouble and painfulnesse? Who is so merciful, as not to say that a whip is the best almes for so lazy and wilfull need? Peace should not be good if it were not hard: Goe, and by this excuse shut thy selfe out of heaven at thy death, and live miserably till thy death, because the good of both worlds is hard to compasse. There is nothing but misery on earth and hell below, that thou canst come to without labour.[70]

The works of Hall, like those of Mornay and La Primaudaye, reveal how much common ground a Calvinist Protestant could find with an ancient Stoic and why some commentators have seen Calvinism as "baptized Stoicism." The Stoic tradition shared with the Pauline-Augustinian that issued in Calvinism a belief in the universal corruption of man, a view of the moral faculty as a divine agency within man, and a belief in self-knowledge as one of the essential avenues to knowledge of the divine. These common beliefs concerning the nature of man and, with some qualification, the human potential inform Renaissance Neostoic writings and a closely related, largely Protestant body of moral literature devoted to faculty psychology.[71] In addition, there were concerns and beliefs shared by the two traditions about the role of man in society, his duties as citizen, ruler, or magistrate. To a large extent, this latter body of beliefs is informed by the former.

As I mentioned earlier, the Protestant view of conscience as God within man, which found classical support in the Stoic doctrine of the spark, was an important doctrinal basis for resistance to absolutism and indeed tyranny in any form. One of the reasons why Renaissance Neostoic writers consistently favored Plato and Socrates over Aristotle is that the latter, largely because of his dogmatic followers, was perceived as representing intellectual tyranny and resistance to the free inquiry after truth. Charron's attitude in this regard is typical. He characterizes as "barbarous" those "of the schoole and jurisdiction of Aristotle, affirmers, positive men, dogmatists, who respect more vtilitie than veritie, according to the vse and custome of the world, than that which is good and true in it selfe." These he contrasts with those rare individuals of "quick and cleare spirit, a strong, firme, and solid judgement," who will not be contented with commonly received notions and opinions. Such men are acutely aware of the deceptiveness of appearances and are willing to seek dispassionately the true causes of things, "louing better to doubt, and to hold in suspence their beleefe, than by a loose and idle facilitie or lightnesse, or precipitation of judgement to feede themselves with lies, and affirme or secure

themselues of that thing whereof they can haue no certaine reason."
Among these very rare individuals are those "of the Schoole of *Socrates* and *Plato,* modest, sober, staied, considering more the veritie and
realitie of things than the vtilitie."[72]

In this passage, Charron is defending his application of the Pyrrho-
nist Skeptical approach to the problem of self-knowledge that he had
learned from Montaigne. But one can see in it as well the idea that
submission to the tyranny of received notions and opinions is associated with idleness, a vice abhorred by Stoics and Protestants alike and
one that the Reformers tended to associate with Roman Catholicism,
especially as it appeared to be sanctioned by the monastic ideal, as
well as by an overreliance on Aristotle and the Schoolmen.

The necessity of resisting tyranny in all forms is a ubiquitous theme
in seventeenth-century English Protestant writings, as it is in the works
of the ancient Stoics. In the latter works, the resistance most frequently
enjoined is the cultivation of *apatheia,* a willed extinguishing of destructive passion that enables one to maintain indifference to any
supposed injury a tyrant can manage to inflict.[73] The Stoic paradox
"Tyrants can kill but never hurt a man" expresses the sage's belief
that the only true injury a man can suffer is the willful abandonment
of his moral purpose. But beyond the injunctions to resist passively
through indifference, there are implicit and explicit injunctions to take
action against tyrants. One of the most celebrated of Stoic heroes is
Cato the Younger, who chose suicide rather than the endurance of
tyranny. The Stoic idealization of Hercules implies action, and as Epictetus argues, one who follows his example may be assured that any
necessary action, such as the slaying of a monster or a tyrant, can be
reconciled with a correct moral purpose.[74] This same idealized Hercules is the hero of Seneca's *Hercules Furens,* a play that includes a
tyrannicide. As Hercules emerges onstage after slaying Lycus, he utters these lines:

> ——There can be slaine
> No sacrifice to God more acceptable
> Than an unjust and wicked King——[75]

Milton quotes these lines in his ringing defense of tyrannicide, *The
Tenure of Kings and Magistrates* (1649). This passage is one of the
few references to pagan authority in *The Tenure.* Among the others
is a reference to Aristotle's definition of a king as "him who governs
to the good and profit of his People, and not for his own ends," which
is also a central theme of *De Clementia.* As Milton explains, he cites
no more ancient authorities, "lest it bee objected they were Heathen."

But he quotes this speech, put in the mouth of "*Hercules* the grand suppressor of Tyrants," as an expression of an attitude generally held by the "prime Authors" Greek and Roman.[76]

"No man who knows ought, can be so stupid as to deny that all men naturally were borne free, being the image and resemblance of God himself." Thus begins the main argument of *The Tenure*. Milton had made the same statement eight years earlier in *Of Prelatical Episcopacy* (1641).[77] His hatred of tyranny in any form, whether it be censorship or "the censorious and supercilious lording over conscience" of meddling divines, called forth his most eloquent prose polemics and is abundantly reflected in his poetry as well. In *The Tenure* he is primarily concerned with establishing the point that the trial and execution of Charles I were in agreement with the principles of Protestantism. In addition to Scripture, his authorities include Luther, Zwingli, Calvin, Bucer, and the English divines who sought refuge in Geneva during the reign of Mary, and he demonstrates that the Scottish Presbyterians, who had hoped to gain power through the secret treaty of Newport, are betrayers of these principles.

That these principles are wholly in harmony with classical Stoic views concerning the relationship between ruler and subjects can be readily seen if one compares *The Tenure* with *De Clementia*. For Milton, as for Seneca, rulers are the servants of the people. Since Seneca was addressing his treatise to Nero, one would hardly expect him to develop a corollary justifying regicide, but the argument that sovereignty belongs to the people and servitude to the ruler is obviously a basis for such a corollary. Milton's arguments were grounded primarily on the ideas of sixteenth-century Calvinists, but his quotation from Seneca suggests that he was probably fully aware of Stoic analogues.

By 1649, the anti-Stoic reaction was well underway, but the Stoic revival had made an indelible impression upon English Protestant thought. The classical Stoic ideas that were most objectionable to the anti-Stoics, such as their view of the passions, had already been refuted by Christian Neostoics, who demonstrated in the process that rejecting a few ideas did not prevent the incorporation of the main body of Stoic beliefs regarding the duty of a wise man to seek out the reason of things and the divinity informing them, to acquire the knowledge of self that is joined with the knowledge of God, and having acquired this knowledge, to labor actively for the welfare of his fellow man.

*   *   *

If, then, we are going to discuss the "penetration of Senecan sensibility" in the drama, we will need to consider how that sensibility was shaped by Reformation, mainly Calvinist, moral theology, as well as the Roman Stoicism that it adapted. It might be objected that the Senecan sensibility that penetrates the drama differs considerably from that which informs Christian Neostoic moral writings, which are focused primarily on the ways in which Stoicism could be adapted to the needs of Christians, while most tragedies in the Senecan tradition are not confined by such reductive moral concerns and indeed throw basic Stoic and Christian assumptions into question. But it should be borne in mind that the audiences for whom both dramatists and moralists are writing are largely the same. Over five decades ago, F. P. Wilson called attention to the fact that the abundance of moral writings reflected the taste of theater audiences:

> The wealth of sermons and moral treatises available to the dramatists was available also to their audience. The sermon was the most popular form of literature of the day. Without an audience interested in serious matters tragedy is not possible.[78]

More recently, Martha Tuck Rozett has offered convincing evidence that the audiences attending the theatres and those who attended sermons "undoubtedly overlapped." Moreover, these same audiences were schooled in rhetorical theory that enabled one to argue opposing views of any question and "produced a mind that instinctively sought out multiplicity and revelled in contradictions." And an essential part of the pleasure they experienced watching a play was due to the encounter of conflicting ideas:

> the plays functioned as media of intellectual and emotional exploration for minds that were accustomed to examine the many sides of a given theme, to entertain opposing ideals, and by so exercising the understanding, to move toward some fuller apprehension of truth that could be discerned only through the total action of the drama.[79]

The audience participated in this exploration and judged the "conflicting truths embodied in the characters and situations of the play":

> To this dialectical process the Elizabethans brought the ability to see themselves and others from opposing perspectives that had been conferred upon them by their Christian inheritance.[80]

Indeed, as we study plays that are informed by conflicts between Stoicism and Skepticism, it is not difficult to find mirrorings of the great debates rending Christendom in the sixteenth and early seventeenth centuries. Christianized Stoicism, with its faith in *recta ratio* and the benevolence of providential design, is used by dramatists, beginning with Kyd, to represent Christian orthodoxy itself. In the worlds the dramatists create, worlds that have much in common with the world of Seneca's tragedies, it is challenged by Skepticism in various forms. Some types of Skepticism, of course, could seem to be harmonious with Christian fideism, as we see in the writings of Montaigne and his Neostoic disciple Charron.[81] Others, such as that voiced by the character D'Amville in *The Atheist's Tragedy* or Edmund in *King Lear*, are clearly antithetical to fideism in any form. Before we discuss the Stoic-Skeptic dialectic in the plays, it will be useful to review the types of Skepticism they represent.

THE SKEPTIC SIDE

It is perhaps a little misleading to suggest that the Stoic revival and the anti-Stoic reaction represent an unequivocally positive view evolving into something negative. The plays I discuss mirror the ambivalence with which Stoicism was viewed even by those who professed to admire its ideals. As Braden observes, "The main line of Renaissance reactions to Stoicism is a complicated mixture of respect and rejection."[82] Hamlet's ambivalence toward it, his oscillations between a yearning to embrace it and a skeptical recognition of its limitations and questionable basic assumptions, is representative of a prevalent mindset.

As I have indicated, criticism of Stoicism is abundantly evident even in the writings of Christian moralists who are trying to adapt and "baptize" it. Its fundamental doctrines and assumptions were also being challenged by other ancient philosophies that were enjoying revivals during the sixteenth century, mainly Skepticism and Epicureanism. As with Stoicism, these revivals, especially that of Skepticism, are intimately connected with the great religious debates of the time. The connections of Skepticism with Reformation and Counter Reformation theology have been discussed by various intellectual historians, and I won't attempt to summarize them here but refer only to those that I find especially relevant to the drama.[83]

The term *skepticism* must always be qualified with care, especially as applied to Renaissance writers. In general, as Ernest A. Strathmann observes, "The varied manifestations of what is popularly called 'skepticism' have in common a tendency to challenge received opinions or the dicta of established authority and to submit them to the tests of reason and experience."[84] The tendency to question all received opinions is, indeed, what all skeptical thinkers, fideistic or atheistic, have in common. What distinguishes the fideistic skeptic, such as Montaigne, from what we call a freethinker, aside from the matter of belief, is an attitude toward reason itself. The atheistic freethinker challenges received opinions but trusts in the efficacy of his own reason to discern the truth in the light of experience. From a traditional Christian perspective, he is St. Paul's "natural man" (I Cor. 2:14), the intellectually arrogant rationalist who will not accept truths inaccessible to reason.[85] As he appears in Renaissance drama he is usually an atheist, a Machiavellian manipulator, and a believer in the complete autonomy of the rational individual:

> Virtue? a fig! 'tis in ourselves that we are thus or thus. Our bodies are our gardens, to the which our wills are gardeners; so that if we will plant nettles or sow lettuce, set hyssop and weed up tine, supply it with one gender of herbs or distract it with many, either to have it sterile with idleness or manur'd with industry—why, the power and corrigible authority of this lies in our wills. If the beam of our lives had not one scale of reason to poise another of sensuality, the blood and baseness of our natures would conduct us to most prepost'rous conclusions.
>
> —*Othello* I. iii. 319–29

Characters like Iago, Edmund or Tourneur's D'Amville are what a Renaissance audience would recognize as "practical atheists." Such self-serving naturalistic skeptical villains, albeit troublesome and destructive, were regarded as less dangerous than "speculative atheists." Don Cameron Allen contrasts these "two faces of atheism" as they were recognized by Renaissance apologists:

> There were practical atheists, who lived intemperately and were careless of salvation. They were rogues and rascals, not especially dangerous to the Christian faith. On the other hand, there were speculative atheists, who often lived decorous lives but who tested every religious notion and were, consequently, very much to be feared. Some of these men, it was said, thought the world eternal or the chance product of a fortunate confluence of atoms. Others believed in a divine creator who used coeternal matter or part of his own substance to make the universe. Some went wrong on Providence, believing in the Nature which supervised birds but not in the Grace which noted the sparrow's fall.[86]

Allen goes on to note that works by "speculative atheists" are rare. The popular image of the atheist that appears on the stage is largely a product of works written to refute atheism, even as the stage Machiavel is partly derivative from anti-Machiavellian treatises. In the process of representing atheism, well-intentioned Christian apologists frequently brought upon themselves the charge of being atheists. Those who relied overmuch on reason in the defense of revealed supernatural religion were often vilified as atheists themselves.[87]

In sharp contrast with atheistic skeptics, both speculative and practical, fideist skeptics place no faith in human reason. Montaigne's *An Apology for Raymond Sebond,* the greatest expression of Renaissance Christian skepticism, turns reason itself into an instrument of misology. His definition of reason equates it with man's capacity to delude himself:

> I alwaies call reason that apparance or shew of discourses which every man deviseth or forgeth in himselfe: that reason of whose condition there may be a hundred, one contrary to another, about one selfe same subject: it is an instrument of lead and wax, stretching, pliable, and that may be fitted to all byases and squared to all measures: there remaines nothing but the skill and sufficiency to know how to turne and winde the same.[88]

Montaigne's view of the unreliability and limitations of man's reason is shared by two other fideists who are not generally regarded as skeptics, Luther and Calvin. Luther condemned skepticism, believing that conscience informed by the reading of Scripture would lead one to certainty in matters of religious truth. He warned Erasmus that "The Holy Ghost is not a Sceptic," and He has not inscribed in our hearts uncertain opinions, but, rather, affirmations of the strongest sort."[89] But his extreme antirationalism, his utter contempt for reason as the malleable "whore of the devil,"[90] is essentially in harmony with skeptical views of reason's unreliability.

And Calvin, who adapts so much Stoicism into his moral philosophy, has no faith in *recta ratio* by itself as an avenue to righteousness. Like Luther, he takes Augustine's interpretations of Paul's teachings concerning the state of fallen man to deterministic extremes. While the natural faculties of fallen man—understanding, judgment, and will—have been corrupted, he possesses enough reason, a vestige of his prelapsarian state, to seek the truth:

> For we perceive in the mind of man some desire of investigating truth, towards which he would have no inclination, but from some relish of it previously possessed. It therefore indicates some perspecuity in the human understanding, that it is attracted with a love of truth; the neglect of which in the brutes argues gross sense without reason.[91]

But this "desire" cannot be fulfilled, "for it", as Calvin goes on to say,

> faints even before its entrance on its course, because it immediately termi-
> nates in vanity. For the dulness of the human mind renders it incapable
> of pursuing the right way of investigating the truth; it wanders through a
> variety of errors, and groping as it were, in the shades of darkness, often
> stumbles, till at length it is lost in its wanderings; thus, in its search after
> truth, it betrays its incapacity to seek and find it.[92]

And since the will is inseperable from reason, it, too, is in bondage to
vanity and sin.

Calvin in effect replaces the Stoic concepts of *recta ratio* and the
divine spark with his doctrine of Divine Illumination from within by
the Holy Spirit. Agreeing with Luther that Scripture is the basic source
of religious truth, he notes that reason is unable to prove to man that
the Bible is the Word of God. Only illumination by the holy Spirit
provides the inner persuasion that assures the elect that Scripture is
the Word of God, enables them to grasp its meaning, compels them
to believe it, and provides the assurance of being among the chosen:

> Such, then, is a conviction that requires no reasons; such a knowledge
> with which the best reason agrees—in which the mind truly reposes more
> securely and constantly than in any reasons; such, finally, a feeling that
> can be born only of heavenly revelation. I speak of nothing other than
> what each believer experiences within himself—though my words fall far
> beneath a just explanation of the matter.[93]

While it would be inaccurate to describe either Luther or Calvin as
skeptics, they clearly share with the skeptic Montaigne a complete
mistrust of man's reason. In his illuminating comparison of the three,
Robert Hoopes concludes:

> Fideism and skepticism, though they represent the principal theological
> and philosophical tendencies operating during the Reformation against
> right reason and the tradition of Christian humanism, are clearly indistin-
> guishable as separate "systems" in the thought of the three men we have
> examined. While they may employ a different dialectic, Christians like
> Luther and Calvin are bound to accept the Pyrrhonic attitude—that man's
> reason is unreliable and therefore he cannot know or do with certainty—
> as justified by the fact of original sin. It is not, however, reason's inade-
> quacy so much as it is its wickedness that offends them. For Montaigne,
> on the other hand, the impotence of human reason is something which,
> by and large, reason itself discovers.[94]

*   *   *

Discussions of Renaissance Skepticism inevitably end up being focused on the *Essais* of Michel de Montaigne. While he is certainly not the only important Skeptic of the time, he is the one virtually everyone read and still reads. Exploring the *profond labyrinthe* of the human condition in the light of his own experience and vast reading, he leads each of us on a journey of self-discovery that is likely to end with the question he had inscribed as a motto on his emblem of a Balance: *Que sçay-je?* What do I know?[95]

The familiarity of English Renaissance dramatists with the *Essais*, especially after Florio's translation appeared in 1603, is abundantly evident. In Jonson's *Volpone*, Lady Pol refers to the Italian dramatist Guarini, who is plagiarized by English writers, "Almost as much as Montagnie" (III. ii. 121). And Anthony Caputi points out that while Marston's early plays are full of Senecan quotation and other borrowings, those written after 1603 reveal a greater debt to Montaigne.[96] Whether or not Shakespeare was heavily influenced by the *Essais* is debatable, but obviously he was familiar with them.[97] Like Montaigne, he tirelessly explored the *profond labyrinthe* that is man and was dissatisfied with conventional explanations of human experience. "There are more things in heaven and earth, Horatio, / Than are dreamt of in your philosophy" expresses the essence of Montaignean skepticism.

Early in his progress, Montaigne was attracted to Stoicism. In "Of Constancie" he contrasts "the wise Stoicke" with one in whom "the impression of passions doth not remaine superficiall . . . but rather penetrates even into the secret of reason, infecting and corrupting the same." Clearly he believes that this penetration can be resisted. The sage responds to violent disturbances or troubling visions as other men do, shrinking and turning pale initially, but then he collects himself and will not permit fear to overmaster his reason: "So likewise in other passions, alwayes provided, his opinion remaines safe and whole, and the situation of his reason, admit no tainting or alteration whatsoever: and hee no whit consent to his fright and sufferance."[98] He accepts without reservation the basic assumptions of Stoic moral psychology, that the passions of the soul cannot overcome reason without the consent of the will and that opinion is to be ordered by reason. In another early essay, "Of Cato the Younger," he praises the great Stoic hero as "truly a patterne, whom nature chose to shew how farre humane vertue may reach, and mans constancie attaine unto."[99]

Don Cameron Allen believes that Montaigne "resigned from the Stoa" the day he had his motto struck. "Stoicism is a disease of young men, and Montaigne had been recovering for some time."[100] Indeed he had, though Allen oversimplifies his attitude toward Stoicism. As

Braden points out, "Senecan quotations turn up throughout the *Essays,* almost to the last page, often linked to austere Stoic affirmations . . . The Stoic will neither wins nor loses; it becomes one partner in an unending dialectic by which Montaigne hopes to avoid either losing himself in the world or isolating himself from it."[101]

It cannot be denied, however, that his attitude toward Stoicism is profoundly critical, even in some early essays, such as "Of Drunkennesse." This particular essay anticipates some of the main themes in *An Apology for Raymond Sebond.* As in the *Apology* he ridicules human pride and pretensions and the illusion that man can transcend his humanity by acquiring so-called wisdom: "Let him be as wise as he can, in the end he is but a man; what is more fraile, more miserable, or more vaine?" Contradicting one of the basic assumptions in "Of Constancie," he rejects the notion that a passion such as fear can always be subdued by reason. Threatened with bodily harm, man will always react fearfully, as Nature dictates, "to reserve these light markes of her aucthoritie unto herselfe, inexpugnable unto our reason, and to the Stoicke vertue: to teach him his mortalitie and our insipiditie."

He also disagrees with the Stoic view that all vices are equally evil: "Vices are all alike, inasmuch as they are all vices: And so doe haply the Stoikes meane it. But though they are equally vices, they are not equall vices." In his view drunkenness is an especially "grose and brutish vice," and he notes that even the Ancients he admires failed to condemn this vice and were guilty of it themselves. "Yea, and some of the Stoikes deeme it not amisse for man sometimes to take his liquor roundly, and drinke drunke, thereby to recreate his spirits. . . . Cato, that strict censurer and severe corrector of others, hath beene reproved for much drinking."[102]

In "Of Cruelty" he speculates that Cato the Younger's suicide may actually have been a source of voluptuous pleasure rather than a deed performed dispassionately in conformity with Stoic principles:

> witnesse Cato the younger; when I see him die, tearing and mangling his entrails, I cannot simply content my selfe to beleeve that at that time he had his soule wholly exempted from all trouble or free from vexation: I cannot imagine he did only maintaine himself in this march or course which the rule of the Stoike sect had ordained unto him, setled, without alteration or emotion, and impassible. There was , in my conceit, in this mans vertue overmuch cheerefulnesse and youthfulnesse to stay there. I verily beleeve he felt a kind of pleasure and sensualitie in so noble an action, and that therein he more pleased himself than in any other he ever performed in his life.[103]

In a similar vein, he shares Plutarch's doubts about the purity of motive in such individuals as Junius Brutus and Torquatus who managed to overcome all natural feeling and killed their children. In such cases, it "remaineth doubtfull whether vertue could reach so farre, and whether such men were not rather moved by some other passion. All actions beyond the ordinary limits are subject to some sinister interpretation."[104]

As Montaigne demonstrates repeatedly, Stoicism, like other philosophies, is grounded on questionable assumptions regarding the extent of human knowledge. The injunction to live according to Nature, for instance, is based upon the assumption that man truly understands what Nature demands. As Montaigne points out, this is a highly questionable assumption. In "On Experience," which summarizes his own conclusions regarding how man should live, he states that he is still seeking to discover "*what shee* (Nature) *inwardly requiers.*" His search is hampered by the confusion and trickery that have been imposed on her. "And that Academicall and Peripateticall *summum bonum* or sovereign felicity, which is, to live according to her rules: by this reason becommeth difficult to be limited, and hard to be expounded. And that of the Stoicks, cousin germane to the other, which is, to yeeld unto nature."[105]

A related injunction, that each man should know himself, is similarly discredited and shown to be based on unexamined assumptions:

Even so in this, for a man to know himselfe: that every man is seen so resolute and satisfied, and thinks himselfe sufficiently instructed or skilfull, doth plainly signifie that no man understands any thing, as *Socrates* teacheth *Euthydemus.* My selfe, who professe nothing else, finde therein so bottomlesse a depth, and infinite variety, that my apprentisage hath no other fruit, than to make me perceive how much more there remaineth for me to learne.[106]

A comparison of this reflection with Seneca's thoughts on the same injunction is revealing:

Toward this (death), at different paces, moves all this throng that now squabbles in the forum, that looks on at the theatres, that prays in the temples; both those whom you love and revere and those whom you despise one heap of ashes will make equal. This, clearly, is the meaning of that famous utterance ascribed to the Pythian oracle: KNOW THYSELF. What is man? A vessel that the slightest shaking, the slightest toss will break. No mighty wind is needed to scatter you abroad; whatever you strike against will be your undoing. What is man?[107]

For Seneca, self-knowledge consists largely in recognizing the brevity and vulnerability of the human condition. For Montaigne, it is a goal that may never be reached. Introspection leads one into the labyrinthine maze of the self. He agrees with Seneca that a recognition of man's weakness and mortality is essential to self-knowledge, but this is only the beginning of the quest.[108]

In his longest essay, *An Apology for Raymond Sebond,* Montaigne uses skepticism to support Catholic fideism and goes far beyond any of his other discussions in revealing the limitations of human understanding. Reading the *Apology* is a humbling experience, as Montaigne intended it to be. He announces at the outset that he means to "trample this humane pride and fiercenesse under foot, to make them feele the emptinesse, vacuitie, and no worth of man: and violently to pull out of their hands the silly weapons of their reason; to make them stoope, and bite and snarle at the ground, under the authority and reverence of God's Majesty."[109]

To begin this stripping process, Montaigne quotes several scriptural and non-scriptural authorities, including the highest of all, the Holy Ghost speaking through St. Paul:

> What preacheth truth unto us, when it biddeth us flie and shun worldly philosophy; when it so often telleth us 'that all our wisdome is but folly before God; that of all vanities man is the greatest; that man, who presumeth of his knowledge, doth not yet know what knowledge is: and that man, who is nothing, if he but thinke to be something, seduceth and deceiveth himselfe?' These sentences of the Holy Ghost do so lively and manifestly expresse what I would maintaine, as I should neede no other proofe against such as with all submission and obeysance would yeeld to his authority.[110]

He is referring to several Pauline texts, one of which, according to Popkin, was to be the favorite scriptural text of the "nouveux Pyrrhoniens":

> Scripture says, "I will destroy the wisdom of the wise, and bring to nothing the cleverness of the clever." Where is your wise man now, your man of learning, your subtle debater of the present age? God has made the wisdom of this world look foolish! As God in his wisdom ordained, the world failed to find him by its wisdom, and he chose by the folly of the gospel to save those who have faith. I *Corinthians* 1: 19–21[111]

Beyond this point he makes no more reference to the authority of Scripture but relies exclusively on reason to discredit itself.

A key part of Montaigne's humbling agenda is his attack on Man's assumption that he is superior to other animals by reason of intellect or understanding. Citing numerous authorities, mostly ancient, he notes that various creatures exhibit foresight, sympathy, and understanding equal or superior to that of humans. He presents a disturbingly persuasive argument that man is morally inferior to other beasts and raises the question of what it is, if anything, that sets him apart, other than his capacity to misuse his intellect through an unruly imagination:

> And if it be so that he alone, above all other creatures, hath this libertie of imagination and this licence of thoughts which represent unto him both what is and what is not, and what him pleaseth, falsehood and truth; it is an advantage bought at a very high rate, and whereof he hath little reason to glorie: for thence springs the chiefest source of all the mischiefs that oppresse him, as sinne, sicknesse, irresolution, trouble and despaire.[112]

The belief that Man is essentially no different from the lower animals was held by atheistic skeptics during the Renaissance who also held "that he is indebted to his nature (not God) 'for the better composition of the two.'"[113] Montaigne's argument appears initially to be moving in this direction. As everyone notices, it is a startling anticipation of Darwin, who makes the same comparisons of the mental powers of Man with those of the lower animals and having argued that his fundamental mental intuitions must be the same concludes that he is "descended from some less highly organized form."[114] Montaigne's purpose is, of course, entirely different from that of Darwin. He is demonstrating that man without God is morally no better, is indeed worse, than a beast. Only by divine grace can he hope to rise above his bestial humanity, and he concludes the *Apology* with a swipe at the Stoics for perpetuating the illusion that Man can transcend his human limitations by his own means:

> For to make the handfull greater than the hand, and the embraced greater than the arme, and to hope to straddle more than our legs length, is impossible and monstrous: nor that man should mount over and above himselfe or humanity; for he cannot see but with his owne eyes, nor take hold but with his owne armes. He shall raise himself up, if it please God extraordinarily to lend him his helping hand. He may elevate himselfe by forsaking and renouncing his owne meanes, and suffering himselfe to be elevated and raised by meere heavenly meanes. It is for our Christian faith, not for his Stoicke vertue, to pretend or aspire to this divine Metamorphosis, or miraculous transmutation.[115]

*   *   *

The sharp differences between Renaissance Stoicism and Skepticism should not obscure what they had in common. As Rosalie Colie observes, "The elements of the two systems concurred very often."[116] Both Stoics and Skeptics enjoined a suspension of judgment with the aim of achieving inner peace. For the Stoics, suspension of judgment was necessary to enable one to order one's opinions rightly and to avoid being carried away by appearances. *Apatheia,* the state in which one has achieved the extinguishing of destructive passion, can only be achieved if one has made a correct judgement about what is and is not within the sphere of the moral purpose. Skepticism, as defined by Sextus Empiricus in the book that brought about the revival of Pyrrhonean Skepticism, "is an ability, or mental attitude, which opposes appearances to judgements in any way whatsoever, with the result that, owing to the equipollence of the objects and reasons thus opposed, we are brought firstly to a state of mental suspense and next to a state of 'unperturbedness' or quietude."[117] This state of quietude, called *ataraxia,* is essentially the same as the tranquillity sought by the Stoics. It is a kind of negative happiness, consisting of freedom from disturbance, even as Stoic tranquillity consists of *apatheia* combined with *eupatheia* or benevolent states of feeling.

As Colie observes, elements of both philosophies can be found in the works of various Renaissance writers and cannot be separated from each other.[118] While both Erasmus and Montaigne, for instance, ridicule the Stoics and profess Skepticism, there are obvious Stoic elements in their works. And while Charron is critical of "dogmatists,"[119] he seems not to recognize that the Stoics were commonly grouped with them.[120] *De la Sagesse,* which begins with the assertion that "la vraye science & le vray estude de l'homme, c'est l'homme,"[121] is full of pyrrhonism but informed overall by Stoic ethics, especially with regard to the passions.[122] And Sir William Cornwallis, while generally inclined toward Stoicism, professes himself to be "halfe a *Pyrrhonian* concerning these Terrene businesses."[123]

The close connection of these two traditionally opposed philosophies during the Renaissance is important to bear in mind as we examine the Stoic-Skeptic dialectic in the drama. As we will see repeatedly, tragic protagonists, like some of the writers I have been discussing, oscillate between the two stances and even manage to combine them.

2

English Seneca

SKEPTICISM IN TRAGEDY

ELEMENTS OF SKEPTICISM AND IRREVERENCE IN VARIOUS FORMS ARE PRESent in most great tragedies. In the process of imitating men better than they are,[1] revealing their capacity to learn and grow spiritually through suffering, tragedians tend to diminish the moral stature of the gods who may be partly responsible for human affliction. Understandably, Plato found the representations of the gods in tragedies, specifically those of Aeschylus, as well as in the poems of Hesiod and Homer, improper and dangerous to the moral development of the young.[2] The Aeschylean tragedies he quotes have been lost, but the representation of Zeus in *Prometheus Bound* through the characters Force and Might can hardly generate reverence, and even if, as some conjecture, the lost sequel depicted a reconciliation of Zeus with Prometheus, the angry force of the indictment of divine injustice in the existing play would be undiminished.[3]

Euripides was popularly accused of promoting disbelief in the gods' existence.[4] While he may or may not have believed in their existence himself, he recognizes the power they have over the human imagination. He is the most obviously skeptical and irreverent of the three great tragedians. Most of the gods in his plays are amoral, unconcerned with justice, and frequently destructive to humans.

In the tragedies of Sophocles the gods do not intervene directly in human affairs. As Kitto observes, they operate on a different plane. They are concerned with justice but not in the way the moral personal God of the Old Testament is shown to be concerned, and δίκη itself in his tragedies seems to be devoid of the moral sense it has in those of Aeschylus.[5] Like the rationalistic Renaissance skeptic, Sophocles attributes to nature what a fideist would attribute to God.

Skepticism and fideism can coexist in tragedy, as we see in *The Book of Job,* a tragic poem that superficially resembles Sophocles' *Oedipus at Colonus.* Like Montaigne using reason to reveal its inade-

45

quacy in the *Apology for Raymond Sebond,* the *Job* poet uses wisdom to reveal its own limitations and the necessity of total submission to the unknowable. The poem may, to use Stanley Cavell's words in another context, be "the working out of a response to skepticism."[6] The skepticism based on reason and experience in Job's great complaints against the palpable injustice of Yahweh refutes the canned wisdom of the comforters before it too is finally refuted in the theophany. In *Hamlet,* too, as I will argue, skepticism prepares the way for faith.

In the tragedies of Seneca, the element of skepticism is very much at odds with faith. As Rosenmeyer shows, Stoic piety and perfectionism are undercut by Stoic science. The Stoic universe that is supposedly ordered by Divine Reason is actually "diseased," and the Nature apostrophized by the Senecan hero or heroine is powerless to respond. "In entreating the far-flung potencies of their world, including the vengeful demons of the underworld, a Senecan Hercules or Oedipus, or a Juno, can no longer hope for the recourse the cry is designed to elicit. Nature is no more reliable, no more powerful, than the agent who appeals to it."[7] The world of these characters is a model for the world of *The Spanish Tragedy* wherein Kyd introduces a dialectic that will inform the major tragedies of his contemporaries that follow. The Stoicism that was being baptized by Christian moralists and theologians is challenged by Skepticism, even as the Stoic moral philosophy of Seneca is challenged in his tragedies by the realities of life in a Stoic universe.

Beginning with *The Spanish Tragedy,* English dramatists not only exploited the sensational possibilities of the Senecan revenge play, but also used it as a vehicle to explore the problems of evil and suffering in a world in which men still cling to the idea of providential order and divine justice in spite of empirical evidence that the gods are indifferent or hostile. Much of the tension in these plays derives from juxtapositions of belief and disbelief in the morality or concern of the powers that shape human destiny. The Stoic-Skeptic dialectic is a recurrent motif, emerging almost inevitably as avenging protagonists find themselves faced with the alternatives of enduring oppressive evils passively or taking action to end them. The option of enduring passively is almost invariably rejected, and avengers take upon themselves a role that is usually not reconcilable with conventional morality or religion. Typically, conventional moral and religious assumptions themselves undergo critical scrutiny, and a twentieth-century reader may be led to interpret the plays as subversive or even nihilistic.

Referring to Marston's *Antonio's Revenge,* Jonathan Dollimore argues persuasively that "revenge action is not a working out of divine vengeance, but a strategy of survival resorted to by the alienated and dispossessed. Moreover, in that action is a rejection of the providential scheme which divine vengeance conventionally presupposed."[8] With part of this, one might agree, but even in the *Antonio* plays, as I will argue, Marston does not wholly reject the providential scheme itself, nor do other dramatists who, like Marston, create skeptical characters who do. The vision of a dramatist is much more encompassing than that of any of his characters, and identifying any one of them as representative of his own point of view is questionable at best. But Dollimore focuses as one must in any discussion of a revenge play on the implications of revenge and how a character who assumes the role of avenger defines himself or herself within the world of a play. There have been numerous discussions of this subject, and the question of how the contemporary audience regarded revenge and revengers is still being debated. The debate itself has been instructive, not only in terms of what has been discovered with regard to contemporary views of revenge, but also in connection with the larger philosophical issues that inevitably emerge in a revenge play. While those issues are the main focus of this study, a brief review of the ethical considerations that create conflicts in revenge plays will help to clarify them as they emerge first in *The Spanish Tragedy* and then in subsequent representatives of the genre.

The Ethical Problems of Revenge

Twentieth-century views of Elizabethan and Jacobean revenge plays have been heavily influenced by Lily Bess Campbell's 1931 article "Theories of Revenge in Renaissance England." Basing her argument largely on works by moral philosophers and theologians, she concluded that dramatists and their audiences were in basic agreement with contemporary moralists that since divine vengeance, though delayed, was inevitable and could be carried out on earth only through the divinely sanctioned means of public vengeance, all private revenge was damnable and unjustified:

> It is, then, apparent, it seems to me, that the great tragic theme of sixteenth- and seventeenth-century teaching is this theme of God's revenge for sin. Writers of tragedies, both dramatic and non-dramatic tragedies, were necessarily preoccupied with this fundamental teaching. And all Elizabethan tragedy must appear as fundamentally a tragedy of revenge

if the extent of the idea of revenge be but grasped. The threefold aspect of revenge must, however, be always held in mind: and revenge must be reckoned as including God's revenge, public revenge committed to the rulers by God, and private revenge forbidden alike by God and by the state as his representative.[9]

Campbell's conclusions were largely accepted by subsequent commentators, including Fredson Bowers, Eleanor Prosser, and Charles and Elaine Hallett, among others.[10] They were, however, challenged by other critics. Philip J. Ayres has noted how a number of revenges are presented in Elizabethan narrative literature as "heroic and praiseworthy."[11] And John Sibly has discussed how the idea of revenge as a sacred duty dramatized in some revenge plays was paralleled by the Oath of Association, signed by many of Elizabeth's subjects, in which they pledged, in the event of her assassination, to pursue her killers "as well by force of arms as by all other means of revenge."[12] Moreover, as Harry Keyishian observes, "we should recall that Drake named the sea vessel he led against the Armada not *Forgiveness* or *The Turned Cheek*, but *The Revenge*.[13]

It should be apparent to anyone who studies *The Spanish Tragedy* closely that it generates a very complex audience response that defies reduction to any sort of conventional moral judgement of its avenging protagonist. Indeed, like subsequent Tudor and Stuart revenge plays, it subjects conventional views of revenge itself to critical scrutiny and raises some of the same questions that exercised the moralists. For them, as for Hieronimo and other revengers, revenge was a vexing ethical problem because conflicting moral and religious imperatives governing it were equally compelling. On the one hand, one who had been injured was enjoined by the Pauline injunction to leave revenge to God and the magistrates who have a divinely sanctioned authority to execute "public vengeance" (*Rom.* 12:17–19 and 13:4). On the other, one had to feel the pressure to act out of a concern for justice and to preserve one's honor.

It is tempting to dichotomize these imperatives and characterize them simply as "Christian" and "pagan-humanist."[14] Nietzsche, with his distinctions between "master morality" and "slave morality," would encourage us to do this.[15] But the Renaissance did not make such neat distinctions between the injunctions of Christian morality and the demands of honor. Honor was not an exclusively secular concern. William Ames, a Calvinist theologian, asserts that one is obliged in conscience not to permit an injury to his honor ("credit") to go unpunished:

He who is much wronged by any in his credit, and is to stand upon his credit with other men, insomuch that hee may not exercise his function as long as his credit is tainted is bound by that commutative Iustice whereby he stands ingaged to others, to seek Revenge.[16]

The "revenge" he speaks of here is of course "public revenge," to be sought at the hands of a magistrate, for, like all Christian moralists, he condemns private revenge in principle. The moral importance he attaches to maintaining "credit" is typically Christian. In a discussion of the necessity of "providing good things, not only in the sight of God, but also in the sight of all men," Luther quotes Augustine:

A man who is not concerned to have a good reputation is lacking in good feeling. For you personally a good conscience is sufficient, but for your neighbour your good reputation is a necessity.[17]

A good Christian is obliged to maintain his or her honor in the sense of reputation and to render honor where it is due. In this connection, Richard Hooker observes that it is a great injustice to neglect the giving of honor, for "unto whom we deny all honour, we seem plainly to take from them all opinion of human dignity, to make no account or reckoning of them, to think them so utterly without virtue, as if no good thing in the world could be looked for at their hands."[18]

The Christian imperative to preserve honor differs significantly, of course, from what has come to be called the Renaissance Code of Honor. This latter body of values and concomitant imperatives, including the mandate to avenge injuries and insults, derives mainly from Aristotle's *Ethics, Politics,* and other writings. Other classical works, such as Cicero's *De Officiis,* also influenced its development, but it is mainly Aristotelian.

According to Aristotle, honor (τῑμή) is "the greatest of external goods," "the prize of virtue," "the end of virtue."[19] But he denies that honor should be identified with happiness or "the good" that men seek, because honor is dependent on those who bestow it rather than on those who receive it, and "the good we divine to be something proper to a man and not easily taken from him."[20] Men seek the honor that is given to them by men of wisdom because it assures them of their own virtue. He goes on to say that while a man who possesses true greatness of soul (*megalopsychia*) regards all external things with something akin to disdain, he claims honor, the greatest of all external goods, as his desert. He condemns unduly humble men more severely than vain-glorious men because their reputations cause them to refrain from undertaking noble actions.[21]

Though Aristotelian *megalopsychia* is the antithesis of self-denying Christian humility, Christian writers could find support in Aristotle for the view that maintaining one's reputation is a moral imperative. Where they differ radically from Aristotle is in their adherence to Christ's teaching in the Sermon on the Mount that one must not return injury for injury, a teaching also articulated by Socrates in *The Republic*.[22] Aristotle observes that the good-tempered man realizes that there are times when the endurance of insults is base and that he must either become angry or suffer a loss of reputation and additional injuries as well:

> For those who are not angry at the things they should be angry at are thought to be fools, and so are those who are not angry in the right way, at the right time, or with the right persons: for such a man is thought not to feel nor to be pained by them, and, since he does not get angry, he is unlikely to defend himself: and to endure being insulted and to put up with insults to one's friends is slavish.[23]

An implicit sanctioning of revenge is obvious here, and in the *Rhetoric* he explicitly sanctions it, asserting that "it is noble to avenge oneself upon one's enemies, and not to come to terms with them; for requital is just, and the just is noble; and not to yield is a mark of courage."[24] This appears to be somewhat at odds with what he says elsewhere in the same treatise, that it is "equitable [*epeikes*] to forgive human things" (*Rhet.* 1374b10), but it should be noted that the contexts are very different. In the latter context, he is concerned with equity and the mitigation of strict legal punishment.[25]

Behind Aristotle and heavily influencing his ethical teachings was the great heroic tradition of *arete* and *kleos* (fame) as a measure of honor that informs the Homeric epics, both of which climax with spectacular revenges. As various commentators have remarked, anger (*mênis*) is the first word in European literature.[26] Aristotle's discussion of anger in the passage above expresses the typically Greek view that it is an emotion (*thymos*) with ambivalent possibilities, depending on how a man permits himself to be moved by it. Misdirected, it can diminish a man, as we see in the raging of Oedipus against Tiresias in *Oedipus the King,* or paralyze him, as we see in the withdrawal of Achilles from the war in the *Iliad.* Properly directed, it can magnify him, providing the energy to accomplish great deeds, as we see in the revenge of Achilles upon Hector and the raging of Oedipus against his betrayers and the injustice of his fate in *Oedipus at Colonus* which seems to help establish his worthiness to be apotheosized in the last scene.

The idea that one can be defined by how he expresses his anger and either raised or diminished in honor accordingly becomes a com-

monplace during the Renaissance.[27] Ben Jonson treats it comically in
Everyman in His Humour and *The Alchemist*. Master Stephen in the
former play and Kastril in *The Alchemist* both aspire to be gentlemen
and regard the learning of proper anger as an indispensable social
grace. More seriously, Hamlet berates himself in his second soliloquy
for his lack of "gall" and the rage, "passion," needed to accomplish
his revenge. Later in the play, comparing himself with Fortinbras,
whose mindless commitment to a dangerous enterprise may bring
him honor, he castigates himself for his failure to make a commitment
to his own "quarrel" in which both his "reason" and "blood" should
move him:

> Rightly to be great
> Is not to stir without great argument.
> But greatly to find quarrel in a straw
> When honour's at the stake. How stand I then,
>
> (IV. iv. 53–56)

The idea of remiting anger and forgiving an injury as an expression
of love that cancels a wrong is, of course, wholly Christian. Philip
Vellacott points out that the Greek verb *syngignoskein,* meaning "to
pardon" and *syngnome,* meaning the act of pardon, were not in
Homer's vocabulary, though obviously the memorable scene in the
Iliad XXIV in which Priam kisses the hands that killed his son and
Achilles relinquishes his anger "undoubtedly shows for the first time
a poet's answer to the most painful and eternal of life's questions.
How can anger reach an end?"[28] Revenge was obviously not the
answer, either for Homer or for the tragedians, but the honor imperative that drove one to carry out revenge was, nonetheless, strong,
and though he asserts that the great-spirited man is not revengeful,
Aristotle, like the poets, reveals how concern for one's honor can
leave no alternative.

Christian forgiveness offers a way out of the ethical dilemmas created by the honor imperative, but it is only possible for one who
subscribes to Christian religious beliefs. Moreover, even when one is
a committed Christian, he or she may still be compelled to forbidden
action by the demands of honor, as Dostoevsky shows in the case of
Father Zossima in *The Brothers Karamazov* when, as a young army
officer, he provokes a duel and then experiences a mysterious conversion. Even though he has no intention of firing his weapon, Zossima
must, nonetheless, go through with the duel and possibly make the
other man responsible for his death.

Aristotle made clear distinctions between true greatness of soul and the honor that the world bestows upon men of noble reputation, but the Renaissance Code of Honor that derived largely from his writings and that serves as the sovereign moral imperative of characters in Renaissance drama reveals a strong tendency within a certain type of moral sensibility to equate "honor" wholly with reputation, making it purely a thing external. Nowhere does this appear more clearly than in those plays in which characters attempt to restore lost honor through revenge. Avengers allegedly motivated by "honor" include some of the most despicable villiains in literature—Webster's Aragonian brethren in *The Duchess of Malfi,* Kyd's Lorenzo in *The Spanish Tragedy,* Fletcher's Maximus in *Valentinian* among many others. These characters all subscribe to the belief, articulated by Iago, that "Good name, in man and woman . . . Is the immediate jewel of their souls." Iago, who articulates a totally different view of "reputation" earlier in *Othello,* tries to explain his own motiveless malignity to Roderigo in terms of revenge for the loss of honor when he has been passed over. It is a plausible sounding motive and makes sense even to some modern commentators on the play.[29]

In *Hamlet,* the foil relationship between the two young avengers, Hamlet and Laertes, illuminates the contrast between the type of "honor" that is purely a thing external and honor as integrity. Laertes, whose obsession with family "honor" is evident in his parting counsel to Ophelia (I. iii. 29 ff.), storms into Elsinore and refuses to be calmed at a moment when a man of honor should exhibit rage:

> That drop of blood that's calm proclaims me bastard;
> Cries cuckold to my father; brands the harlot
> Even here between the chaste unsmirched brows
> Of my true mother.
>
> (IV. v. 115–18)

Later he professes to be "satisfied in nature" by Hamlet's apology for the deaths of his father and sister but will not be reconciled with Hamlet until he can consult with "elder masters of known honor" about what he must do to keep his "name ungor'd." In view of the fact that his personal equipage includes a vessel of deadly ointment that could only serve some treacherous purpose, we should not be surprised that this "honor" obsessed young nobleman lets himself become a tool of Claudius.

The integrity of Hamlet, who constantly condemns himself for being deficient in honor, is one of the principal obstacles preventing him from achieving revenge. Unlike Laertes or Fortinbras, he cannot surrender himself blindly in the name of honor to a course of action he cannot square with his conscience. Ironically, he forgoes the perfect opportunity to kill Claudius at prayer because it is not the right moment to execute a ruthless, conscienceless stereotypical "revenge" of the kind Laertes does not hesitate to execute upon him.

The tensions in plays dealing with revenge are by no means all due to conflicts between Christian injunctions and the honor imperative. Indeed even in plays in which the moral framework is unambiguously Christian, there are questions about when and whether private revenge can become justifiable public revenge and vice versa. For instance, in *Richard III,* when the two murderers sent by Richard, Duke of Gloucester, are about to dispatch his brother Clarence, the doomed man reminds them that God Himself forbids murder and will avenge it:

> Take heed; for he holds vengeance in his hand
> To hurl upon their heads that break his law.
>
> (I. iv. 187–88)

The murderers reply that they are, in effect, agents of divine vengeance sent to punish Clarence for his sins of perjury and complicity in the murder of Prince Edward at Tewkesbury. Clarence does not deny his guilt, but he tries to make the murderers see that they cannot justify their crime as an act of divine vengeance:

> If God will be avenged for the deed,
> O, know you yet he doth it publicly!
> Take not the quarrel from his pow'rful arm.
> He needs no indirect or lawless course
> To cut off those that have offended him.
>
> (I. iv. 203–7)

Clarence's statement of accepted Christian principles touching revenge is perfectly correct, but within the context of the play and the York tetralogy as a whole it can be seen that the murderers are also accurately describing their role. England has been scourged by civil war to atone for the murder of Richard II, and now as the country is enduring the final stages of its punishment, the Yorkists, damned "scourges" operating within a providental design, are being scourged by one of their own. While they still rule the country, Clarence cannot be lawfully tried and punished "publicly" for his crimes. This is not to suggest that the murderers are justified in their action. Like their victim, who has dreamt proleptically of his own infernal destination, they are damned by what they've done and know it.

In another history play, *2 Henry VI,* Shakespeare presents a more justifiable instance of private individuals assuming the roles of public avengers. Justification arises from the fact that there is a complete breakdown of law and order, and the play depicts all the consequences of this breakdown. The weak king himself is largely responsible for civil dissension, which is aggravated by political intrigue.

As the country moves inexorably toward civil war, one of the first casualties is the legal process itself. The contest between Horner the Armourer and his man Peter, in II. iii., is virtually a parody of the traditional medieval trial by combat. As it happens, the guilty party, Horner, reveals his treason after being mortally wounded by his much weaker opponent. The pious utterances of the king and the victorious apprentice attribute the outcome to the hand of God Himself, but the audience must wonder if Divine Justice would have been vindicated so handily if the Armourer hadn't been so drunk. Indeed, one of the witnesses, York, tells Peter to "thank God, and the good wine in thy master's way." (II. iii. 91).

Not many scenes later, we see that York himself is instrumental in destroying the legal process. He joins with his enemies the queen and her lover, Suffolk, in sanctioning the murder of good Duke Humphrey of Gloucester. The impotent, hand-wringing king has given them permission to do as they will, even though he realizes that Gloucester is innocent, and they seize the opportunity to eliminate the Protector. When they agree to let Cardinal Beaufort arrange the murder, York says, "And now we three have spoke it, / It skills not greatly who impugns our doom." (III. i. 280–1). There is not even a pretence of respect for law as these ruthless power seekers implement their designs. The murder of Gloucester is the pivotal catastrophe in the tragedy of England itself, marking the complete breakdown of orderly rule.

Ironically, a due process is carried out against Suffolk, but not through the duly appointed agencies of public vengeance. Indeed, perhaps the most lawless elements in the kingdom, pirates who are deserters from the English army, manage to achieve what the king and other sanctioned magistrates could not, the semblance of a trial of Suffolk and the infliction of a just and fitting punishment. A nameless "Lieutenant" charges Suffolk justly with the capital crimes of treason, complicity in murder, and sedition and sentences him to death at the hands of Walter Whitmore.

Given the lawless condition of the kingdom, the "trial" and execution of Suffolk might well be sanctioned by some Renaissance moralists. According to Jeremy Taylor, "In the sea, and in desert places, where there can be no appeals to judges, every man is executioner of the sentence of the law of nations."[30] Because he is a private person, the revenge will in one sense be a private revenge, but it will be what Francis Bacon would term the "most tolerable sort of revenge."[31] Taylor qualifies this precept with great care. Even in lawless circumstances, Christians may proceed "to touch blood" or "to give sentence for the effusion ot it . . . with caution, and a slow motion, and after a loud call, and upon a great necessity; because there are two great impediments: the one is the duty of mercy, which is greatly required and severely exacted of every disciple of Christ; and the other is, that there is a soul at stake when blood is to be shed." Therefore, those who would act as judges of the crimes of others have "a tender employment, and very unsafe" unless they proceed with "a just authority, and a great mercy, and an unavoidable necessity, and public utility, and the fear of God always before their eyes, and a great wisdom."[32]

Francis Bacon's dictum that "Revenge is a kind of wild justice" is frequently quoted in critical studies of revenge tragedy, but too often the rest of his essay on the subject of revenge is not considered. Revenge is "wild" in that it undermines civilized society, which is ordered by laws. The wrong that one revenges may be an offense against the law, but the act of revenge "putteth the law out of office." Bacon never condones private revenge, but he clearly acknowledges that the degree of culpability varies according to circumstances, and "The most tolerable sort of (private) revenge is for those wrongs which there is no law to remedy, but then let a man take heed the revenge be such as there is no law to punish; else a man's enemy is still beforehand, and it is two for one." But private revenge is never the best course of action. A man who "studieth revenge keeps his own wounds green." He should instead, like Job, be willing to accept both good and evil from God's hands. Bacon's essay concludes with a careful distinction between public and private revenges:

> Public revenges are for the most part fortunate, as that for the death of Caesar, for the death of Pertinax, for the death of Henry the Third of France, and many more. But in private revenges it is not so. Nay, rather, vindictive persons live the life of witches, who, as they are mischievous, so end they infortunate.[33]

Bacon's use of the terms *fortunate* and *infortunate* suggests that he is speaking in purely practical, even Machiavellian, terms. If one can rally the support of one's countrymen in an act of revenge, then one might hope to prosper by it. A private revenge on one's neighbor, however, will usually be punished by law. Indeed the emphasis of the essay as a whole is practical, but the moral aspects of the problem are clearly understood. Revenge, as he indicates, is contrary to the teachings of the Bible, but one type of revenge is more "tolerable" than another from a moral as well as a legal standpoint.

Unlike Taylor and Bacon, other Renaissance moralists seem not to recognize that circumstances might arise that would justify the assumption of the role of public avenger by a private individual. William Ames, for instance, argues that a private individual may request that a magistrate inflict punishment on one who has injured him, but he may not inflict punishment himself because "to take vengeance upon another mans offence, belongs only to him who is Superiour in his power: But all private men are by Right equall." Moreover, "a private man cannot by himself set any limits to his revenge."[34] All commentators agree that personal motives and vindictiveness taint and corrupt the process of public vengeance and have the potential to turn it into private revenge. In the words of Ames,

> Publike Revenge, whether it be exercised by a Magistrate, or sought by a private man, if it proceed out of Envy, Hatred, Thirst of blood, or Cruelty, or if by any other meanes it be tainted in the impulsive formall or finall cause, doth in that respect become private and unlawfull.[35]

As noted in the previous chapter, the Neostoic Joseph Hall goes even further and argues that the ideal magistrate is devoid of all feeling, including pity. In this he is following the ancient Stoics, notably Seneca, whose teachings concerning revenge are generally harmonious with those of Christian moralists, albeit colored by the Stoic pride Montaigne condemned. In *De Constantia Sapientis*, an essay in which the ideal of the sage is fully delineated, Seneca develops the proposition that a wise man can receive neither injury nor insult. He considers the case of a just man, Marcus Cato, who was abused by an ignorant mob. In such a case, one should pity the people who fail to appreciate and make use of such a man. Cato himself was not to be pitied because he was impervious to either injury or insult. An injury is always intended to bring evil upon a person. But for a wise man the only evil is baseness, and since a wise man is upright and virtuous, he resists baseness. Also, that which injures must be more powerful than that which is injured; but wickedness is not stronger than righteousness; therefore, a wise man cannot be injured:

> It is impossible, therefore, for any one either to injure or to benefit the wise man, since that which is divine does not need to be helped, and cannot be hurt; and the wise man is next-door neighbour to the gods and like a god in all save his mortality.[36]

A similar argument is based on the proposition that a man can be injured only by one stronger than himself; but only a bad man will attempt to injure a good man, and a bad man is naturally weaker. Therefore, a good man cannot be injured. Seneca realizes that these comforting syllogisms are undermined by certain obvious cases of injustice and injury, such as the trial and death of Socrates. He circumvents these possible objections by arguing that the reception of an injury, like the infliction of one, depends on one's state of mind. A man may become a wrongdoer, may be morally responsible for an injury, simply by intending it. And the wise man who maintains the proper state of mind is invulnerable to an injury. Ill fortune and the deeds of evil men can have no effect on him, for he is protected "by his endurance and his greatness of soul." He is able to endure them in the same way that he endures unpleasant weather and illnesses.[37]

Unlike Aristotle's great-spirited man, Seneca's great-souled wise man is utterly impervious to insults. *Megalopsychia* and Stoic *magnanimitas* mandate radically different responses. *Magnanimitas,* the "noblest of all the virtues," enables the sage to scorn the insults of the proud and the arrogant as things of no consequence. He always remembers that it is only possible to be held in contempt by a superior. But a wise man is superior to all others; therefore, he cannot be held in contempt.[38]

It follows that the wise man is not vengeful, and Seneca develops this point explicitly in *De Ira.* He points out that anger, the "most destructive" of all emotions, is against Nature. It is by its nature a vengeful passion, and he agrees with Aristotle's definition "that anger is the desire to repay suffering." Not only does it make a man vengeful; it also destroys all his natural inclinations to love and help his fellows.[39]

Like St. Paul, Seneca sanctions public vengeance administered by a magistrate, as long as it is carried out with restraint and mercy. He likens the ruler of a state to a physician. In healing an illness, a physician employs the mildest remedies he can. Only when mild remedies fail does he resort to more drastic treatments. Similarly, a good ruler tries to "heal human nature" by the mild means of rebuke and admonition before he resorts to more drastic remedies, such as corporal punishment. He should always strive for equity and never administer an excessive punishment: "Extreme punishment let him appoint only to extreme crime, so that no man will lose his life unless it is to the benefit even of the loser to lose it."[40] When a good ruler does execute a man publicly and covers him with disgrace, he is motivated only by his concern for the common good and takes no vengeful satisfaction in the act. A punishment administered "with discretion" (*cum ratione*) is never motivated by anger, and it"will not hurt, but will heal under the guise of hurting."[41] As Martha Nussbaum observes,

On the one hand, the Stoics are deeply committed to the analogy between wise philosophical treatment and medical therapy; and they accept, as well, the Aristotelian claim that good medical treatment in ethics is searchingly particular, devoted to a deep understanding of each concrete case. On the other hand, the Arisotelian tradition links this medical model with a strong commitment to *epikeia* [equity] in public life. Indeed, *epikeia* means for Aristotle both the searching particularity of good judgment, which goes beyond the generality of law, and also a tendency to mitigation of strict legal punishment in the light of a causal understanding of the particular case. It is, says Aristotle, "equitable [*epeikes*] to forgive human things" (*Rhet.* 1374b 10). The connection between the two meanings of the *epeikes* seems, in fact, to be forged by the medical analogy: for if one approaches a case with the doctor's sympathetic interest in its particularities, one will be more likely to take an interest in the prospects of the offender as a human being, to notice any mitigating factors, and, in general, not to use the hardness of the law as a way of dividing oneself off from the offender.[42]

Epictetus, whose teachings had a considerable influence on Chapman's handling of revenge in *The Revenge of Bussy D'Ambois,* also urges his followers to extinguish anger, the cause of vengeful action. Those who offend or injure us should be pitied rather than punished, and he is even more humane than Seneca with regard to capital punishment:

Ought not this brigand, then, and this adulterer to be put to death? you ask. Not at all, but you should ask rather, "Ought not this man to be put to death who is in a state of error and delusion about the greatest matters, and is ín a state of blindness, not, indeed, in the vision which distinguishes white and black, but in the judgement which distinguishes between the good and the evil?" And if you put it this way, you will realize how inhuman a sentiment it is that you are uttering, and that it is just as if you should say, "Ought not this blind man, then, or this deaf man to be put to death?" For if the loss of the greatest things is the greatest harm that can befall a man, while the greatest thing in each man is a right moral purpose, and if a man is deprived of this very thing, what ground is left for you to be angry at him?[43]

It is the duty one against whom an injury is attempted to aid his assailant in achieving a "right moral purpose," even as Lycurgus the

Lacedaemonian reformed a young man who had half-blinded him and on whom he could have taken vengeance.[44] If one chooses instead to avenge an injury, then he has discarded his own moral purpose:

> "My neighbor has thrown stones." You have not made a mistake, have you? "No, but my crockery is broken." Are you a piece of crockery, then? No, but you are moral purpose. What, then, has been given you with which to meet this attack? If you seek to act like a wolf, you can bite back and throw more stones than your neighbour did; but if you seek to act like a man, examine your store, see what faculties you brought into the world. You brought no faculty of brutality, did you? No faculty of bearing grudges, did you?[45]

In Tudor and Stuart revenge plays, Stoicism frequently appears either literally embodied in the person of a sage, a "Senecal man" such as Chapman's Clermont D'Ambois or Marston's Pandulpho, or as an alternative ethical response in the mind of an avenger. Thus Hieronimo, when he is pondering his course of action after the king has shown his apparent indifference to matters of justice, considers the alternatives of Christian patience and Stoic resignation versus action. And Hamlet, in his "To be or not to be" soliloquy, which may be modeled in part on Hieronimo's soliloquy, juxtaposes Stoic resignation and active commitment against a sea of troubles. In *Hamlet* Stoicism is also literally embodied in the person of Horatio, "more an antique Roman than a Dane," who represents for Hamlet an admirable but unattainable rational ideal, tranquil in *apatheia* and in its certainty of moral purpose. His encomium on Horatio (III. ii. 64–72) expresses both his personal affection for the man and his yearning to emulate the ideal he represents.

The interesting question of whether or not a sage could ever execute blood vengeance without abandoning his moral purpose was being treated at about the same time Shakespeare was writing *Hamlet* by Marston in *Antonio's Revenge*. Marston's depiction of the Stoic Pandulpho's progress from sage to psychopath suggests that he agrees with Shakespeare that vengeful commitment is inherently corrupting, and one who so commits himself must inevitably abandon the role of sage. The question of how a sage would execute blood vengeance without abandoning his moral purpose remained unanswered on the stage until Chapman provided *The Revenge of Bussy D'Ambois* (1610). Clermont D'Ambois remains uncorrupted by destructive passion as he dispatches Montsurry and then commits suicide for the same reason Horatio attempts to kill himself, out of grief for the loss of a friend. Chapman seems to have had *Hamlet* in mind when he wrote *The Revenge,* was probably trying to improve upon it, and perhaps vindicate the Stoic ideal that *Hamlet* throws into question.

Stoicism, then, like Christian moral philosophy, becomes the basis of complex and conflicting dramatic treatments of the ethical problems of revenge. Even as the moral philosophers cannot agree wholly among themselves about whether or not private persons can effect public vengeance or what "honor" demands or whether or not Stoic ethics can be reconciled with revenge, so the dramatists reveal radically differing moral perspectives and attitudes toward revenge. Kyd's perspective in *The Spanish Tragedy,* I will argue, is essentially skeptical, pagan and humanistic. His universe is as hostile to man or at least as indifferent to human suffering as Marlowe's, hence, his treatment of Revenge as literally a force from Hell that good men must resort to if they would see Justice prevail. This is obviously in sharp contrast to the pious orthodoxy of Cyril Tourneur in *The Atheist's Tragedy,* which admonishes us unequivocally that "Patience is the honest man's revenge."

Between these two extremes, or perhaps embracing both of them, is Shakespeare. Hamlet finally achieves, in Gordon Braden's words, "a Stoicism Christianized by an unclassically thorough humility before a greater power," a philosophical stance closer to Montaigne than Seneca.[46] One might add that the skepticism as well as the piety of Montaigne is clearly reflected in the last scenes. All conventional views of human experience are thrown into question in *Hamlet,* including conventional views of how divine vengeance operates in the world through human agencies. We need only consider the implications of his words over the slain Polonius:

> —For this same lord,
> I do repent; but heaven hath pleas'd it so.
> To punish me with this, and this with me,
> That I must be their scourge and minister.

> (III. iv. 172–75)

Supposedly, "scourges" and "ministers" were very different types of avengers,[47] but Hamlet is progressing toward a level of awareness that enables him to perceive the inadequacy of all conventional role definitions. His is a vision that cannot be articulated even in the conventional medium of language. To a point, he can articulate it in the Christian Stoic platitudes he utters to Horatio in the play's final scenes, but then "the rest is silence."

ESCHATOLOGY AND SKEPTICISM IN *THE SPANISH TRAGEDY*

Considering the amount of serious, appreciative scholarship that has been done on *The Spanish Tragedy* in recent years, it is surprising that more attention has not been focused on what is clearly a central crux—the discrepancy between the orthodox Christian Stoic beliefs expressed by the living characters with regard to the process of divine justice and what is revealed in the judgment scenes that frame the main plot. The play begins and ends with eschatological revelations that in no way agree with or fulfill the orthodox Christian assumptions or expectations of the characters who live and die in the intervening acts. This discrepancy is not, I suggest, something that can be accounted for simply as a result of the fact that Kyd juxtaposes a Christian world with a pagan classical underworld conventionally conceived. Rather, it is an essential part of the tragic design that he deliberately emphasizes throughout the play.

In a study of Homer's tragic vision, James M. Redfield remarks: "It is part of the terror of the *Iliad* that it shows us a world in which human action is conditioned by powers and purposes even less moral than our own."[48] He is speaking of Homer's depiction of the Olympian gods as shapers of human destiny, but the "world" he depicts is very like that of *The Spanish Tragedy,* the world introduced in the Induction. In the Induction Andrea's ghost reveals that the souls of the dead are judged in a pagan classical underworld and assigned to various regions, according to their "manner of . . . life and death"(I. i. 37).[49] Like the underworld revealed in Sackville's "Induction" in the *Mirror for Magistrates* and Clarence's proleptic nightmare vision in *Richard III,* it is modeled on the Hades described in book 6 of the *Aeneid.*[50] While the infernal setting is the same, however, the revelations concerning the process of divine judgment in the hereafter are significantly different. For one thing, neither Shakespeare nor Sackville gives us any reason to suspect that there has been any confusion in the process. Clarence foresees the eternal doom that perjury and murder have justly wrought, and while Buckingham may "playn" against Fortune, his complaint will reveal that he is paying the price of serving the ruthless ambition and tyranny of Richard III.

In contrast, the judgment scene Don Andrea's ghost describes must make us wonder if the gods are genuinely concerned about their roles as dispensers of "divine justice," Aeacus and Rhadamanth, two of the three judges of Hades, seem to take their jobs seriously enough, but they are confused by the fact that Andrea has died as both a lover and a warrior and are unable to resolve their argument about whether he should be sent "to walk with lovers"(I. i. 42) or "to martial fields" (I. i. 47). Minos, "mildest censor of the three," persuades them that the case should, in effect, be referred to a higher court, that of Pluto himself. When Andrea presents his "passport" in Pluto's court, the "infernal king" is clearly more concerned about gratifying his Proserpine than resolving eschatological disputes and readily yields to her whimsical plea that she be allowed to "doom" Andrea. At her bidding, Andrea is led back to earth by the allegorical figure Revenge, who indicates that the two of them will be functioning as a "Chorus" while they view the "mystery." In fact, it soon becomes apparent that Revenge is not merely a spectator-commentator but a force operating within all of the principal characters, a "mood soliciting their souls" (III. xv. 19).

This judgment scene in Hell, which serves to introduce the main plot of The Spanish Tragedy, resembles in some ways the rather indecorous scene on Mount Olympus with which Marlowe and Nashe begin their Dido Queen of Carthage. In that scene, the King of Heaven is roused from his pederastic play by an outraged Venus concerned for her son, who is being then victimized by the king's neglected consort. The scene, like the scene in Pluto's court, conveys unmistakably the impression that the gods who are principally responsible for seeing that justice is carried out, either in this world or the next, are in fact not greatly concerned with human affairs. They are not as removed as the gods of Epicurus and Lucretius, but they are difficult to reach, and they are as indifferent to human suffering as the gods in the Iliad or the tragedies of Euripides. Indeed, like the scene in book 4 (ll. 25–58) of the Iliad in which Hera soothes her husband's wounded feelings by permitting the destruction of three innocent cities, or the prologue to Euripides' Hippolytus in which Aphrodite reveals her intention to have her revenge, even if it means sacrificing one of her own devotees, these introductory scenes in Dido and The Spanish Tragedy serve to make us aware that it is only man himself who confers significance and tragic dignity upon human suffering.[51]

Assigning the souls of the dead their places for eternity is, of course, only a part of that great never-ending process that is the design of Divine Vengeance for sin. But having seen in the Induction to The Spanish Tragedy how frivolously this part of the process is handled in Hades, we may be inclined to listen with a skeptical ear to expressions of faith in the process as a whole. We are not led to doubt the reality of, the existence of, the process itself, but the discrepancy between what the Induction reveals and the expressed beliefs of the actors in the scenes that follow serves to impart an ironic perspective, very like that which is imparted in classical Greek tragedies, especially those of Euripides.[52] We are made to realize how completely beyond human imagination the workings of "Divine Justice" really are and how vulnerable a character may make himself by placing faith in the palpable benevolence of its design.

The first expression of faith in the process of divine justice occurs almost immediately after the Induction in the response of the Spanish king to the news that his army has been victorious over the Portingales: "Then bless'd be heaven and guider of the heavens, / From whose fair influence such justice flows" (I. ii. 10–11). In the view of one critic, this pious utterance is a statement of "the moral framework of the play, the belief in Divine Vengeance or God's justice."[53] Actually, it would be more accurate to say that this speech, along with others expressing the same belief, are statements of "the moral framework" of the human characters in the play. They reveal faith in powers unseen, but also, as the Spanish king's speech in particular shows, a very human tendency to assume that the pattern of justice imposed by heaven may be discerned by human beings.

The king's public avowal of faith in the process of divine justice sets up, as has been pointed out, "expectations that he will execute God's justice should the occasion arise."[54] The occasion will not arise until much later in the play, and when it does, the king will, by failing to respond to pleas for "justice" from one who maintains these expectations, precipitate catastrophe. Instead of mirroring heaven's justice, of which he is the divinely sanctioned minister, he will mirror what appears to be heavenly indifference. In this connection, it may be doubly ironic that one of those destined to be destroyed and damned, the king's own brother Castile, utters a speech in response to the King's "showing [in Latin] the King's alignment with God" (I. i. 12–14).[55]

Between this opening scene, which, as Scott McMillin and Jonas Barish have shown,[56] projects both visually and rhetorically an image of political order, and the final catastrophe we experience the agonizing progress of Hieronimo toward revenge. At his hands the Spanish court will be virtually destroyed and suffer the loss of "the whole succeeding hope" (IV. iv. 202). But it is Hieronimo himself who suffers more than any other character, and it is mainly through experiencing his sufferings, even as we maintain the ironic perspective imparted by the juxtaposition of the Induction with the opening scene, that we may come to understand and appreciate Kyd's tragic vision.

For the House of Castile, the tragedy may, as has been suggested,[57] have commenced before the beginning of the action in *The Spanish Tragedy*. For Hieronimo, the tragedy begins with the discovery of his son's body in II. v. Prior to this moment of unbearable discovery, Hieronimo has been introduced as an important official who enjoys the high esteem of the king. Part of this esteem seems initially to be due to his skill in contriving stately entertainments to divert the court, but as later scenes clearly reveal, it is more a result of his reputation for competence and honesty as a magistrate. As a Knight Marshal, he is responsible for administering justice—hearing cases and punishing transgressions—within the immediate vicinity of the court.[58] The seriousness with which he takes his duties is attested by a nameless citizen who tells one of his fellows:

> So; I tell you this: for learning and for law,
> There is not any advocate in Spain
> That can prevail, or will take half the pain
> That he will, in pursuit of equity.
>
> (III. xiii. 51–54)

And Castile speaks of the high regard he has won "By his deserts within the court of Spain" (III. xiv. 61–63). Clearly he is everything a magistrate should be—patient, dedicated, courageous, and impartial—a dramatic embodiment of an ideal that is ubiquitous in the sermon literature of the time.[59]

At the moment of discovering his son's body, however, he is not a presiding magistrate dispassionately dispensing justice but a father half-crazed with grief. As Howard Baker remarks, Hieronimo's role "makes psychological sense; it is real or understandable."[60] Understandably his lamentations over the body of Horatio are mixed with cries for vengeance in any form. At this moment he does not supplicate the heavens for justice, nor does he speak of seeking public revenge. On the contrary, he obviously yearns to administer personally some terrible form of retribution:

> To know the author were some ease of grief,
> For in revenge my heart would find relief.
>
> (II. v. 40–41)

. . .

> Seest thou this handkercher besmear'd with blood?
> It shall not from me till I take revenge.
>
> (II. v. 51–52)

Isabella's response is a pious affirmation that echoes the King's joyful response to the good news from the battlefield:

The heavens are just; murder cannot be hid;
Time is the author both of truth and right,
And time will bring this treachery to light.

(II. v. 57–59)

As has been frequently pointed out, she is uttering Elizabethan commonplaces.[61] Her conventional beliefs will of course fail to sustain her.
She will go mad waiting for the heavens to manifest their justice. For
now, however, her pious utterance serves to divert her husband from
bloody, futile thoughts of personal revenge and to remind him of his
duty as an earthly instrument of heaven's justice. He seems to be
speaking as much to himself as to her when he tells her to "cease"
her "plaints" that they might "sooner find the practice out" (II. v. 62).
He recognizes that he needs time to conduct a thorough investigation.

The fact that Hieronimo has a reputation for being tireless in the
"pursuit of equity" is evidence that he has the patience to listen and
the ability to suspend judgment until all the evidence in a case has
been presented. It is, of course, painfully ironic that the innocent
citizen who praises him for his dedication is among the first to feel the
effects of his despair in the power of his office to implement justice.
Before that happens, however, we are made to experience something
even more painful, the actual process of his disintegration.

The first time we see Hieronimo after the discovery of Horatio's
body, he is a desperate man. The failure of his investigation to yield
any clues has begun to erode his faith in heaven's justice itself: "How
should we term your dealings to be just, / If you unjustly deal with
those that in your justice trust?" (III. ii. 10–11). The psychological
pressure is unbearable, and he recognizes that he is being driven by
the forces that originate in, "do sally forth of hell" itself toward damnable courses of action, "unfrequented paths" that he, a just man dedicated to upholding the laws of a Christian kingdom, fears to tread.
The courses of action that tempt and terrify him are undefined, but
we may guess, on the basis of his dirge over the dead Horatio (II. v.
67–80) that they include suicide and senseless bloodshed to satisfy
his craving for vengeance. He is, of course, destined to follow both
of these damnable "paths," but at this moment he is held back by
the fear engendered by these "fierce inflamed thoughts."

At this moment, Bel-imperia's blood-scrawled letter falls at his feet,
apparently as a direct response to his supplication to heaven to "See,
search, show, send some man, some mean, that may—" (III. ii. 23).
Another man, filled with the same frustrated craving for vengeance,
might seize on this bit of evidence as a basis for immediate action.
But Hieronimo is still, in spite of the unbearable pressure of frustration,

the conscientious magistrate he has always been, and he will wait to gather more evidence "to confirm this writ" (III. ii. 49). He assumes that human, as well as heavenly, affairs are governed in terms of discernible logic, and he cannot perceive any logic either in the contents of the letter itself or in the fact that Bel-imperia would write it. What does seem logical is that the real murderers would be sending him such a letter to trap him by causing him to murder or falsely accuse the king's favorites, Lorenzo and Balthazar.

Before the second incriminating letter falls into his hands with the execution of Pedringano, Hieronimo is shown to be on the verge of despair. His sense of the cruel absurdity of his situation as a toiler "in other men's extremes, / That know not how to remedy our own" (III. vi. 1–2) increases the agony of his frustration. Yet though he has virtually given up hope of receiving justice himself, he will "see that others have their right" (III. vi. 38). He will continue to serve as a minister of heaven's justice in spite of heaven's apparent indifference to his desperate supplications:

> That, winged, mount and, hovering in the air,
> Beat at the windows of the brightest heavens,
> Soliciting for justice and revenge:
> But they are plac'd in those empyreal heights,
> Where, countermur'd with walls of diamond,
> I find the place impregnable; and they
> Resist my woes, and give my words no way.
>
> (III. vii. 13–18)

Like Seneca's Hercules or Oedipus or Juno, he can no longer hope for the recourse his cry would elicit. The far-flung potencies of his world are, if not powerless like Nature in Seneca's drama, so remote and unconcerned that they will not respond.

At this point in the play, it is becoming clear that Hieronimo's sufferings are largely due to the very virtues that have won him such high regard as a magistrate—his dedication to the pursuit of justice, his ability to suspend judgment and, above all, his fidelity to the belief that justice, as the king had put it, "flows" from heaven to earth in a clearly discernible manner. His own office is a channel through which heaven's justice *should* flow. But if the heavens are indifferent, then his office is meaningless. He is apparently about to arrive at this conclusion when the second letter, confirming Bel-imperia's "writ," is delivered to him. Bearing this evidence that has completely restored his wavering faith in heaven's justice, he sets out to present his case before the one who is should be the principal channel through which justice flows into the kingdom:

I will go plain me to my lord the king,
And cry aloud for justice through the court.

(III. viii. 69–70)

As Henry Bullinger insists, in a contemporary discussion of a magistrate's duties, it is essential to the office of a good judge that he be willing to "hear every one" and not let his mind be "busied about other matters."[62] It is, of course, precisely in these ways that the king fails when Hieronimo attempts to present his case. He is so preoccupied with the Portuguese Viceroy's response to his proposal of a marriage that would unite the two kingdoms that he will not even listen to pleading cries for "justice" from the good and faithful servant who has devoted his life to the cause of justice in his kingdom. He also, as has been pointed out,[63] is guilty of another failing that renders a magistrate impotent as a justicer—partiality.

The king's apparent indifference, his amazing ignorance of the fact of Horatio's death, and the machinations of Lorenzo to hinder his efforts to present his suit all combine to convince Hieronimo that the heaven-sanctioned means of obtaining justice on earth are hopelessly corrupt and ineffectual. In his rage he announces his commitment to the lawless "path" of private revenge:

Stand from about me!
I'll make a pickaxe of my poniard,
And here surrender up my marshalship:
For I'll go marshal up the fiends in hell,
To be avenged on you for this.

(III. xii. 74–78)

In surrendering his office, he is abandoning what it represents—justice through the lawful means of public vengeance. That he sees the course of private revenge as damnable is apparent in this speech as well as in what he says when the king commands the courtiers to restrain him: "Nay, soft and fair: you shall not need to strive, / Needs must he go that the devils drive" (III. xii. 81–82).

Hieronimo's awareness of the damnable nature of the course he has chosen should be borne in mind if we are to understand clearly the crucial soliloquy beginning "*Vindicta mihi!*" and concluding with the same decision to revenge (III. xiii. 1–44). Fredson Bowers terms this speech a piece of "un-Christian sophistry," but I find such a label very misleading.[64] "Sophistry" implies hypocritical rationalization, and Hieronimo has been clearly shown to be a man of too much integrity and too much ethical sensitivity to be guilty of that. William Empson is not much closer to the mark when he contends that the "arguments

were meant to seem mad to the audience, or at least tragically de-
luded."[65] The speech is actually similar to Hamlet's "To be or not to
be" soliloquy and may indeed have been a model for it. Like Hamlet's
soliloquy, it begins with a consideration of alternative responses to his
situation—Christian patience or Stoic resignation versus active commitment against a sea of troubles. And like Hamlet's soliloquy, it reveals the speaker's growing awareness of the inadequacy of the
conventional views of human experience represented by these alternatives. By the end of the tragedy Hieronimo will be made to see that
there are more things in heaven and earth than are dreamt of in
anyone's "philosophy." The Christian commonplaces he utters initially are maxims he has accepted all his life, even up to the moment
he cried aloud to his king for justice, but the rage within him will not
permit Christian patience. He does not rationalize. The lines from
Seneca are not arguments to counter the biblical injunctions but *sententiae* he finds expressive of his own vengeful resolution and his
readiness to accept whatever consequences "destiny" decrees. The
question that exercises some scholars, whether or not his revenge
could be justified as an act of public vengeance, simply does not enter
his mind, because he has abandoned his office along with everything
it signifies and has surrendered himself to what he sees as a
damned role.

While Hieronimo has lost all faith in the heavenly sanctioned means
of public vengeance to achieve his end, he is still hungry for and ready
to seize upon any sign that heaven itself may be concerned with the
course of justice on earth. When Bel-imperia chides him for failing to
avenge Horatio, he sees it as clear evidence "that heaven applies our
drift, / And all the saints do sit soliciting / For vengeance on those
cursed murderers" (IV. i. 31–33). This speech invites comparison with
Albany's response in *King Lear* to the news that Cornwall has been
mortally wounded by his good servant during the blinding of
Gloucester:

> This shows you are above,
> You justicers, that these our nether crimes
> So speedily can venge.
>
> (IV. ii. 78–80)

In the context of *King Lear* one must be inclined to label such an
epiphany as illusory *mauvaise foi,* which is not to say that Shakespeare
is denying the existence of a moral order in the universe. There is a
cosmic pattern governing human experience, but it is no more acces-
sible to human reason or satisfying to the human moral sense than

the actions of Yahweh in the *Book of Job* or the amoral powers that control the fate of characters in Sophoclean tragedy.[66] Albany is desperately projecting a design of cause and effect as a way of maintaining a faith in heaven's benevolence that has been shaken by events. Like Hieronimo, he cannot accept the idea that the heavens are indifferent to human suffering.

Watching *The Spanish Tragedy* with the ironic perspective imparted by the introductory glimpses of divine "justicers," we are similarly made to perceive that such desperate grasping at signs of heavenly concern is a wishful imposition of design upon a chaotic reality. Hieronimo is still limited in his perception of reality by a conventional and largely illusory Christian Stoic sense of providential design. A short time later, after Balthazar and Lorenzo have agreed to act in his play, he reflects jubilantly,

> Why so!
> Now shall I see the fall of Babylon
> Wrought by the heavens in this confusion.
>
> (4. 1. 189–91)

The curious reference to the "fall of Babylon" suggests that he, like Hamlet, sees himself as a biblical scourge, a damned instrument of divine justice chosen out for a work of great destruction, and this sense of divine mission seems to account, at least in part, for the unrestrained bloodthirstiness of his subsequent actions.[67]

Hieronimo's vengeance in act 4 exemplifies all of the evils that the Elizabethans associated with private revenge. It is cruel and excessive, including among its victims Castile, whom Hieronimo has no reason to suspect of involvement in the murder of Horatio. This bloody denouement has been very sensitively and persuasively explained and justified "psychologically, theatrically, structurally," in an essay by M. D. Faber and Colin Skinner, who demonstrate how all of the violent action, including Hieronimo's biting out of his own tongue and the murder of Castile, is the inevitable result of Hieronimo's "frustrating, unsuccessful efforts to communicate his grievance."[68] They also make some perceptive observations concerning the probable effects of Hieronimo's tragedy on the Elizabethan audience. I am more concerned here, however, with what follows the denouement—the choric epilogue.

The play concludes as it began, with an eschatological revelation. The Ghost of Andrea expresses its pleasure with everything that has happened, including the miserable deaths of Bel-imperia and Hieronimo:

My Bel-imperia fallen as Dido fell,
And good Hieronimo slain by himself:
Ay, these were spectacles to please my soul.

(IV. v. 10–12)

And he or it goes on to announce that he will "beg at lovely Proserpine / That, by the virtue of her princely doom," he may be privileged
to dispense rewards to "my friends" and "on my foes work just and
sharp revenge"(IV. v. 16). "Obviously," remarks S. F. Johnson, "the
audience is supposed to accept Andrea's dispensations as the judgments of God." And he goes on to suggest that the matter need not
be scrutinized too closely, for, as William Baldwin acknowledges in
the second edition of *The Mirror for Magistrates* (1563) "a poet may
faine what he list . . . and [it] ought to be well taken of the hearers."[69]
Indeed he may, and I would suggest that we the "hearers" have much
to gain by considering the implications of what Kyd has "fained" in
his final judgment scene.

It is, I believe, anything but obvious that Andrea's dispensations are
"the judgments of God." God, or more precisely, "the gods" are
permitting the ghost to take over the divine function of dooming and
rewarding with no restraining guidelines other than its own affection
for friends and vindictiveness toward enemies, some of whom, Castile,
for instance, may not be deserving of the eternal punishment meted
out. The impression conveyed by the Induction, that the gods are not
greatly concerned with human affairs, are utterly indifferent to human
suffering, has been vividly confirmed. Indeed it has already been confirmed in the intervening acts by the spectacle of Hieronimo's tragedy.
A good man, whose only fault has been his unswerving commitment
to justice, has been utterly ruined, forced to damn himself in order to
serve "divine justice." Like Job, he is victimized by his own integrity,
as well as by a playful deity. But Job at least was finally vouchsafed
the hearing he craved. The final cruel irony of *The Spanish Tragedy*
is that Hieronimo will apparently not even be granted the hearing in
the Otherworld that he has been begging for in this one. The gods
have temporarily given up their roles as "justicers," have put the
process of hearing and dooming into the hands of Andrea, who appears by the end of the play to be acquiring the divine attitude of
total indifference to human suffering and whose decisions as a judge
of souls are determined wholly by personal bias and whim. The effect
of this final judgment scene is to intensify enormously the pity and
fear aroused by the tragedy of Hieronimo. G. K. Hunter may be
correct in saying that this last judgment scene "places everyone where
he morally belongs," but it is difficult to accept the idea that the drama

we have beheld was intended by Kyd to be "an allegory of perfect justice."[70]

I would conclude by expressing my agreement with Philip Edwards's observation that "Marlowe never wrote a less Christian play than *The Spanish Tragedy.*[71] No thematic formula that is in harmony with Christian orthodoxy can encompass or explain the eschatological crux. Its purpose may be grasped only if we are willing to see the play as essentially a pagan humanistic skeptical tragedy, closer in spirit and the tragic vision it imparts to Homeric epic or Euripidean tragedy than to the works of Kyd's own time, such as the *Mirror* or even the histories of Shakespeare, which, for all their complexity and openness to conflicting interpretations,[72] are shaped by essentially Christian visions of how the world works. The world Kyd depicts, like the world of *King Lear* or Seneca's tragedies, is "moral" only to the extent that the human beings within it are moral. One might even say that contrary to the orthodox opinion of the Spanish king, justice actually "flows" from this world to heaven, in the form of a projected design of justice that is largely illusory. To say that it is illusory, however, is not to say that it is without moral value. Good men like Hieronimo, or Albany in *King Lear,* in a very real sense vindicate the illusion by their fidelity in clinging to it.[73] Abandoning it frequently means jettisoning all ethical ballast, as we see in the cases of Lorenzo and Shakespeare's Edmund. Hieronimo's very integrity, as well as his tragic destruction, is bound up inextricably with his illusory concept of divine justice. His world is actually a far more terrible world than that of *Lear,* for in *The Spanish Tragedy* there are no redemptive presences, no Cordelias or Edgars; only vengeance-possessed human beings, among whom Hieronimo towers morally by comparison. Projecting a similar world view in the *Tamburlaine* plays, Marlowe celebrated Machiavellian *virtù.* Kyd's vision of the human condition is more genuinely tragic, closer perhaps to the mature vision of Marlowe's *Edward II* or his *Faustus.*

3

John Marston's Sparkling Steel

THE NEOSTOIC CALVINIST

LIKE HIS GREAT RIVAL JOSEPH HALL, JOHN MARSTON REVEALS IN HIS works a mind-set shaped by a combination of Neostoic and Calvinist beliefs. Critics have recognized both the Neostoicism and the Calvinism but see these elements as being at odds with each other. Alvin Kernan, for instance, sees the Marston of the verse satires as a Calvinist whose ridicule of the Puritans is actually directed at himself. He believes that Marston's Calvinism is evident only in the satires and in that he became a Neostoic when he began writing plays.[1] Anthony Caputi rejects this view and finds the Neostoic philosophy of the verse satires consistent with that of the plays.[2]

Apparently Kernan and Caputi assume that one could not be both a Calvinist and a Neostoic at the same time, but as we see in the writings of Calvin and his English disciples, this is not the case.[3] Moreover, the fact that Marston ridicules the Puritans both in his verse satires and his plays does not indicate that there is a conflict with his own Calvinism. By the time Marston began writing his satires, Calvinism had imposed itself on the Anglican reformation so decisively that, in the words of Paul R. Sellin, "the Calvinist temper of the Church of England at the end of the sixteenth century is unmistakably clear."[4] While it is true that some Calvinist doctrines were opposed by Anglican divines such as Donne and Hooker and the Laudian party after 1620, Calvinism ultimately prevailed. Marston eventually entered the Anglican priesthood, and while we have no sermons or theological writings on which to base a characterization of his religious views, the moral beliefs that clearly inform both the satires and his plays are closely in harmony with Calvinist, as well as Neostoic teachings. The transitions in his career from "sharp-fanged satirist" to Neostoic dramatist and finally Anglican divine probably did not involve any major conversions or changes in outlook. Though we cannot be sure, it seems likely that he found the Church, perhaps in spite of but more likely because of its Calvinist temper a congenial home.

The fact that Marston ridicules the Puritans both in his satires and his plays does not necessarily evidence a conflict with his Calvinism. There is a common tendency to identify English Calvinism with Puritanism. But as C. S. Lewis points out, "not all Calvinists were puritans."[5] Even as one would not identify all present-day American political "conservatives" with the so-called Religious Right or other extremist groups, so it would not be accurate to identify all English Calvinists in Marston's time with the Puritan extremists who inveighed against the theaters and vanity in dress and were obsessed with purging churches of popish "idolatry" in the form of graven images. Ronsard coined the term *puritain* in 1564, presumably after witnessing results of zealous activity such as the purging of Rouen Cathedral in 1562.[6] During the turbulent 1640s, the English counterparts of these Calvinist fanatics would exhibit their own zeal by smashing windows in Canterbury Cathedral, stabling their horses in York Minster, and closing the English theaters. It would be absurd to lump together such extremists as these and ardent Calvinists such as Spenser or Sidney as representative of the same kind of "Puritan" mindset.

When Marston satirizes Puritans he is usually targeting the types of vice that were masked by and practiced under a guise of religious zeal—lust, gluttony, greed and the like. In *The Dutch Courtesan,* for instance, he represents all these vices in the Mulligrubs, along with scrupulous puritanical hypocrisy. Mistresss Mulligrub is guiltily aware that their "wines are Protestant," like the Established Church and, therefore, Popish.[7] But she remembers fondly a premarital affair with Master Burnish (III. iii. 5) and is seduced by Cocledemoy as she follows her husband to the gallows, telling him to "make haste" with his taking off (V. iii. 94). Her cheating vintner husband is totally committed to gain, avowing "All things with / me shall seem honest that can be profitable." (III. iii. 58–59). But he is also given to gluttony, as he reveals when he attempts to devour a jowl of fresh salmon he believes has been mistakenly delivered to his house, relishing a feast "at other men's cost."(III. iii. 75). Nowhere, as far as I can determine, does Marston attack the movement to complete the reformation of the Anglican Church by removing "unscriptural and corrupt forms and ceremonies retained from the unreformed church" (O.E.D. A. 1), which is the principal hallmark of English Puritanism per se. He attacks pharisaical hypocrisy, which was most conspicuously and vocally expressed in his world by sanctimonious Puritan extremists obsessed with such "enormities," to use Justice Overdo's term, as excess in dress, the use of tobacco, and the corruption of theatregoers.[8]

The Puritans are actually not a major concern in most of his plays. While his characters refer in passing to Puritan hypocrisy,[9] the plays as a whole are informed by much larger thematic concerns. Beginning with *Antonio and Mellida I & II*, he reveals a Senecan preoccupation with the viability of Stoic ideals in a corrupt world that undermines Stoic faith by its apparent irrationality. In these plays, especially in *Antonio's Revenge*, he represents the Stoic-Skeptic dialectic that Kyd had introduced, and in perhaps his best play, *The Malcontent*, he fuses Stoicism with Christian fideism. In his last play, *Sophonisba*, which T. S. Eliot regarded as his best,[10] he celebrates Stoic integrity and perfectionism within a world as corrupt and threatening as that of *Antonio's Revenge*. It is a final dramatic expression of Marston's idealism, an element that has received comparatively little attention in critical studies of Marston.

Critics have tended to focus on Marston's obvious obsession with the ugly and disgusting. Citing passages from the plays, Samuel Schoenbaum remarks how "his biological interests extend beyond the sexual; he is preoccupied with the waste products of the body, with vomit and spit, sweat and excrement, abscesses and putrefaction."[11] And Theodore Spencer notes how the satires suggest "He was a man who liked to dwell on what disgusted him, whose attraction to sin took the form of violent denunciations of it, to whom loathing and lust were almost synonymous terms."[12] These strictures are reminiscent of what Plutarch said about the Stoics: "Just as the beetles are said to eschew the fine scent and to seek out the stink, so the Stoic love keeps company with what is most ugly and misshapen, and turns away from beauty."[13] And it cannot be denied that Marston exhibits a tendency to "seek out the stink," which may be partly a product of Stoic idealism combined with a Calvinistic recognition of human depravity. Unlike the Stoics Plutarch describes, however, Marston cannot be accused of turning away from beauty, specifically the moral and spiritual beauty that shines forth in a corrupt fallen world.

Caputi is among the very few critics who have recognized Marston's Stoic idealism that coexists with his focus on human corruption. As he notes, "The verse satires are laced with direct and indirect expressions of this idealism; the plays, particularly *Antonio's Revenge* and *Sophonisba*, set it forth more prominently."[14] The most obvious representations of it in the plays are Madonna-like female figures, two of whom are named, perhaps not coincidentally, Maria. In *The Dutch Courtesan*, Beatrice, another suggestively named emblem of female perfection, is placed in polar opposition to the titular protagonist. She, in effect, redeems the character Freevill from his bondage to Franceschina. In *Sophonisba*, Marston celebrates "the Wonder of Women," a Stoic ideal of feminine perfection. In this play too, Madonna-like purity is contrasted with its opposite in the form of

Erictho, an enchantress who confesses her inability "To inforce love." (V.i. 6).[15]

The Madonna-whore syndrome evidenced in these plays might be seen as revealing the limitations of an idealist who cannot accept human imperfection without total condemnation and disgust. But in two of his best plays, *The Malcontent* and *The Dutch Courtesan,* he depicts weak and sinful characters undergoing drastic reformations. If Marston is a cynic, he is not a cynic without hope for humanity. Many of his characters learn through their mistakes, and the Stoic ideal of human perfection, albeit qualified by a Montaignean recognition of man's limitations and need for God's grace, remains a model to be emulated.

Marston, as a Calvinist Neostoic, had a clear sense of the human factors that inhibit the realization of the classical Stoic ideal, mainly the passions, and as he shows repeatedly in his plays, "Man will break out, despite philosophy."[16] Like so much else in his thought, Marston's view of Stoicism parallels that of Montaigne, whose influence on the plays written after Florio's translation appeared in 1603, has been much discussed. Even before 1603, however, in the *Antonio* plays and the satires, one can discern an ambivalence toward Stoicism not unlike that of Montaigne in his early essays. One can see why Marston was so ready to assimilate Montaigne's ideas. As Philip J. Finkelpearl plausibly conjectures, reading Montaigne must have had the effects of reinforcing and clarifying ideas and attitudes Marston had already developed:

> For Marston, reading Montaigne was not a matter of discovering a whole new world. Instead, as is frequently the case when one author has an immense impact on another, Montaigne expressed memorably certain ideas and attitudes which Marston had held at one time or another, and he suggested relationships among these ideas which Marston had not previously perceived.[17]

There have been fine perceptive discussions of Montaignean influences and analogues in Marston's plays,[18] but a great deal more needs to be considered, especially with regard to the fideism that is very like Montaigne's and the Stoic-Skeptic dialectic that continues throughout Marston's dramatic canon and parallels somewhat the same dialectic in the *Essais.* While the focus of this study is how the dialectic informs English Renaissance tragedy, it is illuminating to consider Marston's tragedies in the light of his comedies, especially *The Dutch Courtesan* and *The Malcontent,* as well as *Antonio and Mellida I,* a comedy that maintains a Senecan tragic perspective that is in many ways harmonious with that of its bloody sequel, *Antonio's Revenge*.

DESPITE PHILOSOPHY: *ANTONIO AND MELLIDA* 1 AND 2

Recent critical discussion of Marston's *Antonio* plays has focused on the question of whether the plays should be seen as simply failures marred by linguistic and other excesses or parodies of plays being performed by rival adult companies. In a persuasive and influential article, R. A. Foakes argued that the Induction to *Antonio and Mellida I* makes it "clear that the play to follow will parody old ranting styles, make the children out-strut the adult tragedians, who were still performing the plays of Kyd and Marlowe, and burlesque common conventions."[19] Richard L. Levin repeatedly attacked this interpretation, along with other "new ironic readings" of what had come to be regarded as simply "bad plays," but I don't find his arguments very convincing or illuminating with regard to Marston.[20] Elizabeth M. Yearling provides additional support for Foakes's view that Marston knew what he was doing, though she agrees with some of Levin's points: "Already in the *Antonio and Mellida* Induction he illustrates the idea of stylistic decorum and, despite his own deficiencies and inconsistencies, he clearly condemns the old ranting mode and self-conscious attempts at linguistic affectation."[21]

As is typical with burlesque or parody, the conventions of an established genre are exaggerated and call attention to themselves. Indeed, what Marston is doing with the *Antonio* plays, especially *Antonio's Revenge*, is very like what Anthony Burgess does in his spy thriller, *Tremor of Intent*. Upon the well-worn framework of the James Bond formula established by Ian Fleming, Burgess fleshes out and molds a tale of intrigue that must fire the senses of even the most Bond-weary aficionado of the spy thriller. The typical Bond feats of appetite are duplicated and surpassed, sometimes to a well-nigh ridiculous extent. The protagonist has bedroom adventures that make Bond's conquests seem as crude and unfulfilling as an acned adolescent's evening affair with an issue of *Playboy*. And his gastronomic awareness is such that Bond is by comparison an epicurean tyro.

Similarly, Marston exaggerates the conventions and conflicts of the revenge tragedy as established by Kyd in *The Spanish Tragedy* and, perhaps, a lost *Hamlet*. The difference, of course, is that Burgess's novel is aesthetically far superior to any examples of the genre it parodies, while Marston's revenge play lacks the dramatic sophistication and concentrated tragic power that made *The Spanish Tragedy* a model to be emulated. It is, nonetheless, instructive to consider it in terms of how it reveals in exaggerated form the same conflicts and thematic concerns that inform Kyd's play. And even as Burgess reveals possibilities never thought of by earlier practitioners of the spy thriller, introducing a Dantean eschatology, for instance, and revealing the moral bankruptcy of the modern world, Marston's play is not confined to the elements Kyd had introduced. G. K. Hunter notes how the two *Antonio* plays introduce an original "political image of the court" as part of Marston's stated intention to show "what men were, and are":

> It is then as an image of the "realities" of power (i.e., *Realpolitik*) that Marston defends his *Antonio and Mellida,* and it is in this respect that we ought to see the newness of his play. This not the same thing, of course, as propounding its aesthetic success.[22]

Within the world of these plays dominated by policy, affectation, and corruption, there are, as Hunter observes, only "philosophic and political poses" which shape the whole ten act thematic structure.[23]

In the Induction to *Antonio and Mellida I,* the actor who will play the Stoic sage Feliche says that he doesn't understand the part he has been assigned, nor is he confident that he can play it. He goes on describe a character whose "spirit" represents a Stoic ideal:

> 'Tis steady, and must seem so impregnably fortress'd with his own content that no envious thought could ever invade his spirit; never surveying any man so unmeasuredly happy whom I thought not justly hateful for some true impovershment; never beholding any favor of Madam Felicity gracing another, which his well-bounded content persuaded not to hang in the front of his own fortune; and therefore as far from envying any man as he valued all men infinitely distant from accomplish'd beatitude. These native adjuncts appropriate to me the name of Feliche.[24]

The actor's doubts about being able to play such an unintelligible figure anticipate what will be a central focus in *Antonio's Revenge,* the inability of human beings to maintain a Stoic posture in what one critic calls "a Senecan world of disaster."[25] Marston seems not to have had his bloody sequel in mind at this point, for he announces, through the actor playing Antonio, that Feliche and other characters "but slightly drawn in this comedy, should receive more exact accomplishment in a second part." (Induction ll 135–36). Marston then goes on to reveal, through Feliche, some of the limitations of Stoic perfectionism.

Though supposedly impregnable within the fortress of his own content, Feliche utters torrents of bitter commentary on the characters he observes in the court of Piero Sforza, the "Italianate" tyrant Duke of Venice.[26] Responding to Castilio's self-abasement before Rosaline, he exclaims:

> O that the stomach of this queasy age
> Digests or brooks such raw unseasoned gobs
> And vomits not them forth! O slavish sots!
>
> (II. i. 87–89)

These lines and the remainder of the speech could have been taken from Marston's satires. Like Juvenal, Marston fuses Stoic and satiric voices, and his Feliche vividly illustrates Gordon Braden's point that "Stoic detachment is continuous and deeply involved with the most paralytic kind of anger."[27] Feliche denies that he is a misanthrope, insisting "I hate not man, but man's lewd qualities." (IV. i. 276), but his caustic commentary on the folly around him does not abate. His dramaturgical function in *Antonio and Mellida I* is that of satiric chorus, rather like Thersites in *Troilus and Cressida,* a figure some have suspected to be modeled on Marston himself.

The Stoic posture is also represented in this play by Andrugio, the defeated Duke of Genoa. Deprived of throne, wife, and son, hunted as a criminal, he defies Fortune and asserts his self-sufficiency:

> Fortune my fortunes, not my mind shall shake.
>
> (III. i. 62)

The context of this line in Seneca is Medea's defiant vow to pursue her vengeance. One should not of course expect the original context of a speech quoted by Marston, whether from Seneca or Montaigne, to be strictly relevant to his context, but it is worth noting that both this line and a subsequent lengthy paraphrase of a choric speech in the *Thyestes* (IV. i. 46–66) are expressions of Stoic *virtus* within Senecan contexts of impending disaster. As Hardin craig has noted, "With Seneca the very nature of things was disastrous, and calamity was irresistible and inescapable."[28] Thomas Rosenmeyer relates this partly to Stoic cosmology, as noted earlier, and partly to the Stoic cyclical conception of world history as a series of ages, each terminating in catastrophe as "the whole natural order is reduced to, or exalted into homogeneity, after which a new beginning is made."[29] The catastrophe may be viewed in Empedoclean terms as a triumph of harmony or Love, but in human affairs there is little basis for optimism since, as in Nietzsche's eternal recurrence, there will only be an endless reproduction of the same world peopled by the likes of Nero and following the same course of history. While the Stoic can still maintain a belief in the power of reason to achieve wisdom and perfection, the doctrine of cosmic catastrophe constantly threatens to undermine it. In Rosenmeyer's view, this threat informs the despair of the choruses and speakers in Senecan tragedy:

> But as we scan the writings of the Roman Stoics and watch out for the telltale signs of a deep pessimism, a kind of rogue Stoicism, gnawing away at the assertions of grim confidence, we are not disappointed. To a tragedian, needless to say, this aspect of the Stoic conception of natural history could not be more welcome.[30]

Marston did not express a belief in recurrent cosmic catastrophe, but the bitterness and pessimism of Seneca and the mood of impending disaster are abundantly evident even in *Antonio and Mellida I*. One of the reasons why the happy ending of *Antonio and Mellida I* is so startling and improbable is that Marston maintains a Senecan tragic perspective throughout most of the play.

Andrugio progresses toward "the fulfillment of the Stoic in penury, the kingdom of the self-sufficient man," to use Hunter's phrase,[31] but his progress is attended by much bitter rumination in the vein of Seneca's most despairing dramatic utterances concerning the diseased state of nature and the corruption of man. When his counselor, Lucio, brings him freshly dug up roots to eat he responds:

> O, thou hast wronged nature, Lucio:
> But boots not much; thou but pursu'st the world,
> That cuts off virtue 'fore it comes to growth
> Lest it should seed and so o'errun her son,
> Dull purblind Error. Give me water, boy;
> There is no poison in't I hope; they say
> That lurks in massy plate; and yet the earth
> Is so infected with a general plague
> That he's most wise that thinks there's no man fool,
> Right prudent that esteems no creature just;
> Great policy the least things to mistrust.
> Give me assay. [*They eat.*] How we mock greatness now!
>   (IV. i. 32–43)

Again we should not expect the Senecan context from which Marston takes part of this speech (ll. 36–37) to be strictly relevant to Marston's, but there are, nonetheless, some interesting parallels. In

Thyestes, Thyestes is speaking to young Tantalus, contrasting the perils of "greatness" with the mean and sure estate: "Crime enters not lowly homes, and in safety is food taken at a slender board; poison is drunk from cups of gold."[32] Though apprehensive about the danger to his sons, Thyestes is content: "'Tis a boundless kingdom,—power without kingdoms to be content." (l. 470).

Andrugio, who believes that his son is already dead, has the same view of the perils of greatness and consoles himself with the belief that he too is "content"as he paraphrases a choric speech from the *Thyestes* (342–68):

> Why man, I never was a prince till now.
> 'Tis not the bared pate, the bended knees,
> Gilt tipstaves, Tyrian purple, chairs of state,
> Troops of pied butterflies that flutter still
> In greatness' summer, that confirm a prince;
> 'Tis not the unsavory breath of multitudes
> Shouting and clapping with confused din
> That makes a prince. No, Lucio, he's a king,
> A true right king, that dares do aught save wrong,
> Fears nothing mortal but to be unjust;
> Who is not blown up with the flattering puffs
> Of spongy sycophants, who stands unmov'd
> Despite the justling of opinion,
> Who can enjoy himself maugre the throng
> That sits upon Jove's footstool, as I do,
> Adoring, not affecting majesty,
> Whose brow is wreathed with the silver crown
> Of clear content. This, Lucio, is a king,
> And of this empire every man's possessed
> That's worth his soul.
>
> (IV. i. 46–66)

He is about to be reunited with his son, and a scene of reconciliation with his enemy Piero will soon follow. Thyestes is about to be reconciled with Atreus, whereupon he and his sons will be horribly victimized by his vengeful brother. Young Tantalus tries to relieve his father's anxiety with Stoic injunctions to accept the gifts of a god (l. 471) and trust in the protection God bestows upon those who behave themselves: *"Respiciet deus bene cogitata."* (491). This latter pious injunction is spoken immediately prior to an aside in which Atreus exults over the fact that he has both Thyestes and his sons in his power. Thyestes is about to be tested beyond the limits of Stoic endurance.

Like Seneca, Marston creates a situation in which Stoic assumptions about the human capacity for endurance and self-sufficiency are thrown into question. No sooner does Andrugio utter his great speech on true kingliness than he is, from a Stoic point of view, unmanned by the mere mention of his erstwhile subjects, the Genoese:

> Name not the Genoese; that very word
> Unkings me quite, makes me vile passion's slave.
>
> . . .
>
> Spit on me, Lucio, for I am turn'd slave;
> Observe how passion domineers o'er me.
>
> (IV. i. 68–69, 83–84.)

Given the state of the world in which human beings exhibit nothing but baseness and treachery and only politicians like Piero thrive, how can one be truly "content"? Like the scenes in Piero's court in which Feliche exhibits an inability to live by the Stoic professions he utters (e.g., III. ii. 42 ff.),[33] this one serves to undercut self-conscious Stoic posturing.

Immediately after this breakdown, while he is lamenting his misfortunes, Andrugio is reunited with Antonio, who utters a line that supports Finkelpearl's view that Marston found in Montaigne expressions of his own ideas. In a comical exchange in which father and son come to recognize each other, Antonio says, "He is a fool that thinks he knows himself." (IV. i. 105) Marston probably had not yet read "On Experience," but his line virtually summarizes Montaigne's discussion of the injunction to know oneself.[34] Again it is interesting to compare Montaigne's view of this injunction with Seneca's and to see how Marston's line suggests that his thinking is already closer to that of Montaigne. Having revealed the vulnerability of Stoic self-sufficiency within a corrupted world, he questions as well the Stoic assumption that man is capable of knowing himself.

Another aspect of Stoicism that is criticized both in this play and its sequel is its tendency to encourage passivity. In response to Lucio's observation that he lacks the forces to vanquish his triumphant enemies, Andrugio defiantly asserts his indomitable spirit:

> Andrugio lives, and a fair cause of arms;
> Why, that's an army all invincible.
> He who hath that hath a battalion royal,
> Armor of proof, huge troops of barbed steeds,
> Main squares of pikes, millions of harquebus.
> O, a fair cause stands firm and will abide;
> Legions of angels fight upon her side.
>
> (III. i. 84–91)

The speech echoes and invites comparison with Richard II's attempts to cheer himself in the face of events beyond his control.[35] Like Richard, Andrugio takes comfort in the thought of heavenly assistance but prefers posturing as a victim to taking effective action on his own behalf. When Lucio suggests that he take refuge at the court of some foreign prince until conditions are ripe to "give revenge firm means," he refuses, using the excuse that no one can be trusted "in most princes' courts." (III. ii. 96). Then, like Richard inviting his few retainers to join with him and "sit upon the ground / And tell sad stories of the death of kings!" (III. ii. 155–56), Andrugio invites his companions to join him in a song, a diversion in which he can indulge his grief over the loss of Antonio, as well as his own *De Casibus* tragedy:

> Well, ere yon sun set I'll show myself myself,
> Worthy my blood. I was a duke; that's all.
> No matter whither but from whence we fall.
>
> (III. i. 113–15)

How his actions will "show" himself is not clear. When he reappears in IV. i., he is mainly preoccupied with Stoic posturing. Only after he is reunited with Antonio does he take any action, confronting Piero in his own court to claim the reward Piero has offered for his head. It's not clear that this action is influenced by Antonio, whom Andrugio urges not to "expostulate the heavens' will," even as he invites him to indulge in a passionate outpouring of shared grief (IV. i. 124–35).

To some extent, Marston's handling of Stoicism in this play anticipates his more serious treatment in *Antonio's Revenge.* Anthony Caputi sees the latter play as representing a conflict between "orthodox" or classical Stoicism and "Marstonian Neo-Stoicism." He sees Antonio as a kind of Neo-Stoic activist who convinces the more passively inclined "othodox" Stoics, Pandulpho and Alberto, that they must take retributive action against Piero.[36] In point of fact, Antonio's sentiments throughout both plays are unmistakably anti-Stoic. He has nothing but contempt for the basic principles common to both classical Stoicism and Christian Neo-Stoicism. He is a naive, excessively passionate youth, accurately described by Michael Higgins as "a seventeenth century hero of sensibility."[37] In *Antonio and Mellida I* he is more like the *adulescens* of Roman comedy. In the bloody sequel, as Caputi observes, "Antonio clearly disassociates himself from the burlesque character of *Antonio and Mellida.*"[38]

There are, however, elements of burlesque in *Antonio's Revenge,* as in the play it continues. The dramatic stereotypes of earlier drama, most obviously that of the stage Machiavel, are overdrawn to almost ludicrous extremes. The ghastly revenge that climaxes the action is a scene of complete abandonment more frenzied than the denouement of *The Spanish Tragedy,* and the rhetoric, especially that of the ranting tyrant Piero, is as extravagant as the action. But seeing *Antonio's Revenge* as a parody of earlier revenge tragedies and the drama of Marlowe does not mean that the play is without serious concerns. Burlesque or parody can be another way of treating serious themes, as Shakespeare shows in *Troilus and Cressida* by brutally travestying the conventions of courtly romance and the Greek heroic tradition even as he focuses on themes that inform *Hamlet* and *King Lear.*

As Cyrus Hoy observes, *Antonio's Revenge* "is a remarkable testament to human depravity, and the depravity which it details seems the more profound (and this is true of Elizabethan revenge tragedy generally) for the manner in which the God-given faculty of reason is directed to the gratification of human lust and human greed."[39] What makes it especially remarkable in this regard is that virtually all the characters, excepting only the innocent victims Mellida and Julio, are either depraved from the beginning or become corrupted as the play progresses. Even Maria, one of Marston's madonna figures, a "faithful, modest, chaste" image of matronly virtue who disdains all outward show and is untouched by the "flame of crackling vanity," (I. ii. 46–60) surrenders in the end to the same vengeful bloodlust that possesses her son and the other conspirators, two of whom have degenerated from postures of Stoic constancy.

It is these descents into depravity by the good characters that make the play memorable as a study of evil. The principal villains, Piero and his instrument Strotzo, are so depraved that it's difficult to take them seriously. Even the opening scene in which Piero appears *"smear'd in blood, a poniard in one hand"* followed by Strotzo with his strangling cord has a grotesquely comic quality, as does the scene in which Strotzo, prompted by Piero, enters with a cord about his neck, like Spenser's Despair, and while declaiming his guilt in extravagant terms, facilitates his own strangling (IV. i. 157ff). This latter piece of black comedy may have been modeled partly on the hanging of Pedringano in *The Spanish Tragedy,* an incongrously comic scene that was probably relished by an audience not unused to laughing while a malefactor was taken off.[40]

Initially, the world of the play is one in which characters can be readily defined in strictly opposed moral terms. In extreme opposition to the palpable villainy of Piero and the baseness of his sycophants are set the idealistic Antonio, the chaste and loving Mellida, the madonnalike Maria, and the Stoic sages Pandulpho and Alberto, whose very presence in the corrupt court is, as Hunter notes, rather puzzling.[41] By the end of the play, these polar oppositions have largely disappeared, and the surviving good characters have been morally reduced to a villainous level.

The vulnerability of the Stoic to corruption is a major focus in this play, as it is in *The Dutch Courtesan,* wherein a Stoic "man of snow" is overpowered by lust.[42] Introducing a sage in *Antonio's Revenge* as a spokesman representing an alternative response to oppressive evils recalls the *Vindicta mihi!* soliloquy in *The Spanish Tragedy* (III. xiii. 1–20) in which Hieronimo considers and rejects Stoic resignation as an option, along with the Christian alternative enjoining patience and trust in God's justice. Shakespeare does the same thing in *Hamlet,* introducing a character, Horatio, who embodies the Stoic ideal and represents it to the revenger protagonist. This is one among many startling similarities between Marston's play and *Hamlet* that have prompted critics to attempt conjectural reconstructions of a lost *Ur-Hamlet* on which both plays were presumably modeled.[43] But an important difference is that Shakespeare's Stoic sage remains uncorrupted, while Pandulpho utterly jettisons his moral purpose and surrenders himself to revenge.

As he first appears in *Antonio's Revenge,* Pandulpho is as overdrawn an image of Stoic virtue as Piero is of Machiavellian villainy. When Antonio expresses his fears engendered by "horrid dreams," heavenly "prodigies," and an ominous nosebleed, Pandulpho rebukes him:

> Tut, my young prince, let not thy fortunes see
> Their lord a coward. He that's nobly born
> Abhors to fear; base fear's the brand of slaves.
> He that observes, pursues, slinks back for fright,
> Was never cast in mold of noble spright.
>
> (I. ii. 141–45)

Fear is beneath the sage, and very shortly Pandulpho has the opportunity to exhibit his own mastery of grief as well and to utter another Stoic lecture on fortitude.

The murder of Pandulpho's son, Feliche, provides a spectacular test of the Stoic commonplace that tyrants can kill but never hurt a man.[44] When Pandulpho, Antonio and the rest of the court appear, Piero exhibits the hung up body of Feliche to his father and justifies the murder in terms of family honor, inventing a discovery *in flagrante delicto* of his daughter, Mellida, in the arms of the victim. In response to Forobosco's urging to "Keep league with reason," Piero renounces reason itself:

> There glow no sparks of reason in the world;
> All are rak'd up in ashly beastliness;
> The bulk of man's as dark as Erebus;
> No branch of reason's light hangs in his trunk;
> There lives no reason to keep league withal;
> I ha' no reason to be reasonable.
>
> (I. ii. 222–27)

He is, of course, counterfeiting a passion he doesn't feel, but he is also defining an antirational antithesis to Stoic faith in the rationality of Nature and the belief in right reason. While hardly a statement of a system of beliefs it is a crude expression of a skeptical viewpoint that will be to a large extent vindicated by events in the play. Moreover, the characters who have professed beliefs opposed to it, most notably Pandulpho, will themselves become converted to an equally antirational stance.

The responses of the various characters in this scene to Piero's bloody mischief serve to define them. The death of Andrugio is announced by Strotzo, who, prompted by Piero, feigns "*seeming passion*" and describes the death with an overly elaborate figure that leaves the precise cause unidentified (I. ii. 242–46), whereupon Maria swoons, dutifully yearning to join her husband in death, Antonio pours out his grief and rage, and the Stoics counsel patience and fortitude. Alberto's urging to "be patient," exercise reason and "command affects" infuriates Antonio, who expresses his contempt for what he regards as canned philosophy in terms often applied to the Stoics by their critics:

> 'Slid, sir, I will not, in despite of thee.
> Patience is slave to fools, a chain that's fix'd
> Only to posts and senseless log-like dolts.
>
> (I. ii. 270–72)

Like Job rebuking his comforters, Antonio rejects such "comfort" from one who has not experienced his suffering:

> Confusion to all comfort! I defy it.
> Comfort's a parasite, a flatt'ring Jack,
> And melts resolv'd despair. O boundless woe,
>
> (I. ii. 284–86)

At this point Pandulpho is able to demonstrate his mastery over his own emotions by laughing about the murder of his son. Even Alberto is astonished by this, but Pandulpho explains that if one considers the situation rationally, then there is no cause for grief. If Feliche was innocent, then he is a "thrice blessed soul" (I. ii. 318). If, on the other hand, he was "leper'd" with the crime of dishonoring Mellida, as Piero said he was, then he got what he deserved. Pandulpho then gives his young friends a brief lecture on Stoic fortitude and revenge:

> The gripe of chance is weak to wring a tear
> From him that knows what fortitude should bear.
> Listen, young blood, 'tis not true valor's pride
> To swagger, quarrel, swear, stamp, rave, and chide.
> To stab in fume of blood, to keep loud coil,
> To bandy factions in domestic broils,
> To dare the act of sins whose filth excels
> The blackest customs of blind infidels.
>
>   .   .   .
>
> This heart in valor even Jove out-goes;
> Jove is without, but this 'bove sense of woes;
> And such a one eternity. [To Feliche.] Behold
> Good morrow, son; thou bid'st a fig for cold.
>
>   (I. ii. 321–38)

In sum, nothing can make the truly valorous man surrender to his passions. Having raised his mind above feeling itself, he is braver than Jove, who cannot feel. When he suffers an injury, he neither grieves over it nor rages against his antagonist, and he never degrades himself by seeking retaliation. Vendettas and other "domestic broils" occasioned by the quest for blood vengeance reduce men to a depraved condition wherein they become less than men. He is speaking in general terms but it is clearly understood that blood vengeance on Piero would be an especially filthy "act of sins" since he happens to be a prince.

Subtly undercutting this textbook Stoic posture are the echoes of *The Spanish Tragedy* in Pandulpho's speeches. When he tells Alberto that the two of them "Will talk as chorus to this tragedy" (I. ii. 299), he is echoing Revenge's speech to Andrea in the opening scene of Kyd's play, in effect, rejecting any notion of responding actively to his catastrophe, and when he refuses to vent his passion, "cry, run raving up and down / For my son's loss" (l. 312–15), he is rejecting the role of Hieronimo. But Marston's audience, who were familiar with his model, might have found these echoes ironic. They might have recalled that Revenge is hardly a passive choric figure in *The Spanish Tragedy*. He or it is a "mood soliciting [the] souls" of the revengers, more like a director than a chorus, and his role is eventually taken over by Hieronimo. Pandulpho assumes that he can remain a choric figure, passively witnessing for Stoic fortitude and constancy, but his own passion will not allow this, and he is destined to become, like Hieronimo, an active instrument of vengeance and an embodiment of everything he has condemned in his lecture on fortitude.

Marston continues to define Stoic perfectionism through Pandulpho in the following scene as he and Piero engage in stichomythia consisting mainly of *sententiae* borrowed from the *Thyestes* and *Octavia*. The agon itself is stock Senecan fare, the tyrant attempting to impose his will on one whose only defense is a Stoic sense of moral purpose, and Pandulpho is clearly the victor morally. When the exasperated Piero threatens to use his power to make his "doting stoic" opponent "wretched," Pandulpho defies him and affirms his own power to be where he will: "A wise man's home is wheresoe'er he is wise" (II. i. 163). The essential self cannot be imprisoned, nor can it be banished. Piero banishes Pandulpho and seizes all he has but is frustrated by his failure to "disease" the old Stoic's tranquillity of mind. In their parting exchange, Pandulpho triumphantly asserts his self-sufficiency: "Loose fortune's rags are lost; my own's my own." (II. ii. 170).

The vindication of Stoic morality in these early scenes involving Pandulpho is misleading. The remainder of the play throws it and its underlying assumptions into question. Like Seneca himself, Marston subjects Stoic philosophy to the test of a confrontation with a world that appears to challenge the very notion of rational providential design, the world shaped by "what men were, and are . . . what men must be." The comforting assumptions of Stoic philosophy that underlie all of its heroic injunctions and sustain the posture of the sage are thrown into question by the palpable triumphs of evil which generate a bitter skeptical response that is voiced initially by Antonio.

Having spurned Alberto's Stoic counsel, Antonio peruses Seneca's *De Providentia,* which he finds equally meaningless. Injunctions to surpass God by enduring bravely and to despise fortune and sorrow can only come from one who has not suffered, and like one of the characters in *The Malcontent,* Antonio remarks on how Seneca's luxurious lifestyle was hardly a witness for his philosophy. For someone like Antonio, Stoic passivity is intolerable, and when he visits the imprisoned Mellida, he vows to act, wanting only a course to follow (II. ii. 105–10).

Having been commanded by Andrugio's ghost to avenge his murder, Antonio becomes focused on his task and never swerves from it, though, like Hamlet, he forgoes a perfect opportunity to stab his enemy. Like Hamlet, he lets the opportunity pass with the stated intention of inflicting greater punishment, but unlike Hamlet, he gives us no reason to suspect that this is due to any unstated scruples or rationalization, for no sooner does Piero withdraw than he carries out the brutal murder of Julio. Unlike Hamlet's impulsive thrust through the arras that kills Polonius, this act of butchery is fully premeditated. Neither his professed love for Antonio, his pleas to be spared for his sister's sake, nor the trust he expresses in one who supposedly loves him can save the child, though Antonio does hesitate momentarily for Mellida's sake and needs to be urged on by the ghost.

As he carries out this ritual murder over the tomb of Andrugio, Antonio makes himself one with pitiless all-devouring nature:

> Now barks the wolf against the full-cheek'd moon
> Now lions' half-clamm'd entrails roar for food,
> Now croaks the toad and night-crows screech aloud,
> Fluttering 'bout casements of departing souls;
> Now gapes the graves, and through their yawns let loose
> Imprison'd spirits to revist earth;
> And now, swart night, to swell thy hour out,
> Behold I spurt warm blood in thy black eyes. [*Stabs* Julio.]
>
> (III. i. 187–94)

His lines echo an earlier speech in which he expresses his utter disgust with bestial humanity (III. i. 110–24), which includes nearly everyone around him, the innocent as well as the wicked:

> Piero, Maria, Strotzo, Julio,
> I'll see you all laid—I'll bring you all to bed,
>
> (III. i. 103–4)

But the murder of Julio makes him an embodiment of the depravity and "devilish cruelty" he had denounced.

Having begun his vengeance, Antonio disguises himself as a fool and waits his opportunity to complete it. Responding to Alberto's objection that another disguise, that of a railing malcontent, would be more appropriate and would permit more access to Piero, he defends his choice of disguise, citing the authority of the master of deceit:

> Why, by the genius of that Florentine,
> Deep, deep-observing, sound-brain'd Mach'avel
> He is not wise that strives not to seem fool.
>
> (IV. i. 23–25)

Justifying his actions with reference to Machiavelli simply confirms what the actions themselves have already revealed, that he has descended to Piero's moral level. To make the point even more explicit,

Antonio refutes Maria's objection that the disguise is unseemly by dismissing conventional morality itself:

> Pish!
> Most things that morally adhere to souls
> Wholly exist in drunk opinion,
> Whose reeling censure, if I value not,
> It values nought.
>
> (IV. i. 30–34)

Still defending his disguise, he praises the "beatitude" of folly itself in terms that suggest its essential similarity to Stoic constancy:

> He is not capable of passion;
> Wanting the power of distinction,
> He bears an unturn'd sail with every wind;
> Blow east, blow west, he stirs his course alike.
>
> (IV. i. 39–42)

The lines are ambiguous, conveying at the same time opposing images of weathercock waywardness and steadiness.

Antonio's professed nihilism and capacity for ruthless action coexist rather oddly with an element of piety that enables him to accept the death of Mellida as the will of heaven. His submissive apostrophe to Divine Majesty has an almost Calvinistic ring:

> Ay, Heaven, thou mayst; thou mayst, Omnipotence.
> What vermin bred of putrefacted slime
> Shall dare to expostulate with thy decrees?
> O heaven, thou mayst indeed: she was all thine,
> All heavenly; I did but humbly beg
> To borrow her of thee a little time.
>
> (IV. ii. 1–6)

And he will not let his grief transport him into blasphemy (l. 11). At the end of the play, he, along with Pandulpho, will refrain from suicide because of Christian scruples and will withdraw into a monastery. It is tempting to suggest that this mixture of contraries reflects that of Marston's audience, whose Calvinist piety no doubt enhanced the pleasure of watching the dismemberment of a seminary priest or an unlucky recusant. Perhaps, like Marlowe, Marston was deliberately representing the ruthlessness of his own contemporaries.[45] Or perhaps we are intended merely to see Antonio's piety as a vestige of the idealism he has jettisoned in the pursuit of vengeance.

The once romantic idealist who has become a Machiavellian deceiver and murderer joins forces with the sage who can no longer sustain his Stoic posture or his moral purpose. In the most memorable lines in the play, Pandulpho confesses his human weakness:

> Man will break out, despite philosophy.
> Why, all this while I ha' but play'd a part,
> Like to some boy that acts a tragedy,
> Speaks burly words and raves out passion;
> But when he thinks upon his infant weakness,
> He droops his eye. I spake more than a god,
> Yet am less than a man.
> I am the miserablest soul that breathes.
>
> (IV. ii. 69–76)

Discarding his passive role as sage and choric commentator, he will commit himself to revenge. The fact that this speech was actually uttered by a boy actor must have graphically impressed upon the audience the discrepancy between the superhuman role a would-be sage assumes and what human limitations will allow. For a boy actor to become actually the adult figure he is playing is as impossible as it is for a human being to become morally superior to the gods merely by striking the posture of the sage. It is as though Marston is answering the old Stoic commonplace that all the world's a stage by demonstrating the futility of trying to impose a theatrical reality on human experience. Shakespeare suggests much the same thing in *Hamlet,* a play equally abundant in theatrical reference, by having his protagonist discover the inadequacy of all self-defining conventional roles along with all conventional explanations of human experience.

As Pandulpho and his fellow revengers, Antonio and Alberto, bury Feliche, Pandulpho reveals that he is discarding more than his Stoic illusions of self-sufficiency. In answer to Alberto's observation that his voice is "crack'd," he says,

> Why, coz, why should it not be hoarse and crack'd,
> When all the strings of nature's symphony
> Are crack'd and jar? Why should his voice keep tune,
> When there's no music in the breast of man?
>
> (IV. ii. 91–94)

In most discussions of *Antonio's Revenge,* the real significance of these lines has been overlooked. It has not been noticed that Pandulpho is rejecting a belief that underlies all of Stoic moral doctrine, the belief in the rationality of Nature. He sees only chaos in Nature and, therefore, like his Machiavellian antagonist, finds "no reason to be reasonable."

Having thus rejected all of his inhibiting principles, Pandulpho commits himself wholly to vengeance. He and Antonio are joined by the foolish courtier Balurdo, whom Piero had imprisoned, and by Maria, who has apparently been engaged in preparing the Thyestean banquet (V. iii. 45–46). Once they have Piero in their power they rip out his tongue and present Julio's limbs. Then, determined to kill his soul with his body, they torment him with the prospect of his own damnation. They are quite literally possessed by their vengeful rage, as Antonio makes clear:

> Now, therefore, pity, piety, remorse,
> Be aliens to our thoughts; grim fire-ey'd rage
> Possess us wholly.
>
> (V. iii. 89–91)

Marston's representation of vengeful rage in this frenzied climax is thoroughly Senecan. In De Ira Seneca remarks that "you have only to behold the aspect of those possessed by anger to know that they are insane."[46] But he also observes that this madness is exhibited only by those who possess reason, "for while it [anger] is the foe of reason, it is, nevertheless, born only where reason dwells." Wild beasts become angry but "are neither stirred by injury nor bent on the punishment or the suffering of another; for even if they accomplish these ends, they do not seek them."[47] In Marston's play, as Cyrus Hoy notes, "the God-given faculty of reason is directed to the gratification of human lust and greed."[48] In the final scene, it is also in the service of rage directed at one who has served his own appetites with pitiless calculation. In giving full rein to their rage, Antonio and the other conspirators deliberately relinquish the most redeeming qualities of their own humanity and descend to the demonic, subbestial level of their victim.

Critics have been troubled by the ending of Antonio's Revenge. It is assumed that revengers must be punished and that, like Hieronimo and Titus Andronicus, they must die violently.[49] But Marston frustrates the expectations he raises, even as he did in the first Antonio play, and even Antonio is "amaz'd" when, instead of punishment for the crime they have just confessed, the conspirators are offered "What satisfaction outward pomp can yield, / Or chiefest fortunes of the Venice state" (V. iii. 140–41). However, Antonio makes it clear that such rewards do not tempt them. They have already made "other vows" to withdraw from the world into monastic seclusion and spend

the remainder of their lives in prayer. Only Christian constraints prevent them from committing suicide:

> We know the world; and did we know no more
> We would not live to know . . .
>
> (V. iii. 146–47)

From one perspective, it is a curiously optimistic conclusion to a
drama of human depravity. If Marston were truly cynical and pessimistic about mankind, he would have the conspirators capitalizing on the
gratitude of the Venice state. As it is, he suggests that humans are
capable of learning through suffering and even transcending the corrupting effects of their own evil deeds. In *The Malcontent,* which can
also be seen as a dramatization of classical Stoic beliefs concerning
vengeance, the aroused conscience plays a vital role in bringing about
the reformation of several characters. In *Antonio's Revenge,* the
avengers are clearly prompted by a moral sense to seek atonement
that has survived their vengeful abandonment. It is a puzzling and
paradoxical expression of Marston's idealism.

A HEARTY FAITH TO ALL: *THE MALCONTENT*

Marston's handling of vengeance in *Antonio's Revenge* is thoroughly Senecan. His very different handling of the materials of the
revenge play in *The Malcontent* may reflect the influence of Plutarch,
another classical moral philosopher sometimes erroneously referred
to as a Stoic but who, in fact, despised the Stoics and sought to refute
both them and the Epicureans in a number of treatises.[50] Many of
Plutarch's ideas, especially with regard to ethics and the providential
ordering of the universe, are, in fact, wholly in harmony with those
of the Stoics, whom he seems to have misunderstood and frequently
misrepresented in his *Moralia,* which was translated into English by
Philemon Holland and published in 1603, the same year many believe
Marston wrote *The Malcontent.* For all his antipathy toward the Stoics,
Plutarch was a major source of Stoic ideas during the Renaissance.
His essay *On Stoic Self-Contradictions* is full of quotations from Stoic
writers, chiefly Chrysippus, whose works have been lost.

It seems likely that Marston read this particular essay, which begins
with an exhortation to maintain consistency in one's life and teaching.
Philosophers especially are obliged to be consistent, and he goes on
to criticize the Stoics in particular for their failure in this regard. While
Zeno, Cleanthes, and Chrysippus wrote much about the active life of

public service, they themselves "tasted the lotus of leisure" in their academic retreats:

> Consequently it is not unevident that they lived consistently with the writings and sayings of others rather than with their own, since their lives were passed altogether in that tranquillity which is commended by Epicurus and Hieronymus. Chrysippus himself at least in his fourth book on Ways of Living thinks that the scholastic life is no different from the life of pleasure.[51]

In *The Malcontent,* a character denounces Seneca for this same inconsistency:

> Out upon him! He writ of temperance and fortitude, yet lived like a voluptuous epicure and died like an effeminate coward. (III. i. 25–27)[52]

This disparaging reference may reflect Marston's own critical attitude toward Stoicism, beyond what the breakdown of Pandulpho in *Antonio's Revenge* reveals in terms of the difficulty in maintaining a perfectionist stance in a hostile, disordered world, but it should be noted that the remark is uttered by Pietro, the usurping Duke of Genoa, who will himself be subjected to a Stoic therapy that will heal his soul.

An essay that seems to have exerted a more pervasive influence on this play, however, is Plutarch's "On the Delays of the Divine Vengeance," a work that makes one wonder why Plutarch was so hostile to the Stoics, since it agrees completely with Stoic moral philosophy. In "The Divine Vengeance," Plutarch vindicates divine providence against the charges that its delay in bringing punishment to evildoers makes the punishment ineffectual and, moreover, promotes disbelief in the gods. He argues that God's delay in punishing the wicked can be seen as one of the ways in which He serves as an example to men. He would have us be guided by reason rather than emotion "and would teach us not to strike out in anger at those who have caused us pain."[53] Another reason He delays in some cases is that the offender may become repentant and cured of his viciousness. We need only consider how changeable human nature is. Plutarch offers several illustrative examples of famous men who experienced radical moral transformations; then he draws an analogy between an Egyptian law that provides that a pregnant woman under sentence of death shall not be executed until her child is born and the practice of God and sensible men of delaying vengeance until the good that is in an evildoer manifests itself. Still another reason that God may delay His vengeance in some cases is that He may wish to use evil men as scourges, allowing them to inflict His punishment on other men before He punishes them for their wickedness.

After citing a fourth plausible reason for God's delay—His desire to inflict punishment at a fitting time and in a fitting manner—Plutarch observes that all of his arguments have been based upon the assumption that there is a delay in most cases, whereas it may easily be demonstrated that there is usually no delay, that punishment follows immediately upon a crime. The punishment he means is the torment inflicted by the aroused conscience, which includes remorse, nightmares, apparitions, and evil portents. and inevitably evildoers must also be tormented by the realization that their wickedness is futile.

Because of these miseries of the soul that attend every wicked deed, evildoers are filled with a yearning to be freed of their sense of guilt:

> so the thought that the soul of every wicked man revolves within itself is this: how it might escape from the memory of its iniquities, drive out of itself the consciousness of guilt, regain its purity, and begin life anew.[54]

As noted earlier, Marston expresses his belief in the moral healing power of the aroused conscience in both his dramatic and nondramatic works. In Satire VIII of *The Scourge of Villainy* he, like Malevole in *The Malcontent,* rails against the "base slauery" of the souls of men to lust and "sensuall luxurie." Wantonness and the pursuit of amorous pleasures have shrouded reason, "the fairest splendour of our soule," and subordinated it to passion:

> But now affection, will, concupiscence,
> Haue got o're Reason chiefe preheminence.

(176–77)

He concludes by invoking "the purer part of conscience":

> Returne, returne, sacred *Synderesis,*
> Inspire our truncks, let not such mud as this
> Pollute vs still. Awake our lethargie,
> Raise vs from out our brain-sicke foolerie.

(211–14)

In Satire XI he again decries the "preheminence" of sense over reason and describes the effect on Synteresis:

> So cold and dead is his *Synderesis,*
> That shadowes by odde chaunce sometimes are got,
> But o the substance is respected not.

(236–38)[55]

He is apparently describing what William Ames would call a "seared" or "cauterized" conscience:

> This sort of Conscience is found chiefly in those, who after they haue been *enlightened,* against their Conscience, doe giue themselues to a wicked life.
> In these the Synteresis it self, or *Law of Conscience,* hath its course stopped, & for (a) time is in a manner extinguished, *Jude.* 10. Whatsoever they *know naturally,* as beastes which are *without reason,* in those things they corrupt themselues. This suppressing of the naturall practicall knowledge, which is ingraffed in all men, is by the Philosophers called απολί-θωσις because such kind of men are changed as it were into stones, as in the Scriptures they are said to haue a *hard* and *stony* heart, by other Philosophers it is called θηριότης and θηριωδεία, because such men become altogether brutish.[56]

There are several types of conscience represented in *The Malcontent.* The villain Mendoza, the sycophant Bilioso, and the old panderess Maquerelle have evidently "seared" their consciences. They are beyond reformation, and a ruler bent on promoting the moral welfare of his citizens must either banish such as these or sentence them to death. Persons with fearful or accusing consciences,[57] like Pietro and his faithless wife Aurelia, can be moved to repentance, and Marston suggests that it is the duty of one who is in a position to administer punishment to show them their errors and let their consciences incline them toward a correct purpose. Marston's position in this regard is Stoic as well as Christian. As I noted earlier, the concept of moral stewardship, generally regarded as a Calvinist notion with Scriptural roots, could find a great deal of support in the writings of the ancient Stoics, who generally shared the belief that while one should be primarily concerned with preserving one's own moral purpose through self-discipline, one should also strive to restore one's less disciplined fellows to a correct moral purpose as well and thus bring about an improvement of the community as a whole.[58]

Caputi discusses how Marston's view of the role of the satirist resembles the Stoic conception of the teacher as moral healer,[59] but he doesn't relate this point to *The Malcontent,* perhaps because initially Malevole appears to be the very antithesis of a moral healer. Disguised as a railing malcontent, with complete freedom of speech, he intends to torment the man who usurped his throne. He begins by informing Pietro that he is a cuckold and incensing him to take revenge on Mendoza with his own hands. Having thus revealed himself as an Iago-like Machiavellian manipulator, he announces his vengeful agenda in a soliloquy that sounds not unlike one of Iago's:

Lean thoughtfulness, a sallow meditation,
Suck thy veins dry, distemperance rob thy sleep!
The heart's disquiet is revenge most deep:
He that gets blood, the life of flesh but spills,
But he that breaks heart's peace, the dear soul kills.—

　　　　　. . .

Duke, I'll torment thee: now my just revenge
From thee than crown a richer gem shall part.
Beneath God naught's so dear as a calm heart.

(I. iii. 152–69)

A Jacobean audience, accustomed to sermons and explications of Scripture, would recognize that "heart" here is synonymous with conscience.[60] Malevole, like other revengers in the drama and Nashe's Cutwolfe, intends to take his revenge on his antagonist's soul. Pietro is a weak but ethically sensitive man whose conscience is already weighted with the damnable act of usurpation. Malevole apparently hopes to goad him into the additional crime of murdering Mendoza, after which Pietro's tormenting conscience will drive him to total despair and the damnation of his soul.

But again, as in the *Antonio* plays, Marston frustrates the expectations he raises. Instead of an avenging fiend, Malevole becomes a minister of spiritual restoration who effects a bloodless purgation of the Court. In the process he himself undergoes a moral transformation and acquires qualities that enable him to function more effectively as a just ruler. When his faithful retainer Celso enters, Malevole, formerly Duke Altofronte, recalls how he had fallen from power. Like Prospero, he had been too trusting: "I wanted those old instruments of state, / Dissemblance and suspect." (I. iv. 9–10). He has learned from his bitter experience, and as the play progresses he exhibits both Stoic *virtus* and Machiavellian *virtù,* which enable him to capitalize on the opportunities fortune provides.[61]

In an illuminating chapter of his book on Marston, George Geckle points out how the "central dramatic symbol" of *The Malcontent* is "the highly traditional Wheel of Fortune, a symbol around which both the structure of the play and its most serious themes literally revolve."[62] He is certainly correct in seeing Fortune as a central focus in the play and noting how the principal characters define themselves to a large extent by their attitudes toward it. But his characterization of Malevole is a bit oversimplified:

The man who trusts in God, avoids vice, and manages to transcend Fortune's influence is Malevole. Whereas Mendoza, following Machiavelli, makes no distinction between Fortune and Providence, Malevole becomes acutely aware of the crucial difference. He chooses to combat Fortune not with fortitude or *virtù* but with prudence and, ultimately, spiritual devotion.[63]

Certainly he places his faith in heaven, and his faith is ultimately vindicated, but he also capitalizes on opportunities, manipulates the other characters, and exhibits those qualities associated with skillful statecraft that Machiavelli refers to either collectively or singly as *virtù*.[64] He is, in fact, as William Babula argues, a Machiavel. He is also a satirist, who rails at the vices of the Court, but as Babula notes, "His role as a Machiavel gives him the effectiveness that the ranting satirist lacks."[65] Indeed he exercises prudence, or, in his own words, "mature discretion," which is "the life of state" (IV. v. 146), and thus is able to carry out the reform of his state.

Geckle's view of Mendoza is also rather questionable. It's not that he fails to make a distinction between Fortune and Providence. Providence does not enter his thoughts. He glories in the gifts of Fortune and attributes his success to shamelessness (II. i. 29) and "impudence" (II. v. 94). Machiavelli, too, seems to have thought little about Providence. He didn't deny its existence, but it was irrelevant to his projects of formulating a science of statecraft and explaining human history. He would, however, have regarded someone like Mendoza as a fool for trusting Fortune so completely, believing that "the prince who bases himself entirely on fortune is ruined when fortune changes."[66] Fortune is a woman to be overmastered by the adventurous possessor of *virtù*.[67]

In spite of his assumed name, Malevole is a benevolent Machiavel who combines *virtù* with Stoic faith and is able not to transcend Fortune's influence but to capitalize on opportunities as they are presented. Machiavelli, it will be recalled, thought that such great leaders as Moses, Cyrus, and Romulus should be admired both for the opportunities they had and their abilities to exploit them:

And in examining their life and deeds it will be seen that they owed nothing to fortune but the opportunity which gave them matter to be shaped into what form they thought fit; and without that opportunity their powers would have been wasted, and without their powers the opportunity would have come in vain.[68]

Benevolent Machiavels are not numerous in Renaissance English drama, but Malevole is hardly unique. Shakespeare's Henry V could have been modelled on Machiavelli's successful prince, and his Duke Vincentio in *Measure for Measure* is a politic manipulator who knows how to use a subordinate effectively to carry out a hateful task and enhance his own image in the process.[69]

Geckle is certainly correct in observing that Malevole places his trust in God. Like Mendoza, he frequently refers to Fortune but obviously maintains the orthodox Christian view that she or it is in the service of Providence. When it is apparent that everything is in place for him to regain power, he tells Celso,

> I'll give thee all anon. My lady comes to court; there is a whirl of fate comes tumbling on; the castle's captain stands for me, the people pray for me, and the great Leader of the just stands for me. Then courage, Celso! For no disastrous chance can ever move him That leaveth nothing but a God above him.
>
> (V. v. 84–89)

Such fideism is not what one usually hears from a Machiavellian manipulator, but again it is not unique. Henry V succeeds at Agincourt by brilliant strategy and the English longbow but forbids his troops under pain of death to attribute the victory to anything but divine favor. And Marlowe's Navarre in *The Massacre at Paris,* the champion of Protestant Christianity in France, frequently expresses his total faith in Providence but remains focused on politic concerns. Perhaps we are intended to take such pious speeches in the mouths of Machiavellian princes as expressions of the same mindset as Cromwell's when he enjoined his troops to "Trust in God but keep your powder dry."[70]

As is typical in a revenge play, those whom the revenger intends to punish intrigue against and punish each other, accomplishing much of the revenger's task without his or her direct intervention. But in this play the revenger uses the opportunities provided not to punish but to reform. He begins with the hapless Ferneze, whom Mendoza has tried to murder. Finding that the man has survived his rapier wound, Malevole conveys him into hiding, but not before he seeks to shame him:

> Thy shame more than thy wounds do grieve me far;
> Thy wounds but leave upon thy flesh some scar,
> But fame ne'er heals, still rankles worse and worse;
> Such is of uncontrolled lust the curse.
> Think of what it is in lawless sheets to lie;
> But, O, Ferneze, what in lust to die!
> Then thou that shame respects, O, fly converse
> With women's eyes and lisping wantonness!
>
> (II. v. 144–51)

Earlier he had railed at courtly vice in general and lust in particular, but clearly in this speech he is no longer just railing but attempting to persuade the man to change.

His effort to reform Ferneze is perhaps not entirely successful, as we may infer from the man's attempt to seduce Biancha later in the play (V. vi. 84–92), but he does succeed in applying Stoic therapy to Pietro, achieving a perfect Stoic "vengeance." When Mendoza hires him to assassinate Pietro, Malevole uses the opportunity to resume his vexing of Pietro, which has been temporarily interrupted. He reveals his mission to Pietro, and by means of a disguise, enables the wretched usurper to learn the truth about his court. As Pietro expresses his anguish and revulsion, Malevole adds to his torment by reminding him that he is a cuckold, but his reasons for doing this have changed. He is no longer trying to goad Pietro into murdering Mendoza. When Pietro complains that he is being tormented excessively, Malevole replies, "Tut, a pitiful surgeon makes a dangerous sore: / I'll tent thee to the ground." (IV. v. 64–65). As Caputi observes, the medical analogy comparing the role of the Stoic teacher-philosopher to that of a physician in a hospital is commonplace in Stoic and Neostoic writings,[71] but it seems likely that Marston was thinking of Seneca's use of it in *De Ira*, when he likens the ruler of a state to a physician who tries to heal human nature by means of rebuke and admonition before he resorts to more drastic remedies, such as corporal punishment. Like a physician, he heals "under the guise of hurting".[72] He helps Pietro relate his afflictions to his sins, and after they are informed that Pietro has lost the throne, Malevole offers him Stoic consolation by pointing out that he has lost nothing of value (IV. v. 105–18). Moved by his "tenting" (probing) and the belief that his afflictions are justly ordained retribution, Pietro repents his usurpation and vows to aid Altofront in regaining the throne. For Malevole, Pietro's transformation is proof of the beneficence of providence and the wisdom of patience and "discretion":

> Who doubts of providence,
> That sees this change? A hearty faith to all!
>
> .   .   .
> Let's close to counsel, leave the rest to fate;
> Mature discretion is the life of state.
>
> (IV. v. 137–46)

By "healing" Pietro, Malevole also indirectly aids Pietro's unfaithful wife, Aurelia, whose conscience has driven her into despair because she believes Pietro has committed suicide to escape the intolerable disgrace of being a cuckold. Addressing Mercury in the concluding masque, she says,

> Are you god of ghosts? I have a suit depending in hell
> betwixt me and my conscience; I would fain have thee help
> me to an advocate.

(V. vi. 59–61)

Pietro rescues her by accepting her repentance, even as Malevole had rescued him.

By eschewing blood vengeance and aiding his enemy to achieve a correct moral purpose, Malevole follows the teachings of Seneca and Epictetus, but, as I indicated earlier, the thematic development of the play as a whole suggests the influence of Plutarch's "On the Delays of the Divine Vengeance". Admittedly, most of Plutarch's ideas in this essay are commonplaces of both Stoic and Christian moral philosophy. What leads one to believe that *The Malcontent* may be a dramatization of the ideas is that Marston has brought together the same arguments Plutarch uses to support the wisdom of delayed vengeance, and he has also demonstrated that the anguish of guilt is an adequate retribution for sin. Delay permits Pietro and Aurelia to see the folly of their wickedness and repent. Delay also permits the villain Mendoza to act as a scourge, inflicting punishment on Pietro, Aurelia, and Ferneze. Moreover, because of the delay, vengeance is inflicted on all malefactors at a fitting time and in a fitting manner. Had Malevole chosen to carry out a swift revenge on his enemies, he would have incurred the wrath of the great Duke of Florence, who had enabled Pietro to usurp the throne. Because he is reinstated as a ruling magistrate, Malevole is able to decree just punishments not only for his own personal enemies but for other persons who have degraded the Court. And at the same time that Marston demonstrates the wisdom of delayed vengeance he also shows, through Pietro and Aurelia, that ample punishment is inflicted from within by the aroused conscience.

The moral framework of *The Malcontent* is actually much the same as that of Tourneur's *The Atheist's Tragedy*, a play that rewards study mainly because of how it seems to mirror contemporary responses to some major works, notably *King Lear* and Chapman's *Bussy* plays, but also because it presents in a stridently didactic manner some of the conflicts and themes that inform other plays more subtly. The hero, Charlemont, is, like Malevole, a Christian Stoic who refrains from taking vengeance on his enemy, the atheist D'Amville, and places his faith in providence. His faith is finally vindicated when

D'Amville brains himself with a headsman's axe and dies acknowledging a power higher than Nature:

> There was the strength of natural understanding.
> But Nature is a fool. There is a power
> Above her that hath overthrown the pride
> Of all my projects and posterity,
>
> (V. ii. 257–60)[73]

The difference, of course, is that Charlemont takes virtually no active role in opposing evil. He is a passive Stoic, while Malevole is an activist, and his antagonist, as Protestant orthodoxy would dictate, is apparently damned in spite of his conversion *in articulo mortis*. It is tempting to see in Marston's play reflections of a Neostoic-Calvinist belief in the efficacy of moral stewardship. It may also be seen, perhaps, as another expression of Marston's idealism that coexists with and somewhat tempers his representations of human depravity.

Scenes Exempt from Ribaldry or Rage: *Sophonisba*

Reading the epilogue to *Sophonisba*, one gathers that Marston would have agreed with T. S. Eliot's assessment that the play is his best:

> If wordes well senc'd, best suting subject grave,
> Noble true story may once boldly crave,
> Acceptance gratious, . . .[74]

What is remarkable, considering his earlier plays and nondramatic works, is the complete absence of satire or any elements that might be construed as burlesque. Nothing undercuts the decorous celebration of Stoic virtue triumphant. Caputi is probably right in his surmise that Marston was becoming disenchanted with the satiric attitude and was perhaps on the verge of "a re-evaluation that led him ultimately to renounce the theatre for the church."[75]

Equally remarkable is the completely uncritical attitude toward classical Stoicism evidenced in this play. In *Antonio and Mellida I* the Stoic posture of Andrugio is repeatedly undercut, and in *Antonio's Revenge,* a Stoic-Skeptic dialectic emerges in the form of catastrophic challenges to the assumptions voiced by the Stoic characters and the nihilism those challenges beget. In *The Dutch Courtesan,* Stoic *apatheia* is shown to be humanly impossible. In *The Malcontent* Stoic *virtus* is morally effective only because it is combined with *virtù* in the person of one who sees the world as it is and rails passionately against its corruption. Malevole is hardly a passive or dispassionate witness for Stoic virtue, and implicit in Marston's representation of him is the idea that Stoic pefectionism unmixed with wisdom derived from bitter practical experience is of little value in the real world.

In the illuminating introduction to his critical old-spelling edition of *Sophonisba,* William Kemp agrees with Philip Finkelpearl that it is "a play about perfection" and goes on to observe that "In no way does *Sophonisba* represent a revision of the attitudes Marston dramatizes in his other plays."[76] This is true, and when we compare it with the other plays, which appear to be so dissimilar, we can acquire a clearer grasp of Marston's vision of the human condition and human possibility.

The world of *Sophonisba* is as fallen and subject to depravity as that of *Antonio's Revenge.* In the opening speech the villain Syphax defines himself as the antithesis of the inner-directed Stoic ideal. Rejected by the virtuous Sophonisba, he is determined to avenge himself on his successful rival, Massinissa. The rejection itself is actually a less compelling motive than the fact that the world is aware of it:

> *Reputation!*
> Wert not for thee Syphax could beare this skorne
> Not spouting up his gall among his bloud
> In blacke vexations: Massinissa might
> Injoy the sweets of his preferred graces
> Without my dangerous Envy or Revenge.
> Wert not for thy affliction all might sleepe
> In sweete oblivion: But (O greatnes skourge!)
> *We cannot without Envie keepe high name*
> *Nor yet disgrac'd can have a quiet shame.*
>
> (I. i. 12–21)

Syphax goes on to define himself further as a Senecan tyrant for whom "*Passion* is *Reason* when it speakes from Might." (l. 76).

Against this dark backdrop, the virtue of Sophonisba shines forth in the bedroom scene that immediately follows. As has been noted, Marston clearly disagreed with Montaigne in the matter of love and marriage.[77] In Montaigne's view, "A good marriage (if any there be) refuseth the company and conditions of love; it endevoureth to present those of amity."[78] Love actually gets in the way of a successful marriage:

I see no mariages faile sooner, or more troubled, then such as are concluded for beauties sake, and hudled up for amorous desires. There are required more solide foundations and more constant grounds, and a more warie marching to it: this earnest youthly heate serveth to no purpose. Those who thinke to honour marriage, by joyning love unto it, (in mine opinion) doe as those, who to doe vertue a favour, holde, that nobilitie is no other thing then Vertue.[79]

Clearly rejecting Montaigne's assumptions, Marston has his virtuous heroine frankly deplore the hypocritical "custom" whereby a bride is expected to feign reluctance to enjoy her wedding night:

> We must still seeme to flie what we most seeke
> And hide our selves from that we faine would find us.
>
> (I. ii. 13–14)

When the bridegroom enters the chamber and removes the white ribbon signifying her chastity, she passionately avows her love:

> What I dare thinke I boldly speake.
> After my word my well bold action rusheth.
> In open flame then passion breake.
> Where Vertue prompts, thought, word, act never blusheth.
>
> (I. ii. 48–51)

This is consistent with Marston's treatment of sexual passion in *The Dutch Courtesan* as a force that cannot be ignored or transcended, but in *Sophonisba* he is going even farther by actually celebrating it in the context of lawful marriage.

By endowing his chaste Stoic heroine with warmth and unashamed passion, Marston makes her more attractive and believable, and her dutiful acceptance of her husband's departure on their wedding night to lead an army against the enemies of Carthage becomes magnified as an act of patriotic sacrifice. She is a vision of human possibility, the purest expression of Marston's idealism, which, though tempered by realism, clearly informs *The Malcontent* and is present, albeit subtly, even in *Antonio's Revenge*. Quite literally, her surpassing goodness, mirrored by that of her heroic mate, is a "wonder" within the corrupt venal world of the play.

Carthage itself hardly deserves such loyalty and sacrifice. No sooner has Massinissa departed, having placed duty to the state before everything, than he is betrayed by by the Carthaginian leaders, who intend to hand Sophonisba over to Syphax and have Massinissa poisoned. Their dupicity is so appalling that Gelosso, a senator of Carthage, is moved to wonder if there are gods in the heavens: "Let me not say Gods are not." (II. i. 34). His moment of doubt passes, however, and what follows is a debate between Gelosso, a voice of Stoic piety, and Cartholo, a fellow senator, who represents the kind of ruthless amoral politic mind-set commonly referred to as Machiavellian, but which, as Kemp persuasively argues, Marston probably modeled on those of Seneca's villains.[80] When Gelosso warns the Carthaginian leaders of the danger of heavenly wrath, Cartholo dismisses the idea of divine concern or involvement in human affairs as a poetic fiction and goes on to assert that "Nothing in Nature is unservisable, / No, not even Inutility it selfe." (II. i. 55–56), a line taken from Montaigne.[81] Applying this axiom, Cartholo defends lying, betrayal, and murder on utilitarian grounds. Gelosso refutes this by pointing out that one who breaks faith with himself will break faith with a prince; then he reaffirms his faith in providence: "Plots before Providence are tost like dust." (II. i. 87). When the Carthaginian leaders persist in their treachery, he calls on Jove to annihilate Carthage's shame in a cosmic conflagration:

> Leape nimble lightning from Joves ample shield
> And make at length, and end, the proud hot breath
> Of thee contemning *Greatness,* the huge drought
> Of sole selfe loving vast *Ambition.*
> Th'unnaturall scorching heate of all those lamps
> Thou reard'st to yeeld a temperate fruitfull heat
> Relentlesse rage whose hart hath not one drop
> Of humane pittie: all all loudly cry
> Thy brand O Jove, for know the world is dry.
> O let *A Generall End* save Carthage fame.
> When worlds doe burne unseens a Citties flame.
> Phoebus in me is great: Carthage must fall.
> *Jove hats all vice but vows breach worst of all.*

(II. i. 159–71)

As Kemp points out, Sophonisba, Massinissa, and Gelosso are committed to moral absolutes, whereas their enemies serve only expediency and appetite: "For every assertion by the protagonists that man's conduct must be governed by superhuman ethical standards, the antagonists declare that transient desires such as political advantage and sexual gratification are the only imperatives man need acknowledge."[82] Not surprisingly, the antagonists also define themselves as atheists, both practical and speculative. Cartholo reveals his speculative atheism, or perhaps Epicureanism, in the debate with Gelosso, partly to justify gratifying the lust of Syphax, whose actions and bestial mind-set grossly manifest his practical atheism. Confronted by such outrageous Godlessness, even Gelosso is momentarily shaken by doubt. Like Hieronimo and Albany in *King Lear,* he yearns for some sign whereby heaven will vindicate its justice and manifest concern.

In one way, the good characters are as outer directed as their antagonists. The sovereign value governing their behavior is honor in the sense of good fame. Urging her husband to leave their marriage bed and take the field against Carthage's enemies, Sophonisba places fame and glory in battle above any other prize to be desired by either a soldier or his wife:

> Fight for our country, vent thy youthfull heate
> In fields, not beds. The fruite of honor, *Fame,*
> Be rather gotten then the oft disgrace
> Of haplesse parents, children. Goe best man
> And make me proud to be a soldier's wife
> That valews his renoune above faint pleasures.
>
> (I. ii. 217–22)

She preserves her own good fame in a series of tests, beginning with the Carthaginian leaders' politic decision to hand her over to Syphax in exchange for his military support. Though she is powerless to resist being handed over, she manages eloquently to shame them and refute their excuses for treachery. Her arguments are grounded morally on the absolute necessity of maintaining good faith and the principle that only a just state will receive divine favor and prosper. For her, as for Gelosso and Malevole in *The Malcontent,* piety and wise statecraft are inseperable. Defeat is preferable to dishonor. Moreover, she rejects the assumption that expediency is the best policy. Assuring the politicians that she cares only for what's "safe to Carthage," she appeals to ideals and values that are virtually unintelligible to such cynical power seekers:

> But tis not safe for Carthage to destroy,
> Be most unjust, cunninglie politique,
> Your heads still under Heaven. O trust to fate,
> *Gods prosper more a just then crafty state.*
> *Tis lesse to have a pitied losse*
> *Then shamefull victory.*
>
> (II. i. 112–17)

Like the hapless Melians in Thucydides' *History,* who oppose the ruthless policy of the Athenians with essentially the same arguments,[83] she is destined to be a victim, but even as she is victimized, she asserts her freedom and manages to triumph over her foes. The issue of freedom is brought up in the same debate with Chartolo, who, contradicting somewhat his earlier denial that the gods are involved in human affairs, claims that the Carthaginian leaders have been forced into their treachery by divine foreknowledge governing fate. Sophonisba refutes this bit of bad faith by adapting to a pagan polytheistic context the Boethian doctrine that God sees the future in His eternal present without abridging human free will:[84]

> Gods naught foresee, but see, for to their eyes
> Naught is to come, or past. Nor are you vile
> Because the Gods foresee: For Gods not we
> See as thinges are. Things are not, as we see.
>
> (II. i. 133–36)

Then, having utterly vanquished Cartholo in debate, she makes light of her own "affected wisdom" and submits herself to tyranny masking as *raison d'état*. The lines she utters as she is led out by the Senators define her as an image of Stoic perfection—defying "blacke chaunce" to do its worst, regarding death as "no evill," and ready for whatever trials will enhance the glory of her virtue. The spectacle of her virtue is such that Gelosso is moved to exclaim,

> A prodegy! Let nature run crosse legd,
> Ops goe upon thy head, let Neptune burne,
> Cold Saturne cracke with heate for now the world
> Hath seene a *Woman*.
>
> (II. i. 155–58)

Indeed her unfailing goodness, so far beyond the capacity of ordinary human beings, defies nature itself, which, as Gelosso's next lines indicate, is subject to cosmic conflagration. Her absolute commitment to virtue sets her above not merely other human beings but the gods themselves, as Massinissa tells Scipio later in the play (III. ii. 50–59).

Marston clearly believed in Stoic perfection as a viable, albeit rarely achieved, ideal. At first glance, this would seem to be at odds with what he shows in his earlier plays. But it should be noted that the perfection embodied in Sophonisba differs significantly from the ideal projected and aspired to by Andrugio and Pandulpho in the *Antonio* plays or Malheureux in *The Dutch Courtesan*. To maintain that ideal or posture one must be capable of *apatheia,* the complete eradication or transcendence of passion. The assumption that passion was inherently corrupting and should be extinguished was, of course, the Stoic doctrine most often attacked by anti-Stoic Christian moralists, who were fond of pointing out that Christ Himself exhibited passion, weeping over Lazarus and enraged by the money changers in the temple.[85]

But as I noted in an earlier chapter, Renaissance Neostoics, such as Marston, were able to reject such objectionable doctrines and still incorporate or adapt the main body of Stoic doctrines and beliefs. Sophonisba is a passionate heroine throughout the tragedy, a woman who dies to preserve the honor of the man she loves. Without this capacity to love and feel as a woman, she would not be complete, would indeed be less than perfect.

Her death by suicide is her final triumph, making her worthy, in Massinissa's eyes, of apotheosis:

> Covetous,
> Fame-greedy Lady, could no scope of glory,
> No reasonable proportion of goodnes
> Fill thy great breast, but thou must prove immense,
> Incomprehence in vertue? What wouldst thou,
> Not onely be admirde, but even adorde?
> O glory ripe for heaven!
>
> (V. iii. 107–12)

And Scipio, entering in triumph, surrenders to the dead woman his crown, robe, and scepter.

Earlier, she preserves Massinissa's honor and her own by resisting two attempts by Syphax to rape her. What necessitates her suicide is her husband's vow of allegiance to Scipio. For her, as for Gelosso and her husband, keeping faith is a sovereign imperative:

> Speach makes us men, and thers no other bond
> Twixt man and man, but words: O equall Gods
> Make us once know the consequence of vowes—
>
> (II. i. 119–21)

The Christian constraints that prevent the conspirators in *Antonio's Revenge* from committing suicide are irrelevant, indeed unintelligible, in the world of *Sophonisba,* but it is worth noting that suicide was, like revenge, a vexing ethical question in Marston's time. Donne's *Biathanatos,* regarded by some as a skeptical and relativistic treatment of the subject, has been shown by two recent coeditors to be a coherent and consistent argument, utilizing traditional principles of Christian casuistry, against any absolute prohibition of suicide.[86] Montaigne's "A Custome of the Ile of Cea" is a partial defense of suicide. He says that "The voluntariest death is the fairest" but then goes on to exalt endurance as nobler than escape through suicide: "There is more constancie in using the chaine that holds us than in breaking the same; and more triall of stedfastnesse in Regulus than in Cato."[87] As noted earlier, he seems to have revised his opinion of Cato and to suspect the purity of his motives in committing suicide. In his book *Suicide and Despair in the Jacobean Drama,* Rowland Wymer notes how, "as an apparently virtuous and honourable suicide," Cato "became a site for conflict within the imperfect Renaissance synthesis of Christian and pagan values."[88]

It is revealing to compare Sophonisba's suicide with that of another woman in a Jacobean Roman play, Fletcher's *Valentinian.* In Fletcher's play, the character Aecius, more a Jacobean Christian moralist than an antique Roman, tries to dissuade Maximus from encouraging his ravished wife, Lucina, to commit suicide, using arguments that echo those of St. Augustine when he condemns the suicide of Lucrece in *The City of God.* Augustine observes that Lucrece "with the Roman love of glory in her veins, was seized with a proud dread that, if she continued to live, it would be supposed that she willingly did not resent the wrong that had been done her."[89] Aecius tells Maximus that such deaths are "superstitious." Idolatrous and irrational, they propitiate the idol of public opinion at the cost of violating God's law.

No such scruples occur to either Sophonisba or Massinissa. He does not question her decision. Indeed he administers the poison himself. Marston has clearly distanced the world of his play from the world of Christian values and constraints. The love of glory, which Augustine condemns, is a spur to greatness for Marston's virtuous pagans. Of course he would agree with his great rival Joseph Hall that "not Athens but *Jerusalem*" must provide the lessons that lead to true spiritual fulfillment, but this isn't an issue. Like Dante's just pagans, Sophonisba and the other good characters manifest the highest fulfillment of the human potential through the exercise of natural virtue. Significantly, they also manifest faith in providence and witness for values and principles that Stoicism shares with Christianity. If their ignorance of Revelation and their inability to imagine the Christian scheme of salvation would condemn them to Limbo, they are, nonetheless, like Dante's Virgil and his Cato, exemplars to inspire a Christian audience.

4

The Dialectic of Virtue in Chapman's *Bussy* Plays

Taken together, George Chapman's *THE TRAGEDY OF BUSSY D'AMBOIS* (1607) and *The Revenge of Bussy D'Ambois* (1613) provide the most complex representation of the Stoic-Skeptic dialectic in English Renaissance drama. The Stoic ideal, especially as it is delineated in the latter play, has been generally recognized and frequently discussed. A few critics have assumed that it is also embodied in Bussy D'Ambois,[1] but a more widely held view is that Bussy and his "Senecal" brother, Clermont, are antithetical figures. The effort to define them, either in opposition to each other or as complementary versions of Stoicism, has led to a tendency to regard the plays as consisting mainly of ethical ideas, and this has led, in turn, to a didactic reductivism that deprives them of their richness and subtlety.[2]

Both plays seem to invite such reductivism, being centered around protagonists who define themselves in terms of a commitment to virtue that sets them apart from other men. But neither their own self-dramatizations nor the responses of the other characters who seek to define or explain them can account for all the qualities they manifest. Along with Chapman's other heroes, as Millar MacLure observes, "They are, finally, mysteries, not test cases exhibiting the problems of the individual versus society or the operation of certain laws of human behaviour."[3]

FORTUNE, NOT REASON: *BUSSY D'AMBOIS*

Certainly the most mysterious of his protagonists is Bussy, whose professed ideals and modes of conduct are so radically opposed that we are left with a sense of an irreconcilable conflict or gulf between thought and action not unlike that which divides a very different kind of protagonist, Hamlet. The difference, of course, is that Hamlet is aware of the gulf and strives to bridge it, whereas Bussy remains secure in a self-image that is largely illusory but which enables him to act without inhibition. Yet Bussy, for all his limitations in self-awareness, is not a simple figure. Like Hamlet, he embodies the contradictions and paradoxes that issue from the labyrinthine maze of the psyche, and his tragedy, like Hamlet's, throws conventional views of experience into question, creating a skeptical sense of the limitations of human understanding. As A. R. Braumuller observes, "Chapman refuses to allow the audience any grip on Bussy's nature. Just as the court has trouble defining the hero, so, too, the audience cannot fit him into the tidy categories their theatrical experience or their knowledge of humankind has prepared for them."[4]

The play's opening soliloquy, spoken by Bussy, appears to affirm unequivocally the worth of Stoic virtue in a corrupt world dominated by so-called great men who affect a pretentious manner but lack any inner substance.[5] All they really possess are the advantages spawned by Fortune, yet they maintain a hugely exalted sense of their worth. Bussy goes on to reflect on the transitoriness of mortal life in general and how its brevity begets a sense of unreality:

> Man is a torch borne in the wind, a dream
> But of a shadow, summ'd with all his substance.
>
> (I. i. 18–19)

Those who opt to sail the dangerous seas of the active life, driven by world-circling ambition and the thirst for "glassy glory," can avoid a disastrous ending to their voyage only by relying on virtue as a guide.

"Virtue" in the context of this speech is clearly equivalent to Stoic *virtus*.[6] Bussy's own poverty, indicated by the stage direction, signifies his true inner worth. He has little but is much. In contrast, the great ones who are preoccupied with outward show are "monstrous." Only the virtuous inner-directed man is in harmony with nature, and Bussy is defining himself as such a man. Implied is the Stoic view that his poverty is actually an advantage. Material possessions impede one's progress on life's journey and make one less prepared to encounter the attacks of Fortune. "Lighten your baggage for the march," enjoins Seneca.[7]

As Peter Bement notes, the setting in which Bussy utters this speech, his "green retreat," links him with the contemplative life, and he exhibits many of the qualities associated with the malcontent stereotype:

> He loves meditation, solitariness, and darkness, affects the malcontent's shabby external appearance, which conventionally indicates unsociableness and preoccuption with thought and the inner life.[8]

The setting also serves to emphasize his harmony with nature, which, for a Stoic, means a life according to reason. One who is focused on the spark within is necessarily alienated from the unnatural "monstrous" world that won't be ruled by reason and has no regard for virtue.

The world as seen by Bussy from his detached retreat is clearly dichotomized in Stoic terms. The realm of virtue and reason is within individuals such as himself who maintain an uncompromising stance in opposition to the corrupt outer-directed world subject to "all the spawn of Fortune." (l. 13). The term *monstrous* applied to these subjects of Fortune signals another dichotomy that excludes these same subjects from nature itself. From the Stoic point of view expressed in this speech Fortune and Nature are opposed forces, each compelling total allegiance, like God and Mammon in the Christian scheme.

What becomes immediately apparent, however, is that such dichotomies do not survive well in the world outside fugitive and cloistered green retreats. Given the unmistakable Stoic character of this speech, it is readily understandable that some critics see Bussy himself as a Stoic. But for Bussy, as for Hamlet, Stoicism is an ideal to be admired and even emulated, if the conditions of life in the world would permit it. Perhaps if Hamlet could have remained in the academic womb in Wittenberg, he might have been able to live the Stoic ideal he sees and praises in Horatio. Under the pressures he encounters at Elsinore, he cannot assume the detached posture of the sage, nor can Bussy maintain it once he is lured out of his retreat by Monsieur.

Chapman, like Marston and Shakespeare, questions the viability of the Stoic stance, not merely in terms of the difficulty of maintaining reason's supremacy over passion but also in terms of its basic assumptions concerning the rationality of nature and the role of Providence. The brief meteoric career of Bussy at the French court which ends in disaster becomes an occasion for skeptical meditation by two characters who are identified as "Fate's ministers."

One of these ministers of Fate, Monsieur, lures Bussy out of his green retreat with the intention of making him the antithesis of the virtuous Stoic ideal he has just professed. He recognizes Bussy as a type and cynically assumes that he can be turned into an instrument in the service of his own ambitions:

> A man of spirit beyond the reach of fear,
> Who discontent with his neglected worth
> Neglects the light and loves obscure abodes;

> But he is young and haughty, apt to take
> Fire at advancement, to bear state and flourish
> In his rise therefore shall my bounties shine.
>
> (I. i. 46–51)

He exhibits Satanic genius in his seduction of Bussy. Dismissing Bussy's professed scorn for the great as gross envy, he goes on to undercut Bussy's claim, implied by his malcontented withdrawal, to a moral high ground. Citing three great examples from antiquity, he exalts the active life in terms of altruism and duty:

> . . . for as the light
> Not only serves to show, but render us
> Mutually profitable, so our lives
> In acts exemplary not only win
> Ourselves good names, but do to others give
> Matter for virtuous deeds, by which we live.
>
> (I. i. 76–81)

Strongly reminiscent of Cassius's seduction of Brutus in *Julius Caesar* and Ulysses' great speeches on honor to Achilles in *Troilus and Cressida,* his speech insidiously conflates the spheres of public duty and the self-promotion mandated by *superbia.* To a point, he knows his man.

Bussy appears to be unmoved by Monsieur's argument. His response shows that he has no illusions about the court. It is a "wellhead" of corruption within which one must be false and frivolous, waste his life in the service of the vicious, and utterly disregard the law of God. Unruffled and clearly unimpressed by the sincerity of this condemnation of his politic world, Monsieur does not bother to refute it but simply reextends his invitation:

> Thou has the theory; now go there and practice.
>
> (I. i. 105)

"Practice" is of course laden with sinister suggestion, connoting mainly treacherous manipulative politic activity (O.E.D. 6 b.), and Bussy's soliloquy following Monsieur's exit indicates that he takes it in this sense. But his initial response is not prompted by moral revulsion. He is concerned about his appearance. While it might be a small thing in itself, Bussy's distress about how he would appear in court "in a threadbare suit" signals a vulnerability to direction from without and preoccupation with things external that clashes with the virtuous self-image he has just projected in his soliloquy, suggesting a discrepancy between how he perceives himself and reality.[9] He goes on to inveigh against the falseness of courtly values and how fine clothes "Attract court loves, be in-parts ne'er so gross," but his initial response throws into question the adequacy of his own inner qualities to sustain him in the world of the court, as does his responsiveness to Monsieur's repeated invitation to enjoy the rewards Fortune bestows. Within the frame of reference he had expressed in the first line of the play, the whole "state of things" ruled by Fortune is devoid of reason and, therefore, contemptible.

The soliloquy that follows Monsieur's exit presents a revealing psychomachia. Bussy clearly understands the implications of the choice he is making to accept the goods of Fortune in the form of Monsieur's largesse. He knows that Monsieur intends to use him for politic ends and that letting himself be used to serve "policy" will be a betrayal of his ideals and integrity:

> He'll put his plow into me, plow me up.
> But his unsweating thrift is policy,
> And learning-hating policy is ignorant
> To fit his seed-land soil; a smooth plain ground
> Will never nourish any politic seed;
> I am for honest actions, not for great.
>
> (I. i. 123–28)

In these lines we see yet another dichotomy. "Learning-hating policy" juxtaposes the world he is about to enter and all its meretricious values with "Learning." The full implications of this dichotomy are more readily grasped with reference to Chapman's concept of Learning as he presents it in various dramatic and nondramatic works. Millar MacLure provides a useful, illuminating summation mainly with reference to a seldom read work, *The Tears of Peace*. In this poem, Chapman asserts repeatedly that Learning is the art of living well, which means imposing the rule of the soul and eradicating the unruly "Humors, perturbations and Affects" of the body:

> But this is Learning; To have skill to throwe
> Reignes on your bodies powres, that nothing knowe;
> And fill the soules powers, so with act, and art,
> That she can curbe the bodies angrie part;
> All perturbations; all affects that stray
> From their one object; which is to obay
> Her Soveraigne Empire . . .
> to make her substance still contend
> To be Gods Image.
>
> (ll. 504–14)

> . . . th' effect
> Proper to perfect Learning [is] to direct
> Reason in such an Art, as that it can
> Turne blood to soule, and make both, one calme man.
>
> (ll. 556–59)[10]

The enemies of Learning are "chiefly the 'Active men,' who 'consume their whole life's fire' in mounting after power, the tragic heroes; the 'Passive men,' who are 'in meates, and cuppes laborious,' and 'bangle in the Ayre, / To stoope at scraps,' the comic gulls and perhaps even their tormentors the intriguers; and the 'Intellective men,' who pursue the shadow of knowledge only."[11]

As Bussy sees clearly, there is no room for Learning in the self-seeking, power-hungry, greatness-obsessed world of "policy." Policy hates Learning for the obvious reason that Learning deprives it of the very elements it requires to dominate individuals. One who possesses learning is free, subject only to the divinity within the rational soul, "(Being substance of Gods Image sent from heaven.)"[12] The politic "great" are in bondage to their passions and appetites.

But his reflections beyond this moment of clear moral vision reveal that Monsieur's specious equation of self-promotion with public duty has had the desired effect of muddling his thinking. In spite of what he knows about the court, he entertains the illusion that, sped by Monsieur's politic "plow," he "may bring up a new fashion / And rise in court for virtue."(ll. 129–30). His supreme confidence in his own worth, his *superbia* grounded on a sense of his own *areté*, allows him to see himself as an exception to the rule he articulates: "Man's first hour's rise is first step to his fall" (l. 141).

The line is prophetic, for he is stepping into a world that will destroy him physically, but whether or not he falls into corruption in the process is a vexing question. In trying to answer it, we may find the business of trying to apply conventional moral standards rather frustrating. Nor are the dichotomies Chapman presents in Bussy's opening soliloquies altogether helpful. Bussy's declared commitment to virtue is in harmony with nature and at odds with the unnatural "monstrous" world of the court. But he readily adapts to this world and proves to be adept at playing its games. His actions as duelist and adulterer would seem to be blatant betrayals of the ideals he professes, and understandably some critics assume that he is corrupted. In his very sensitive discussion of the play, Peter Bement notes how in the first act "Chapman's use of the imagery of light and dark . . . makes it clear that, whatever else Bussy might achieve in his venture at court, in opting for the active life he chooses not only a vicious environment, but also his own eventual corruption by it."[13] Another critic sees him as a "faultless" figure of "impeccable virtue" who remains pure and uncorrupted.[14]

The question is vexing because Bussy himself is so convinced of his innocence, and other characters, notably the king, who, albeit weak and ineffectual, seems capable of appreciating moral goodness, accept Bussy's view of himself. He claims to be a law unto himself, subject to no king or body of laws that govern other men. The duel he provokes by his insolent behavior, courting the Duchess of Guise and insulting her husband, makes him guilty of what the king sees as "willful murders" he cannot pardon. Monsieur's defense of Bussy in terms of the honor imperative would seem to be the only one possible: "But my friend only sav'd his fame's dear life / (Which is above life)" (II. i. 174–75). But instead of seconding it or maintaining a discreet silence while Monsieur speaks for him, Bussy asserts his right to live by his own law:

> Let me be king myself, as man was made,
> And do a justice that exceeds the law.
> If my wrong pass the power of single valor
> To right and expiate, then be you my king
> And do a right, exceeding law and nature.
> Who to himself is law, no law doth need,
> Offends no law, and is a king indeed.
>
> (II. i. 198–204)

This astonishing claim of autonomy, which, even more amazingly, the king accepts, is based on the belief that he has a right to "make good what law and nature / Have given me for my good." (ll.193–94) The exact sense of these lines is not clear, but taken in the light of his earlier speeches and the king's subsequent defense of him as "A man so good that only would uphold / Man in his native noblesse."(III. ii. 90–91) it would seem that he is speaking of "law" in terms of the natural law that governed man before his fall and asserting his own prelapsarian innocence that sets him apart from fallen creatures lacking inner direction and, therefore, subject to artificial law. Guided by "law and nature," he may " do a justice that exceeds the law." Given the Stoic frame of reference of his opening soliloquy, it is tempting to see an equation of law and nature in terms of the inner light of reason that puts one in harmony with the higher law of reason that governs the universe. But the more obvious sense is that he is claiming autonomy as natural man by reason of what he sees as his unfallen state. His innocence is, in fact, a willed illusion. The process of his corruption began as soon as he entered the court. But the king, surrounded by so much corrupt "greatness," is so eager to discover "goodness" that he accepts the illusion and permits Bussy to claim prerogatives.

Even as Bussy refuses to be judged by conventional standards, his tragedy resists reduction to tidy moral formulae. Bement notes how the imagery of light and dark in the first act which made clear the opposition of the virtuous inner-directed life in a dark retreat to the vicious life in the daylight of the court becomes inverted:

> The darkness that pervades much of the remaining four acts presents certain difficulties because it seems completely to invert the connotations that night had had in Act I.[15]

He explains this in terms of Chapman's distinction between the darkness of inwardness and "the false 'shadow night'"described in *The Shadow of Night*. The inverted imagery of light and dark in *Bussy D'Ambois* reflects the moral confusion of the characters in the world of the play.

> . . . the perverse world in which all but hermits and contemplatives must live—a world in which the night of "blindnesse of the minde" has destroyed the twin pillars of truth, learning and religion. It is at night that Bussy's pursuit of active virtue comes to grief.[16]

Indeed the fallen world Bussy has entered is one in which both the characters and the audience have difficulty maintaining their moral bearings. While Bussy's claim of moral autonomy may excuse his acts of homicide in the eyes of the king, his affair with Tamyra can hardly be justified in similar terms. The justification offered by Friar Comolet in his role as go-between is about what one would expect from a spiritual advisor in this morally bankrupt environment. Only a lover like Bussy, gifted with "wit and spirit," can satisfy Tamyra, and it is a given that she must be satisfied:

> You know besides that our affections' storm
> Rais'd in our blood, no reason can reform.
> Though she seek then their satisfaction
> (Which she must needs, or rest unsatisfied),
> Your judgement will esteem her peace thus wrought
> Nothing less dear than if yourself had sought.
>
> (II. ii. 140–45)

But given the contemptible willingness of her husband to tolerate Monsieur's advances to her, she can hardly be blamed for putting his honor in jeopardy.

As they are brought together by the pandering Friar, both Bussy and Tamyra practice various deceptions. Coached by the Friar, Bussy feigns ignorance of her real feelings for him and pretends that he is there mainly to reassure her that her honor is untouched by the death of her admirer, Barrisor, at his hands. She, in turn, strives to "seem" aloof and unmoved by desire, even as she manages to inform the Friar that conditions could not be more propitious for a liaison. But having announced that her husband is away for the night, the doors are locked, and the servants are asleep, she expresses anxiety about the divine witness whose scrutiny and judgment cannot be evaded:

> . . . yet there is One
> That wakes above whose eye no sleep can bind.
> He sees through doors, and darkness, and our thoughts;
> (II. ii. 215–17)

Divine judgment for sin and the suspicions that such a nocturnal visit might arouse are her main concerns, and Bussy steps forward to reassure her: "Madam, 'tis far from that." (II. ii. 222). In fact, it is precisely "that." He is telling her what she wants to hear, even as he anticipates the joys of illicit love consummated.

We may reasonably infer from the stage direction introducing the next scene ("*Enter* D'Ambois, Tamyra, *with a chain of pearl.*") that their consummation has provided Tamyra the satisfaction of her affections' storm. The token represents her acceptance of Bussy as her lover. But she is frenzied with guilt and fear as she reflects on the consequences she may face. Her honor and life are in danger. Moreover, she is tormented unbearably by her conscience. Now, instead of her affections' storm she is buffeted by tempests of remorse:

> So confident a spotless conscience is,
> So weak a guilty. O, the dangerous siege
> Sin lays about us, and the tyranny
> He exercises when he hath expugn'd!
> Like to the horror of a winter's thunder
> Mix'd with a gushing storm that suffer nothing
> To stir abroad on earth but their own rages,
> Is sin when it hath gathered head above us:
> No roof, no shelter can secure us so,
> But he will drown our cheeks in fear and woe.
> (III. i. 10–19)

Bussy's response to this is consistent with his earlier claim of autonomy as unfallen natural man. Not unlike Marx attacking the morality of the bourgeoisie as a device to oppress the proletariat,[17] he dismisses sin as a pernicious fiction imposed upon the ignorant by deceitful politicians for the sake of gain:

> Sin is a coward, madam, and insults
> But on our weakness, in his truest valor;
> And so our ignorance tames us that we let
> His shadows fright us; and like empty clouds,
> In which our faulty apprehensions forge
> The forms of dragons, lions, elephants,
> When they hold no proportion, the sly charms
> Of the witch Policy makes him like a monster
> Kept only to show men for servile money.
>
> (III. i. 20–28)

As Richard S. Ide remarks, "his attitude approximates the naturalistic notion that a mistaken conception of honor as a symbol of social consensus fosters an inhibiting social code, something like the Ten Commandments, which is imposed on man to blunt the confident assertion of natural desires."[18] It also approximates the naturalism voiced by Edmund in *King Lear* in his apostrophe to Nature. Edmund is, as W. K. Elton calls him, a "*raisonneur* of naturalism," and the implications of his apostrophe challenge all the assumptions of the accepted social code: "Since nature is not bound by mere custom, which is seen to rule the world in place of nature, what is natural determines what is lawful. Hence, free reign is given to sensuality and libertinage with such absolute powers as a providential God, in practice, less invoked."[19]

As Edmund demonstrates, such a philosophy readily sanctions Machiavellian ruthlessness and treachery, since appetitive gratification and the acquisition of power are the only things that matter. And Bussy, too, readily embraces "policy" when it is advised by Behemoth (IV. ii. 157–58). He fancies that he can outpolicy the master of policy himself, Monsieur:

> I'll soothe his plots and strow my hate with smiles
> Till all at once the close mines of my heart
> Rise at full date and rush into his blood.
> I'll bind his arm in silk and rub his flesh
> To make the vein swell that his soul may gush
> Into some kennel where it longs to lie:
> And policy shall be flank'd with policy.
>
> (IV. ii. 175–81)

But he is not capable of putting into practice this Machiavellian agenda, since it requires the cool reptilian rational control of an Edmund, which Bussy lacks. As he repeatedly demonstrates in the court, he cannot dissemble or hide his feelings. But the fact that he embraces in theory the very policy he condemned in his second soliloquy reveals the extent of his corruption.

"Nature," as Elton observes, is a "slippery word" in Renaissance discourse,[20] and in the world of Chapman's *Bussy* plays it is especially elusive because some of its meanings appear to be uniquely Chapman's. This is not true of Tamyra's understanding of the word. She equates nature with fate, the "urgent destiny" that overrules her by means of her carnal weakness as a woman:

> What shall weak dames do, when th' whole work of nature
> Hath a strong finger in each one of us?
>
> . . .
>
> Our bodies are but thick clouds to our souls,
> Through which they cannot shine when they desire.
>
> (III. i. 66–79)

Hers is a familiar excuse and one that is wholly unacceptable from an orthodox Christian point of view.[21] But it agrees with what her spiritual advisor, the Friar, who seems to have spent his novitiate at Rabelais's Abbey of Thélème, had said to Bussy about her need to be satisfied.

More complex views of "Nature" are uttered by Monsieur as he observes the man he has attempted to make his creature move completely beyond his control and eventually toward destruction. Monsieur's attitude toward Bussy is a complex mixture of admiration and scorn, and some critics have felt that his speeches defining Bussy are inconsistent and out of character. Reacting to Bussy's refusal to cease courting the Duchess of Guise and his defiance of the Guise himself, Monsieur likens him to the most ungovernable and unpredictable force in nature:

> His great heart will not down; 'tis like the sea
> That partly by his own internal heat,
> Partly the stars' daily and nightly motion,
> (Their heat and light), and partly of the place
> (The divers frames), but chiefly by the moon,
> Bristled with surges, never will be won
> (No, not when th' hearts of all those powers are burst)
> To make retreat into his settled home
> Till he be crown'd with his own quiet foam.
>
> (I. ii. 153–61)

The play abounds in sea imagery, and in her very sensitive analysis of its images Gunilla Florby notes how, beginning with Bussy's image of trust in the guiding hand of virtue to lead one safely into port and Monsieur's likening of the deeds of kings to the sea "That shuts still as it opes and leaves no tracts / Nor prints of precedent for mean men's facts." (I. i. 39–40) the sea images undergo change. Referring to the splendid simile above, she observes: "The passage is at once highly poetic and didactic, attempting a scientific explanation of the sea at the same time as it is a tribute to Bussy's greatness."[22] Indeed the simile is richly suggestive, evoking the destructive power and mystery of the sea, whose movements can be explained only partly with reference to external forces. Unfathomably, it is moved from within itself by its own energy and the conformations on the floor of its abysmal depths. There is none of the cynicism of Monsieur's first assessment of Bussy. Clearly, he realizes that the man is no typical malcontent to be controlled by bounty and advancement.

Later in the play, he pays another tribute to Bussy's greatness of spirit in what would seem to be a very unlikely context. Having been advised of Bussy's affair with Tamyra, Monsieur teasingly asks Bussy how Montsurry might react if someone made cuckold's horns at him and if he himself identified her lover. Intending to defend his mistress's honor, Bussy instead virtually confirms the report by the violence of his reaction. He threatens to mutilate Monsieur and, if "wrong'd so and provok'd" by the accusation of being her lover, would be undeterred by Monsieur's royal blood or any prerogatives of corrupted kingship in avenging himself. Monsieur's response to these threats and insults is an encomium one would hardly expect from an offended prince:

> Go, th' art a devil! Such another spirit
> Could not be still'd from all th' Armenian dragons.
> O my love's glory, heir to all I have
> (That's all I can say, and that all I swear),
> If thou outlive me—as I know thou must,
> Or else hath Nature no proportion'd end
> To her great labors: she hath breath'd a mind
> Into thy entrails of desert to swell
> Into another great Augustus Caesar
> (Organs and faculties fitted to her greatness),
> And should that perish like a common spirit,
> Nature's a courtier and regards no merit.

                                        (IV. i. 97–108)

As Florby remarks, "The sudden shift from Bussy's invective to Monsieur's effusive praise is bewildering." She explains it in terms of the "choral" nature of the speech. Like a chorus in classical tragedy, Monsieur is uttering a "self-effacingly impersonal interpretation of events and characters."[23] This explanation is plausible. Chapman is so preoccupied with defining Bussy that he sacrifices verisimilitude by making the other characters express attitudes toward him they might not be expected to feel. But perhaps we should not see the speech as being entirely out of character, even though Monsieur has changed from Bussy's benefactor to his enemy and is now bent on his destruction. Bussy's great spirit generates admiration in all beholders, including an enemy who does not hesitate to destroy goodness or greatness for the sake of policy. Like Webster's Bosola and more than a few assassins in real life, he is not inhibited by admiration for his intended victim.

Of particular interest in this speech is Monsieur's statement that Bussy's premature demise would reveal that Nature works without purpose when she creates a great man. This anticipates the exchange of choric speeches in the last act that prepares the audience for Bussy's death. "Fate's ministers," Monsieur and the Guise, who have conspired to bring about his murder, place the blame for it on Nature, who had prodigally gifted Bussy only to destroy him.

As Bussy willfully proceeds toward his destruction, Nature itself becomes the primary focus. Given the Stoic frame of reference in Bussy's early soliloquies, one might expect speeches about Nature to contain some Stoic ideas. In fact, the choric exchange between Monsieur and the Guise expresses a view of Nature that is completely antithetical to Stoic beliefs. While it might be objected that the two speakers are vicious conspirators lacking any sort of ethical ballast and therefore dubious moral observers, Chapman has not, in fact, given us any reason to question their reliability as choric commentators.

Monsieur begins the exchange by observing that what they are about to witness will prove that Nature operates without reason or design:

> Now we shall see that Nature hath no end
> In her great works responsive to their worths,
> That she that makes so many eyes and souls
> To see and foresee is stark blind herself;
> And as illiterate men say Latin prayers
> By rote of heart and daily iteration,
> Not knowing what they say, so Nature lays
> A deal of stuff together, and by use,
> Or by the mere necessity of matter,
> Ends such a work, fills it, or leaves it empty
> Of strength or virtue, error or clear truth,
> Not knowing what she does; . . .

$$\text{(V. ii. 1–12)}$$

He goes on, using still another of the play's many nautical images, to liken the gifted man to a ship laden with powder for its defense that a sudden spark will explode. Empty ships are safe from such disasters, even as vacuous men without any inner substance are unthreatened. He conveys the same idea in a subsequent speech, likening the virtuous man to a solid tree that will be uprooted by the winds, while hollow tees, like hollow men, will survive because they do not resist the winds of chance:

> So this whole man
> That will not wind with every crooked way
> Trod by the servile world shall reel and fall
> Before the frantic puffs of blind-born chance
> That pipes through empty men and makes them dance.
>
> (V. ii. 41–45)

Monsieur's view that Bussy is a "whole man" is not shared by the Guise, who regards him as gifted with virtue and learning but "headless." But the Guise agrees with Monsieur that one who judges from experience, "like a worldly man," must conclude that "Nature works at random." She doesn't bother to complete or perfect what she begins, and Bussy's deficiency manifests the randomness of her works.

As Florby observes, "Chapman makes Nature take on some of the traditional characteristics of Fortune." While traditionally, Fortuna and Natura were represented in opposition to each other as twin agents of Providence, Chapman effects "something of a merger between the two."[24] He makes Nature "stark blind" and irrational, like Fortune, and represents her creation as a completely random purposeless activity. "For this concept of Nature," says another critic, "which is neither Christian nor Stoic, no definite parallel has yet been found; her creation 'at random' and 'by use, / Or by the mere necessity of matter,' however, is a general approximation of Epicureanism."[25] It can also be seen as an approximation of the type of skepticism that was generally termed *atheism* in Chapman's time. Monsieur and the Guise, as self-serving villains, would obviously fit into the category of practical atheists, and their choric exchange indicates that they are of the speculative type as well. The fact that they see the world in Epicurean terms is consistent with their atheistic Skepticism. Epicureans were not, strictly speaking, atheists, but what they had in common with atheists was a denial of providential involvement in human affairs. Providence is replaced by Fortune.[26]

By identifying Nature with Fortune and omitting any reference to Providence, Chapman imparts through these ministers of fate a profoundly skeptical perspective of the hero and his tragedy.[27] From this perspective, it can be seen that the play's first line virtually contains the whole play: "Fortune, not reason, rules the state of things." Uttering the line, Bussy did not envision anything like his own victimization by the irrational forces that rule. He was and continues to be completely confident in the power of his own virtue to sustain him.

Monsieur and the Guise do not, however, have the last word. The catastrophe they have introduced brings about a radical shift in the mood of the play. The skeptical pessimism of these choric speeches is answered by a powerful affirmation in the form of Bussy's heroic death, which finally validates his Herculean stature. Throughout the play, there are allusions and parallels suggesting his Herculean character.[28] In the final scene, Chapman adapts lines from Seneca's *Hercules Oetaeus* and makes the parallel explicit as Bussy dies, in words spoken by the ghost of the Friar:

> Farewell, brave relics of a complete man,
> Look up and see thy spirit made a star;
> Join flames with Hercules and, when thou sett'st
> Thy radiant forehead in the firmament,
> Make the vast crystal crack with thy receipt,
> Spread to a world of fire, and the aged sky
> Cheer with new sparks of old humanity.
>
> (V. iv. 146–52)[29]

As Eugene Waith points out in his study of the type in Renaissance and Restoration drama, the Herculean hero sins and transgresses, but his extraordinary greatness permits him to escape condemnation.[30] And as Chapman well knew, this freedom from ordinary moral constraint had been granted to Heracles himself by Homer. The great bow of Odysseus, we are told, was the gift of his friend Iphitus, who was subsequently murdered by Heracles, who coveted his horses:

For Heracles killed him in his own house, though he was Iphitus' host, caring no more in that cruel heart of his for the vengeful eye of god than for the hospitality he had given him—feasted the man first, then killed him, took the mares himself, and put them in his own stables.[31]

But as Odysseus tells us earlier in the poem, Heracles was still apotheosized and banquets at ease with the immortal gods. Chapman's hero grants himself the same degree of autonomy, and the Friar's speech seems to validate his Herculean prerogative.

Bussy's death scene is full of reference to fire. He likens himself to warning fire, to "a falling star / Silently glanc'd, that like a thunderbolt / Look'd to have stuck and shook the firmament." As Florby notes, "The falling star sadly recalls his resolute mood on leaving his old obscure way of life: 'men that fall low must die, / As well as men cast headlong from the sky" (I.i.142–43), while the thunderbolt reminds us of the bearer of Jove's thunder in act 3.[32] Florby dismisses these "fiery phenomena" as "largely conventional, representing insuppressible passion" as in the Nuntius speech in II.i., but I believe that Jean Jacquot is right in seeing a Stoic frame of reference evoked by this fiery imagery.[33] Chapman seems to be deliberately evoking the fiery death of Hercules on the pyre that preceded his apotheosis, as well as the Stoic idea of conflagration. As Seneca, or his imitator, presents it through the report of Philoctetes, Hercules imagines that his father is summoning him to heaven and welcomes the flames with a perfect Stoic composure that astonishes witnesses:

> The whole crowd stands in speechless wonder and the flames have scarce belief, so calm his brow, the hero so majestic. Nor does he speed his burning; but when now he deemed that courage enough had been shown in death, from every side he dragged the burning logs which the fire least fed upon, and into that blazing mass he strode and sought where the flames leaped highest, all unafraid, defiant.[34]

While hardly a figure of Stoic composure, Bussy is, nonetheless, Herculean in the greatness of spirit he exhibits as he dies. In his last speech, he echoes not only the *Oetaeus* but a passage in *Revelation* which describes signs that the world is ending: "And the second angell blew / & as it were a great mountayne burning with fyre was cast into the see / & the third parte of the sea turned to bloud / . . . And the thyrde angell blew / and ther fell a greate starre from heauen burnynge as it wer a cresset / and it fell in to the thyrde parte of the ryers / & in to fountaynes of waters / & the name of the starre is called Wormwood. And the thyrde part of the waters was turned to wormwood. And many men dyed of the waters/because they were made bitter."[35] The sight of Tamyra's wounds causes Bussy's "sun," or reason, to become "blood," or passion, and his passions to flow like lava into the sea and embitter it:

> Melt (like two hungry torrents, eating rocks)
> Into the ocean of all human life,
> And make it bitter, only with my blood.
>
> (V. iv. 137–39)

By echoing both the *Oetaeus* and *Revelation* in this context, Chapman evokes both Stoic and Christian apocalyptic images of conflagration. And this vision of cosmic catastrophe is not wholly at odds with the skeptical pessimistic pronouncements of Monsieur and the Guise. As Rosenmeyer observes, the threat of cosmic catastrophe generates a profound pessimism that undermines Stoic faith in Nature itself: "It is as if nature in all of its functions had catastrophe embedded in it. A proper vision of that nature can only be an apocalyptic one. It casts shadow over even the most sanguine homilies of consolation and encouragement."[36] By evoking this same apocalyptic vision, however, Chapman actually strengthens the affirmation of his hero's greatness in much the same way that Seneca does in the *Oetaeus*. The agonizing death of Hercules is a prelude to apotheosis, and Bussy's greatness of spirit similarly transforms catastrophe into triumph, even as Bussy, the falling star Wormwood, becomes a star in the firmament in the Friar's final speech, which is a kind of epitaph in celebration.

While the echoes of Seneca show that Chapman had the *Oetaeus* in mind when he was writing Bussy's death scene, it seems likely that he was also influenced by the death of another Herculean dramatic hero, Marlowe's Tamburlaine. Throughout both *Tamburlaine* I and II, Tamburlaine exhibits the same "absence of self-awareness endemic to the ironic-tragic hero," to use Allen Bergson's phrase, that one sees in Bussy. Like Bussy, he avoids it largely by maintaining a headlong commitment to action that leaves little opportunity for reflection. Also, like Bussy, he is significantly diminished in the eyes of the audience by unfolding events. The action of part 2 especially forces the audience to perceive, again using Bergson's phrase, "the growing discrepancy between protestation and act."[37] Yet the play moves inexorably toward a triumphant conclusion. The final test of Tamburlaine's aspirations and his illusions is his own approaching death. Still wont to refer to death as his lackey, he finally accepts his own mortality, but only as a prelude to apotheosis. His very defiance in maintaining the illusion of godhood in the face of death must itself kindle some admiration and sympathy. And as we listen to the catalogue of his achievements together with a list of works planned but undone we experience a resurgence of the old triumphant mood of part 1. Tamburlaine's achievement *has* been glorious and godlike, vindicating in a very real sense his godlike self-image. Tamburlaine must finally be judged by, to use Travis Bogard's phrase, "the strength of his faith in the ideal."[38]

Bussy, too, must finally be judged by his fidelity in clinging willfully to an ideal, a heroic self-image based on illusion. Like Coriolanus, he betrays all the ideals he professes but maintains a kind of integrity by avoiding *anagnorisis*. Paradoxically, the ironic perspective created by the obvious discrepancies between his professed ideals and actions does not undercut but actually strengthens the affirmation of his Herculean greatness of spirit. The audience is invited to judge him by conventional standards but at the same time is forced to acknowledge their inadequacy. For Chapman and Marlowe, as for Flaubert, illusion is the real truth.[39]

THIS SENECAL MAN: *THE REVENGE OF BUSSY D'AMBOIS*

In treating *Bussy D'Ambois* and its sequel, *The Revenge of Bussy D'Ambois,* as two parts of a continuous drama, I am agreeing with critics who reject the older view that there is little or no relationship between the two plays.[40] Millar MacLure points out some of the obvious differences between the two works but then goes on to say, "these differences tend to conceal a fundamental continuity between the two plays."[41] He summarizes what he sees as the main thematic and structural parallels but doesn't fully illuminate the continuity, and since he is providing a comprehensive survey of Chapman's dramatic and nondramatic works in relation to his life, it is understandable that he doesn't allow space for an in-depth comparison. There have been some other perceptive discussions, notably that of Peter Bement, but the fullest and most penetrating study of the relationship of the two plays is certainly that of Gunilla Florby.

Florby points out the increased emphasis on the appearance-reality theme and the destructive effects of ungoverned passion in the revised 1641 quarto of *The Tragedy of Bussy.* She believes that this change in emphasis anticipates the thematic concerns of *The Revenge.* Basing her argument on a close scene-by-scene analysis and comparison of the two plays, she concludes,

> that to gain its full impact, *The Revenge of Bussy D'Ambois* must be viewed against the background of *The Tragedy of Bussy D'Ambois.* As Clermont is matched against Bussy in a series of parallel situations and as unresolved questions are brought up again in the sequel, the effect is something of a debate between the two plays, an extension of the various debates carried on in *Bussy D'Ambois.*[42]

Indeed the two plays have a dialectical relationship to each other. In *The Tragedy of Bussy,* as we have seen, Chapman introduces his hero within a Stoic frame of reference that seems to be undercut by subsequent events and a catastrophe that throws Stoic assumptions about Nature itself into question. But the skeptical pessimistic perspective itself is then undercut by a triumphant conclusion in which the greatness of the hero is affirmed, albeit equivocally and ironically given the absence of *anagnorisis*. The question of whether or not the hero has maintained his virtue is finally left unresolved. In *The Revenge of Bussy* the dialectic of virtue continues, and although it finally seems to be resolved unequivocally in Stoic terms, Chapman again maintains a skeptical perspective. Like *The Tragedy of Bussy, The Revenge* resists didactic reductivism. As Florby remarks, it "should be read as a critique of Stoicism rather than as a collection of precepts."[43]

Florby and Bement are among the very few critics who have appreciated the complexity and subtlety of this play. Other scholars have been puzzled or distressed by it, and the consensus seems to be that it is not well integrated, that Chapman chose to write a revenge play because the type was in vogue but that it was a genre ill-suited to his didactic purposes.[44] Of course, one can hardly quarrel with the judgment that *The Revenge of Bussy* is theatrically inferior to *The Tragedy of Bussy* and the *Byron* plays. However, the fashionable assumption underlying much of the disparaging criticism, that Chapman didn't really know what he was doing in *The Revenge* and combined essentially incompatible ethical and dramatic ingredients, is highly questionable. If we examine the play carefully, we can see that the didactic import of the characterization of the hero is comprehensible only with reverence to the revenge motif. Paradoxically, Clermont's progress toward private revenge, explicitly forbidden by his Christian-Stoic principles, coincides with his intellectual and spiritual progress toward a clearer understanding of the basic premises of his ethical credo.

It is generally acknowledged that Clermont's ethical credo derives almost wholly from the *Discourses* of "the good Greek moralist," Epictetus. And it is fairly obvious that Chapman's reading of Epictetus altered his conception of the tragic hero considerably. In MacLure's view, "It seems safe to say that Chapman's wonder at the Herculean hero, imbued with 'spirit' and outward fortitude, diminished as he read more Epictetus . . . and began to meditate upon Homer's 'fashion of an absolute man' in the *Odyssey*."[45] Actually, it would be safer to say that Chapman's reading of Epictetus gave him a totally different conception of the "Herculean" hero. Bussy and Byron, the incontinent, outer-directed heroes of his earlier tragedies, are "Herculean," but in a Marlovian sense. Like Tamburlaine, they have a great deal in common with the characterization of Achilles in the *Iliad*.[46] Clermont D'Ambois exemplifies an entirely different type of Herculean hero. He is a "Senecal" avenger, and in creating him Chapman seems to have been principally inspired by the idealized image of Hercules presented by the Stoic moralists. Homer's Odysseus may have been an additional source of inspiration, but he appears to have influenced Chapman less than the Stoic image of the world cleansing Hercules, especially as it is presented by Epictetus.[47]

Hercules is one of Epictetus's favorite mythical exemplars, even as he became a favorite of moralists and other writers during the Renaissance.[48] In the *Discourses* he and Odysseus both serve as models of preeminent heroic virtue of the kind denoted in Greek by *areté* and *virtus* in Latin.[49] A concomitant of this heroic virtue is a degree of wisdom and understanding that permits the hero to see beyond all accepted conventions and human opinion in determining proper courses of action. Upon first looking into the *Discourses* we may be a bit puzzled by Epictetus's choice of Herculean and Odyssean exploits for admiration, but we soon see that his choice is dictated largely by a desire to emphasize the freedom these heroes possessed by reason of their godlike understanding. What appears to suggest incontinence and callousness in Hercules, "his habit of marrying when he saw fit, and begetting children, and deserting his children, without either groaning or yearning for them, as though leaving them to be orphans," is actually evidence of his superior understanding:

> It was because he knew that no human being is an orphan, but all have ever and constantly the Father, who cares for them. Why, to him it was no mere story which he had heard, that Zeus is father of men, for he always thought of Him as his own father, and called Him so, and in all that he did he looked to Him.[50]

Similarly, Odysseus, by reason of "his judgement about the things which are under our control," was able, without any loss of honor, to entreat the Phaeacian maidens for food, "which is regarded as being the most disgraceful thing for one person to ask of another."[51]

Obviously, Epictetus is not rationalizing the conduct of Hercules and Odysseus in the sense of dredging up laudable rational motives for discreditable actions; rather, he is demonstrating that the godlike understanding of these heroes enabled them to act justly in ways that would be disgraceful for other men. Unlike other men, they were able to comprehend what is truly pleasing to God, and they governed all their actions accordingly. The restrictions that govern ordinary men they adhered to or disregarded according to their own apprehension of the divine pleasure. Divine scrutiny was the only "external" restraint they acknowledged. Hercules wandering up and down the world, cleansing it of viciousness, "had no dearer friend than God"; and Odysseus, like Socrates, belonged to that class of men who say to God, "Nor when I move am I concealed from thee."[52]

One who possesses this understanding is totally resigned to the divinely ordered decrees of Fate and freed of all anxiety because he has complete confidence in his ability to reconcile any situation with his moral purpose. There is no possibility that circumstances would ever cause him to abandon his moral purpose, for his reason and his virtues enable him to bring any adventure to a just conclusion:

> Is not the future outside the sphere of the moral purpose now?—Yes— And is not the true nature of the good and evil inside the sphere of the moral purpose?—Yes—And are you permitted, then, to make a natural use of every outcome? No one can prevent you, can he?—No one.— Therefore, say no longer to me, 'How is it to take place?' Because, whatever takes place, you will turn it to good purpose, and the outcome will be a blessing for you. Or what would Heracles have been had he said 'How am I to prevent a great lion from appearing, or a great boar, or savage men?' And what do you care for that? If a great boar appears, the struggle in which you are to engage will be greater; if evil men appear, you will clear the world of evil men.[53]

In *The Revenge of Bussy D'Ambois*, Chapman is exploring the implications of this doctrine in connection with the ethical problems of revenge. In his earlier non-dramatic works, as Ennis Rees has remarked, notably in the *Hymnus in Noctem,* he had expressed the belief that God's justice may be implemented in the world by certain divinely commissioned superior beings.[54] It is, however, one thing to call upon Hercules to "cleanse this beastly stable of the world" and quite another to assert that a private citizen of preeminent virtue and superior understanding is entitled to assume Godlike magisterial prerogatives. Clermont's uncertainty about the justice of taking vengeance on Montsurry for Bussy's murder may mirror, to an extent, Chapman's own uncertainty about the possibility of reconciling private revenge with Stoic principles.

Curiously, the proposed vengeance seems, in Clermont's view, to be far less justifiable than the Duke of Guise's infamous St. Bartholomew's Day Massacre. Concerning this latter ghastly piece of vengeance, he has no doubts whatever:

> Had Faith and true Religion beene prefer'd
> Religious Guise had neuer massacerd.
>
> (II. i. 233–34)[55]

He finds sanction for the Guise's action in Epictetus's exoneration of the Greeks who razed Troy. According to Epictetus, the Trojans alone were responsible for their destruction, and since they had become bestial by approving the treachery of Paris, their deaths were no more significant than the slaughter of so many dumb beasts.[56] Similarly, according to Clermont, if one is guided by "a manly reason" one can see that the Guise is equally blameless in the deaths of the Huguenots, who had become bestial by corrupting the truth. He was a blameless instrument of divine justice.[57] Clermont cannot, however, apply the "moral" to his own case until much later in the play. But it is likely that Chapman placed this curious defense of the Guise early in the play to prepare the audience for Clermont's subsequent acceptance of his own role as avenger. The reasons Clermont cannot at this time see his own role as analogous to that of the Guise are clear enough. Whereas the Guise, as a magistrate, had the duty of taking public vengeance thrust upon him, Clermont's planned vengeance on Mont-surry cannot be viewed as anything but private revenge, which he finds totally repugnant:

> I repent that euer
> (By any instigation in th'appearance
> My Brothers spirit made, as I imagin'd)
> That e'er I yeelded to reuenge his murther. /
> All worthy men should euer bring their bloud
> To beare all ill, not to be wreakt with good:
> Doe ill for no ill: Neuer priuate cause
> Should take on it the part of publike Lawes.
>
> (III. ii. 109–16)

Private revenge is directly opposed to his principles as a Christian Stoic. As noted earlier, the ancient Stoics agreed wholly with St. Paul in condemning private revenge even as they sanctioned public vengeance, and Epictetus, "the good Greek moralist" who is Clermont's principal guide, argues at considerable length that it is the duty of one who has received an injury to aid his antagonist in achieving a correct moral purpose. If he chooses instead to avenge the injury, then he has discarded his own moral purpose. Thus it would seem that Clermont must either disregard his vow to Bussy's vengeance-hungry ghost or totally abandon the credo he lives by.

The arguments of his vengeance-hungry sister, Charlotte, do little to incline him toward carrying out the revenge. Wholly outer-directed, she argues in terms of Clermont's personal honor and the honor of their family. Like Laertes in *Hamlet* and such villainous Jacobean avengers as Fletcher's Maximus and Webster's Aragonian brethren, she equates honor completely with reputation and believes that its preservation justifies any type of blood vengeance as long as it is swift and "equal":

> One wreak't in time
> Preuents all other. Then shines vertue most
> When time is found for facts; and found, not lost.
>
> (III. ii. 104–6)

Clermont, however, maintains the proper Stoic contempt for all things external, including honor that is dependent upon good opinion, and is consequently unmoved. He has just completed a long discourse on the folly of valuing worldly honor and is repelled by the thought of making himself "equall" with villains by avenging "a villanie with villanie."

Charlotte's attempts to persuade him in terms of expediency are as fruitless as her efforts to shame him. She points out that not only does the passive endurance of a wrong make men "die honorless," but it invites additional injuries as well. Clermont replies that they must avenge their wrongs "so as we take not more." He is speaking as a Stoic, and what he means is that they must avenge in such a way that they do not injure themselves by destroying their moral purpose. At this point, he cannot see how such a disaster can be avoided, and he repents his commitment to Bussy's ghost, which opposes his principles as both a Christian and a Stoic:

> All worthy men should euer bring their bloud
> To beare all ill, not to be wreakt with good:
> Doe ill for no ill: Neuer priuate cause
> Should take on it the part of publike Lawes.
>
> (III. ii. 113–16)

He has no way of knowing that he will, in fact, by his revenge effect a moral transformation in Montsurry and that his virtuous example could, if he opted to live instead of committing suicide, have a salutary effect on the king and perhaps the country as a whole.

This debate and his earlier debate with Monsieur (I. i. 180–293) serve essentially two purposes. Together with the scenes in which he is shown coping with misfortune after his capture at Cambrai, they help to establish Clermont as a Stoic "invincible man." They also serve to elevate him above all conventional retaliatory motivation. Passion and a sense of injured honor are the principal motivations of most avengers in the contemporary drama, and Clermont cannot be moved by either against his reason. In addition, the debate with Charlotte shows that he, unlike many Jacobean avengers, Beaumont and Fletcher's Melantius in *The Maid's Tragedy*, for instance, is too sensitive ethically to rationalize private revenge as public vengeance. The debate with Monsieur also, as several critics have noted, serves to

contrast Clermont with Bussy. It is a deliberate reversal of the scene
in *The Tragedy of Bussy* (III. iii. 392 ff.) in which Bussy and Monsieur
give full vent to their feelings toward each other. In both plays, the
altercation begins with a request by Monsieur for a frank appraisal of
his character. In *Bussy,* however, the exchange terminates with Monsieur expressing confidence in Bussy's "love" for him. Bussy's lack of
self-control reassures Monsieur. Clermont's restraint and cool irony
have exactly the opposite effect. He cannot be manipulated and is,
therefore, to be regarded as an enemy.

The connection between Clermont's capture and release and his
renewed commitment to revenge has not been remarked by most
commentators. R. H. Perkinson observes correctly that his experience
corresponds roughly to Hamlet's escape from shipboard, but he does
not pursue the point.[58] The events do, in fact, correspond closely
because both Hamlet and Clermont are moved by their narrow es-
capes to acceptance of their roles as avengers, and in both cases the
acceptance is but a part of a renewed acceptance of the total design
of Providence.

Immediately prior to his capture, Clermont is in a state of agitation
that ill-becomes an adherent of Epictetus's teachings. The rumors of
a trap laid at Cambrai cause him anxiety, and he is extremely distressed by what he considers a failure to adhere to his principles:

> I had an auersation to this voyage,
> When first my Brother mou'd it; and haue found
> That natiue power in me was neuer vaine;
> Yet now neglected it. I wonder much
> At my inconstancie in these decrees,
> I euery houre set downe to guide my life.
>
> (III. iv. 8–13)

This severe self-reproach has puzzled many critics, but the reasons
for it are actually quite obvious. For one thing, he has shown "incon-
stancie" to his principles by committing himself to a personal revenge.
Moreover, he has been inconstant simply by being so apprehensive
about the future and about his ability to maintain his moral purpose.
According to Epictetus, such anxiety betokens an infirm moral purpose.[59] Clermont is not, however, able to overcome his anxiety until
after he is treacherously seized at Cambrai.

The king, heeding the counsels of his Machiavellian parasites, or-
ders Clermont's arrest for treason, although it is obvious to everyone
that his only offense is his friendship with the Guise. Clermont struggles magnificently with his treacherous captors before he is finally
subdued. Then, finding escape impossible, he composes himself to

endure his misfortunes. Imprisonment and death, the probable consequences to be faced, are the sort of disasters for which his "learning"
has prepared him. Unlike his commitment to revenge, they present
no complex ethical challenges, and we may safely surmise that he is
almost relieved by the turn of events. His captors are impressed by
his composure, and he favors them with a long discourse on the
wisdom of total resignation to "great Necessity," the divinely ordered
decrees of Fate:

> Good sir, beleeue that no perticular torture
> Can force me from my glad obedience
> To any thing the high and generall Cause,
> To match with his whole Fabricke, hath ordainde,
> And know yee all (though farre from all your aymes,
> Yet worth them all, and all mens endlesse studies)
> That in this one thing, all the discipline
> Of manners, and of manhood is contain'd;
> A man to ioyne himself with th'Vniverse,
> In his maine sway, and make (in all things fit)
> One with that All, and goe on, round as it;
> Not plucking from the whole his wretched part,
> And into straites, or into nought reuert,
> Wishing the compleate Vniverse might be
> Subiect to such a ragge of it as hee:
> But to consider great Necessitie
> All things, as well refract as voluntarie,
> Reduceth to the prime celestiall Cause,
> Which he that yeelds to with a man's applause,
> And cheeke by cheeke goes, crossing it no breath,
> But like Gods Image, followes to the death,
> That man is truely wise, and euery thing,
> (Each cause, and euery part distinguishing)
> In Nature, with enough Art vnderstands,
> And that full glory merits at all hands,
> That doth the whole world at all parts adorne,
> And appertaines to one celestiall borne.
>
> (IV. i. 131–57)

T. S. Eliot's comments on two lines of this speech put it in perspective as an expression of Stoic alienation, as well as fortitude and
resignation:

A man does not join himself with the Universe so long as he has anything
else to join himself with; men who could take part in the life of a thriving
Greek city-state had something better to join themselves to; and Christians
have had something better. Stoicism is the refuge for the individual in an

indifferent or hostile world too big for for him; it is the permanent substratum of a number of versions of cheering oneself up. Nietzsche is the most conspicuous modern instance of cheering oneself up. The stoical attitude is the reverse of Christian humility.[60]

Indeed, as Eliot reminds us, Stoicism, like Epicureanism, is a philosophy of alienation. Its cosmopolitanism could justify a retreat from the active life and even relieve one of allegiance to governments or states while enjoining acceptance of the social order and whatever it imposed.[61] Like Epicureanism, it appeared in the Greek world shortly after Philip of Macedon crushed the Greek city-states at the Battle of Chaeronea in 338 B.C. No longer could a Greek identify himself with his *polis,* and these philosophies, especially Stoicism, enabled the individual to cope as an individual in a threatening alien world. Unlike the Epicurean, of course, the Stoic was consoled by faith in the rational ordering of the universe, but the spectre of cosmic conflagration, as already noted, obviously limited the extent to which one could cheer oneself up, even as Nietzsche's parallel doctrine of eternal recurrence is hardly consoling to moderns.

Chapman does not refer to cosmic catastrophe, except perhaps as I have noted in the last scene of *Bussy D'Ambois.* But this speech and Clermont's other discourses in the Stoic vein should be taken in the context of the play as a whole, which celebrates the Stoic ideal but also reveals its limitations. Throughout most of the play Clermont witnesses for Stoic perfectionism but then decides that life cannot be borne without his friend the Guise, and, as Florby notes, "the play ends on a note of calm hopelessness."[62] His suicide is a final expression of his sense of intolerable alienation and futility.

While Clermont is lecturing his captors on Stoic resignation, the Guise has been bullying the weak king into ordering his release. The order for his release is brought by Renel, who also brings letters from the Guise and from Tamyra, who is eager to have her lover's murder avenged. Renel says that he must "prepare" Clermont for this task. Clermont replies, significantly, "I see all, and will haste as it importeth." (IV. v. 90) He expresses no enthusiasm for the revenge, but he no longer repents his commitment, and it may be safely assumed that it is at this point that he accepts revenge as unavoidable. The punishment of Bussy's murder is apparently a part of the design of "great Necessity."

In analyzing Clermont's progress toward revenge, most commentators attach undue significance to the second appearance of Bussy's ghost. According to Parrott, Clermont reassumes the role of avenger "simply in obedience to the rules of conduct that guide his life, restated by the ghost and applied to his present situation in a speech remarkable for its close-packed and logically developed thought. It closes by repelling Clermont's reason for abstaining from revenge by the argument that the individual is bound to act where public justice has failed."[63] In point of fact, the ghost's speech contradicts the most basic tenets of Clermont's philosophy by urging him to disregard both reason and "Necessity." R. H. Perkinson recognizes that the speech directly contradicts the Stoic doctrine regarding Necessity, but he, like Parrott, feels that it is decisive in moving Clermont to vengeance. He notes that Chapman's reading of Bacon's *Advancement* may have caused him to reject the Stoic doctrine of the cycle of decay and the physical aspect of the Stoic Necessity which nullify the idea of progress.[64] This is an interesting theory, but it should be noted that there is no evidence within *The Revenge,* either before or after the ghost's appearance, that Clermont has discarded his belief in the wisdom of total resignation to "great Necessity."

More recently, Peter Bement has argued that Umbra Bussy is "the authentic voice of Chapman the Stoic moralist, urging the abandonment of false opinion and a limited concept of reason in favour of the true centre of Stoic ethics, obedience to God [the Law of Nature] and the recognition of Necessity." He goes on to say that the ghost is enjoining Clermont to reform the world and "reintroduce the natural justice of the universe into a world so in need of reform that both law and religion are corrupt, and each injustice flies in the face of universal order."[65]

The speech in question is in the final act, which begins with a soliloquy in which Umbra Bussy affirms the inevitability of divine retribution, but as his subsequent words to Clermont indicate, divine justice is meaningful only to the extent that it necessitates the punishment of an enemy. Like Queen Margaret in *Richard III* and the ghost of Andrea in *The Spanish Tragedy,* the ghost of Bussy is capable of appreciating the design of divine justice only in terms of the contingent satisfaction of his own retaliatory desires. Moreover, his speech can be read as an outrageous piece of sophistry, and Clermont is far from convinced by it that "justice" demands the revenge. Even death seems not to have brought Bussy any closer to *anagnorisis,* though, ironically, it is Clermont he accuses of ignorance:

> Danger (the spurre of all great mindes) is euer
> The curbe to your tame spirits; you respect not
> (With all your holinesse of life and learning)
> More then the present, like illiterate vulgars;
> Your minde (you say) kept in your fleshes bounds,

Showes that mans will must rul'd be by his power:
When (by true doctrine) you are taught to liue
Rather without the body, then within;
And rather to your God still then your selfe:
To liue to him, is to doe all things fitting
His Image, in which, like himselfe we liue;
To be his Image, is to doe those things,
That make vs deathlesse, which by death is onely
Doing those deedes that fit eternitie,
And those deedes are the perfecting that Iustice,
That makes the world last, which proportion is
Of punishment and wreake for euery wrong,
As well as for right a reward as strong:
Away then, vse the meanes thou hast to right
The wrong I suffer'd. What corrupted Law /
Leaues vnperform'd in Kings, doe thou supply'
And be aboue them all in dignitie.

(V. i. 78–99)

Bement may be partially correct in his surmise that the ghost is the voice of Chapman urging the abandonment of false opinion and a limited concept of reason, for indeed Clermont is destined to progress to a higher level of awareness as he manages eventually to reconcile revenge with his Stoic principles. But the fact that it is uttered by Bussy, who died for adultery at the instigation of the wronged husband, albeit in a treacherous and cowardly fashion, prompts us to question its total authenticity. Bement is aware of this objection but dismisses it as "irrelevant because all that happened in another play."[66] True, but as Ennis Rees remarks, "the essentially selfish bias of his speech in general, to say nothing of the last four lines in particular, is sufficient to remind us strongly of the old Bussy."[67] Like the ghost's speech to Hamlet in Gertrude's closet, it has an effect but is not the principal impetus to the completion of the vengeance, which, as Renel's speech indicates, has already been set in motion.

Clermont is understandably skeptical about "the iustice"as the ghost "(esteemes it) of his blouds reuenge" (V. i. 117–18). Indeed he could hardly be expected to accept the notion that one may transcend one's limitations by disregarding reason. Equally questionable is the assumption that one necessarily gains more than regal "dignitie" by implementing divine justice on earth. It was generally agreed in Chapman's time that one who served God in this way, i.e., as a "scourge," was more liable to gain eternal damnation than dignity.[68] But as I have noted in an earlier chapter, the question of whether or not public vengeance could ever be justly administered by a private citizen was by no means settled, and Clermont is still willing to place the matter entirely in the hands of "Fortune" by meeting Montsurry in a duel. That murder merits punishment cannot be denied, and although he eschews the kind of "villainie" that would ensure Montsurry's punishment, Clermont is willing to serve as an agent of retribution if "great Necessity" has so ordained it.

Clermont says little specifically about the revenge after this apparition. He and the Guise discuss the difficulty of practicing virtue in a world dominated by "policy," and the orthodox Stoic sentiments Clermont expresses clearly show how little the ghost's denunciations of his philosophy have affected him. Apparently, the Guise is more alarmed by the apparition than is Clermont, even though he has not been able to see it. Like the mysterious voice at the barricadoes, it seems to presage disaster. Clermont tries to reassure him with a Stoic aphorism, which at first glance seems to have only slight relevance either to the Guise's situation or to his own:

> Ensue what can:
> Tyrants may kill, but neuer hurt a man;
> All to his good makes, spight of death and hell.
>
> (V. i. 138–40)

The idea that a tyrant cannot harm a man who is concerned only about his moral purpose is elaborated at considerable length by Epictetus.[69] However, neither the Guise nor Clermont is aware that the king is plotting the Guise's assassination, so they have no way of knowing how appropriate a consolation it is. The second part of the aphorism, that a man may turn every situation to his moral advantage, is also elaborated by Epictetus and illustrated, as I have noted, with reference to the labors of Hercules and the trials of Odysseus. This sentiment, too, is apparently meant to comfort the Guise, but Clermont also seems to be reassuring himself about what he now sees as an unavoidable commitment to revenge.

A short time later, even as the Guise is being assassinated, Clermont fulfills his commitment. Miraculously, his duel with Montsurry becomes a perfect Stoic "revenge" whereby he manages to "wreak" the "ill" of Bussy's murder "with good." He enables Montsurry to experience a marvelous spiritual transformation that elevates him from a murderous coward to a magnanimous Stoic with an uncorrupted moral purpose. Initially, Montsurry is, by the standards implied in Epictetus's defense of the Troy-sacking Greeks, less than human, and his destruction would be no great matter. Like the Trojans and the Huguenots, he has already suffered the only genuine evil a man can suffer, the willful abandonment of his moral purpose, and all that remains of him is bestial. But when Clermont offers Tamyra a dagger to punish his groveling bestial remainder, Montsurry's shame begets anger and a desperate physical courage. Then, after a fierce exchange with Clermont, his fury subsides, and he reveals that a magical change is taking place within him:

> If you were not a D'Ambois, I would scarce
> Change liues with you, I feele so great a change
> In my tall spirits breath'd, I thinke, with the breath
> A D'Ambois breathes here, and necessitie
> (With whose point now prickt on, and so, whose helpe
> My hands may challenge, that doth all men conquer,
> If shee except not you, of all men onely)
> May change the case here.
>
> (V. v. 75–82)

His hatred of Clermont has been completely replaced by admiration, and his attitude toward the outcome is one that approximates Stoic resignation. He has not quite achieved a sense of resignation to "Necessity" that would allow him to be totally indifferent about the outcome. He recognizes that he is in the power of "Necessity," but he is still hopeful that fortune will favor him. Clermont, whose attitude is one of perfect resignation and, therefore, complete indifference to the outcome, apprehends what is occurring and replies,

> True as you are chang'd,
> Her power in me vrg'd, makes y'another man,
> Then yet you euer were.
>
> (V. v. 83–85)

He perceives that he has become an agent of regeneration, restoring Montsurry to manhood and a moral purpose. He feels compelled "in fate" to continue the duel, but he promises Montsurry,

> and since so brauely
> Your Lordship stands mee, scape but one more charge,
> And on my life, Ile set your life at large.
>
> (V. v. 106–8)

One wonders why he continues the duel at all. Perhaps he wishes to confirm Montsurry in his newly acquired courage. Perhaps he is afraid that Charlotte, who has entered disguised as a man and tried to take his place in the duel, may undo everything and return Montsurry to his former baseness. In any case, Montsurry receives his death wound in the next exchange, and as he dies he reveals another newly acquired virtue, magnanimity:

> Farewell, I hartily forgiue thee—Wife,
> And thee; let penitence spend thy rest of life.
>
> (V. v. 111–12)

By this "Noble and Christian" death, Montsurry "makes full amends and more" for all his previous viciousness.

In Florby's view, Clermont's revenge, albeit performed "with unprecedented gentleness," is "un-Stoic behaviour," and as she goes on to say, "clearly revenge must be regarded as being against his Stoic principles."[70] I would agree if the Stoic principles Chapman is dramatizing were confined to those explicitly stated by Epictetus and did not include as well the moral implications of the Herculean ethical attitude he describes. It is certainly true that nothing could challenge the ethical integrity of a Christian Stoic as effectively as the necessity of effecting private blood vengeance. In committing himself to vengeance, Clermont must either simply disregard explicitly stated principles of his ethical credo and thus abandon his moral purpose altogether, or he must find sanctions for vengeance transcending them. Throughout the play he must resist all the worldly and supernatural forces that incline him toward the former alternative while he strives to comprehend how he will bring this repugnant, yet necessary, action within the sphere of his moral purpose. The effort eventually leads him beyond explicitly prescribed codes of conduct to an understanding of the supraconventional moral autonomy alloted to the virtuous man by Epictetus. The regeneration of Montsurry is proof that any necessary action can be made compatible with the moral purpose if one has the requisite virtue and remains uncorrupted by passion.

Such a doctrine, asserting that a good man may reconcile virtually any form of well-intentioned world-cleansing activity with a correct moral purpose, is, of course, potentially very dangerous. Shakespeare's Stoic Brutus could be viewed as a commentary on it. The "noblest Roman of them all" progresses toward a classical Stoic suicide with his moral purpose and his illusions intact, and Rome progresses toward yet another civil war with devastating moral consequences. That Chapman was aware of the dangers and possible misinterpretations may, I think, be inferred both from Clermont's hesitancy and his subsequent refusal to take action against the king after the Guise's murder. Private revenge is so directly contrary to explicitly stated Stoic and Christian principles that even a man as preeminently virtuous as Clermont must hesitate until it has been unavoidably thrust upon him. And even the moral purpose of "this Senecal man" cannot be stretched to encompass a regicide.

Like Marston's Sophonisba, Clermont passes every test of his Stoic virtue, and like her he ends his own life in classical Stoic fashion. But while Sophonisba's suicide is a final triumphant assertion of fidelity to principle, Clermont's is in significant ways a betrayal of what he has professed and practiced. Although Chapman's audience was certainly familiar with the classical Stoic doctrine that it is better to kill oneself than to surrender to destructive passion and abandon one's moral purpose, they were probably surprised by Clermont's suicide especially if they were as familiar with Epictetus's teachings as Chapman apparently expected them to be. As Florby points out, "In Epictetus's scheme of things the death of a friend is emphatically no reason for killing oneself."[71] While we may enjoy friendships, "rejoice in those who dwell with us, yet we must not grieve at those who depart."[72] The only thing that matters is preserving one's moral purpose, and surrendering to grief for the loss of a friend manifests an infirm moral purpose. Moreover, as Florby also notes, suicide is permitted by Epictetus, but only when God commands it.

> And thereupon it were my part to say: "Men, wait upon God. When He shall give the signal and set you free from this service, then shall you depart to Him; but for the present endure to abide in this place, where He has stationed you. Short indeed is this time of your abiding here, and easy to bear for men of your convictions. For what tyrant, or what thief or what courts of law are any longer formidable to those who have thus set at naught the body and its possessions? Stay, nor be so unrational to depart."[73]

This is not to say that Chapman failed entirely to prepare the audience for Clermont's suicide. By the end of The Revenge it is clear that he and the Guise have become completely dependent upon each other. As he approaches the ambush laid for him, the Guise is assailed by fear and filled with shame because of it. He despises his "imperfect bloud and flesh," "this same sincke of sensualitie" that holds him in bondage:

> I hate my selfe, that seeking to rule Kings,
> I cannot curbe my slaue. Would any spirit
> Free, manly, Princely, wish to liue to be
> Commanded by this masse of slauerie,
> Since Reason, Iudgement, Resolution,
> And scorne of what we feare, will yeeld to feare?
>   (V. iv. 10–15)

Infatuated by Clermont's virtuous example, the Guise has sought to emulate it, and he imagines how his master would "chide / This soft-nesse from my flesh, farre as my reason" (V. iv. 21). In spite of the omens and warnings of danger, he is resolved to go forward "to set my true man cleere." As the context makes clear, he identifies his "true man" completely with his reason. The utter contempt he ex-presses for the rest of his being and the shame his fear begets derive from the Stoic assumption, targeted by Montaigne, that a passion such as fear can always be subdued by reason. According to Montaigne, a man threatened with bodily harm will always react fearfully, as Nature dictates, "to reserve these light markes of her aucthoritie unto herselfe, inexpugnable unto our reason, and to the Stoicke vertue: to teach him his mortalitie and our insipiditie."[74] It is as though Chapman is dramatically illustrating Montaigne's point.

Ironically, this very assertion of rational Stoic manhood is what impells the Guise to walk into the trap. Inspired by imagining how his master, Clermont, would deal with treachery, "tossing soules into the skie" like Hercules, he sees himself as similarly invincible and dismisses the fear that might have saved his life. Then, mortally wounded by the royal guards, he denounces the king's hypocritical treachery and prophesies bloody consequences for France. But his last thoughts turn to Clermont, whose suicide he seems to anticipate:

> Clermont, farewell: O didst thou but see this!
> But it is better, see by this the Ice
> Broke to thine owne bloud, which thou wilt despise,
> When thou hear'st mine shed. Is there no friend here
> Will beare my loue to him?
>
> (V. iv. 66–70)

With the death of the Guise, *The Revenge* becomes a critique as well as a celebration of the Stoic ideal. Under the influence of Clermont's philosophy, the Guise has been transformed from the murderous Machiavel of *The Tragedy of Bussy* into the apprentice sage of *The Revenge,* but like Brutus in *Julius Caesar,* he pays a terrible price for adhering to a Stoic model of disembodied reason.[75]

The Guise's dependence upon Clermont is matched by Clermont's dependence upon him. Indeed the relationship sustains Clermont in the corrupt, alien world of the court, and while the Guise has regarded him as an infallible guide to virtue, Clermont's final words indicate that he sees the Guise as his "master" and "Lord." He is the Guise's "creature" (V. v. 193). In his last soliloquy, Clermont asks rhetorically if his death should be inconsistent with a life "neuer liu'd / To please

men worldly . . . th' end being proofe and crowne" (V. v. 162–66).
There is a subtle irony in Clermont's expression of this commonplace.
While he sees suicide as the proof and crown of a life lived in accord
with Stoic principles, the audience must have seen it as the consequence of a failure to adhere to those very principles he has been
professing throughout the play. He is overwhelmed by grief for the
loss of his friend, even as Achilles was for the loss of Patroclus, an
example he referred to earlier and regarded as cautionary:

> When Homer made Achilles passionate,
> Wrathfull, reuengefull, and insatiate
> In his affections; what man will denie,
> He did compose it all of industrie,
> To let men see, that men of most renowne,
> Strong'st, noblest, fairest, if they set not downe
> Decrees within them, for disposing these,
> Of Iudgement, Resolution, Vprightnesse,
> And certaine knowledge of their vse and ends, /
> Mishap and miserie no lesse extends
> To their destruction, with all that they pris'd
> Then to the poorest, and the most despis'd?
>
> (III. iv. 14–25)

He utters these lines after condemning himself for feeling anxiety
about the journey to Cambrai, even as the Guise condemns himself
for the same feelings unbecoming a Stoic moments before he dies.
But in both cases the anxiety is justified, and in his last moments
Clermont is unable to see that he has truly become "insatiate / In
his affections."

Because his decision to kill himself is prompted by a transport of
emotion rather than cool judgment, he does not see any alternatives.
The alternative of enduring and continuing to witness fruitfully for
Stoic virtue without the Guise does not occur to him, but this is not
to say that it doesn't exist as a possibility in the world of the play.
When the king and his courtiers enter and find the dead Clermont
surrounded by grieving women, he expresses a surprising degree of
regret:

> Wee came indeede too late, which much I rue,
> And would haue kept this Clermont as my crowne.
>
> (V. v. 216–17)

Given the treachery and weakness Henry has exhibited throughout
the play, even having Clermont arrested for treason, it's rather difficult

to accept this as sincere. But it should be remembered that Clermont's virtuous precepts and example have had a well-nigh miraculous effect on the Guise, utterly transforming him, not to mention his influence on Montsurry, and Chapman may be suggesting that if Clermont had opted to live he might have effected a similar regeneration in the king that would have benefited the whole country.

No apologist for Chapman can deny that the play's faults are numerous. Chapman was writing for a select, highly literate audience, and he depended on their thorough grasp of Stoic moral theory, both the explicit statements of doctrine and their subtler implications.[76] He expected aphorisms to stir recollections of lengthy discourses that would, in turn, illuminate the meanings of scenes. The result is that one cannot fully appreciate the hero's inner struggles unless he is fairly well read in the *Discourses* of the "good Greek moralist" and other classical writers, especially Plutarch. But the play should be given its due as a skillfully, though perhaps too subtly, crafted philosophical drama.

Chapman obviously had *Hamlet* in mind when he was writing it and seems to have been trying to improve upon Shakespeare's play. At first glance it would appear that the treatments of Stoicism in the two plays differ radically. Having centered his play around a figure who embodies the ideal Hamlet praises and longs to emulate, he seems to be refuting Shakespeare's implicit view that such a model cannot be attained in the real world, a view he himself had implied in *The Tragedy of Bussy*. But the concluding scenes of *The Revenge*, especially his handling of the Guise's death and the suicide of Clermont, are hardly vindications of the Stoic ideal. The mood of these scenes, the "calm hopelessness," to use Florby's phrase, is close to that of the pessimistic skeptical mood established by the choric speeches introducing the death of Bussy. Clermont's suicide is a result of his failure to comprehend a higher duty to live and witness combined with an inability to sustain himself against the assaults of passion. He is impelled by a yearning to escape, elaborately and beautifully expressed in the image of the ship leaving the island (V. v. 175–90). To remain behind is "To feede theeus, beasts, and be the slaue of power." (191). The beauty of the speech does not negate the sense of futility and defeat it conveys, even as Horatio's farewell to Hamlet does not negate the sense of irreparable human loss, along with the feelings of futility generated by the emergence of Fortinbras as heir to the throne of Denmark. In both plays, Stoicism gives way finally to profound skepticism and pessimism.

As a final note, it would seem that the skeptical tone of *The Revenge of Bussy D'Ambois* troubled Chapman's contemporary Cyril Tourneur, whose *The Atheist's Tragedy* may be a commentary on both *Bussy* plays, as well as others, such as *King Lear,* in which skepticism is presented persuasively. Responding to an article by Henry Hitch Adams arguing that Tourneur's Charlemont is modeled as a "static revenger" on Clermont,[77] Clifford Leech agrees that Tourneur's play is related to *The Revenge of Bussy* but rejects Adams's argument concerning the nature of the relationship. In Leech's view, "*The Atheist's Tragedy* presents a christianization of themes which Tourneur found . . . , not only in *The Revenge of Bussy* but in *Bussy D'Ambois* itself."[78] Tourneur's atheist is as unhampered by conventional morality as Bussy, whose surname, D'Ambois, is echoed by D'Amville, but he is clearly damned from the outset, even "as if Tourneur, in revulsion from the Senecanism of Chapman, comes with a sentence of damnation for d'Ambois himself."[79] Comparing the ghostly visitations in Tourneur's play and *The Revenge of Bussy* , Leech observes that "Umbra Bussy is no messenger of God but a voice demanding that scales must be balanced. It speaks of God, of the need 'to do all things fitting His image, in which, like Himself, we live,' but this God is remote, unsectarian. Tourneur's 'King of kings' is the Christian God, and in the words used by Montferrers' ghost he is presented in Calvinist terms."[80]

I agree completely with Leech and would only add that Chapman's God in *The Revenge* seems to be as unconcerned as the Epicurean God implied in *The Tragedy of Bussy* or the playful whimsical dispensers of divine justice in *The Spanish Tragedy.*

5

Nobler in the Mind: The Dialectic in *Hamlet*

LET US IMAGINE A RENAISSANCE NEOSTOIC, SUCH AS SIR WILLIAM CORN-
wallis the Younger, or Philippe de Mornay, or Joseph Hall, watching
an early performance of *Hamlet* at the Globe sometime between 1599
and 1602. Mornay would be on an embassy from France, busy about
promoting the interests of the Protestant cause and perhaps his Calvinist disposition would keep him away from the theater, but then
again the memory of his good friend Sir Philip Sidney, who had a
taste for Senecan tragedy, might influence him to attend. Joseph Hall,
who had only recently given up the writing of Juvenalian formal verse
satire and was about to enter the Anglican Church, might have had
similar Calvinistic scruples. Sir William Cornwallis, whose essays are
full of Shakespearean echoes, would have had no such scruples and
probably did attend it, perhaps in company with his friend John
Donne.

The Neostoic playgoer would certainly recognize the familiar outline
of the model that emerges from Seneca's moral writings, the sage.
He would perhaps discern part of it in the "To be, or not to be"
(III. i. 55–88)[1] soliloquy as Hamlet considers the option of passively
enduring the slings and arrows of outrageous fortune. He would certainly recognize it fully sketched out in the encomium on Horatio (III.
ii. 63–72). It would, presumably, be gratifying to the moral sense of
this playgoer to watch Hamlet progress from envy and admiration for
the Stoic ideal to the Stoic faith he expresses in the final scene. Hearing "the readiness is all," he might reasonably conclude that Hamlet's
anagnorisis has led him to Christian Stoic faith. Cornwallis might turn
to Donne and quote from Seneca's *De Providentia* as a kind of summation: "What is the duty of a good man? To offer himself to Fate."

Donne might nod thoughtfully in reply, but it is doubtful whether
he would agree that the tragedy's meaning could be reduced to this.
For he would have been unable to miss the skepticism implicit in the
dramatic contexts within which Hamlet utters Stoic commonplaces
and expresses his admiration for the Stoic ideal. As the author of the

skeptical *Satire III,* and one for whom the new philosophy put all in doubt, he would certainly perceive that Hamlet's expressions of Stoic faith in the last scene do not fully answer the questions he has raised in earlier meditations, especially in the "To be, or not to be" soliloquy. He might also point out that not all the spokesmen for Stoicism in the play are trustworthy.

Stoic perfectionism is first introduced in the play as a viable ideal by Claudius, who represents himself in his address to the court as a ruler-sage whose reason has enabled him to order his own passions and those of his queen and subjects with "discretion." He projects the Stoic ideal again moments later when he reproves Hamlet for exhibiting "unmanly grief" and failing to accept the will of heaven with a properly disposed heart and mind:

> Take it to heart? Fie! 'tis a fault to heaven,
> A fault against the dead, a fault to nature,
> To reason most absurd, . . .

(I. ii. 100–2)

As Robert Miola points out, Claudius is a perversion of the Stoic model: "His reason serves his passion instead of checking it and degenerates into mere trickery. The Stoic watchwords—'reason', 'thinking', and 'judgement'—echo in various forms in his speech, ironic reminders of the ideal and witnesses to its perversion."[2]

The type of Stoicism Claudius enjoins is an avenue of retreat from political activism, emphasizing passivity, acceptance, and the cultivation of *apatheia.* Its defining quality is constancy, maintained by the practice of two of the cardinal virtues, temperance, and fortitude, and manifesting itself in heroic endurance rather than the performance of great deeds. In his *De Constantia Sapientis,* Seneca exalts Cato above more active heroes, defending his assertion "that in Cato the immortal gods had given us a truer exemplar of the wise man than earlier ages had in Ulysses and Hercules."[3] Renaissance Neostoics who rejected the active life could justify escaping its pressures and corrupting effects by maintaining a view of Stoic cosmopolitanism that relieved them of allegiance to governments or states and enjoined passive acceptance of the existing social order and whatever it imposed. Justus Lipsius is representative of this type of Neostoicism. His *De Constantia* urges the wise man to withdraw from courts and cities into rustic seclusion. Any attempt to change or reform society will destroy constancy.[4] Claudius compels Hamlet to remain in his court, but tries to persuade him to embrace a Stoic constancy that amounts to passivity.

A very different kind of Stoicism, enjoining participation and service, is set forth by Guillaume Du Vair in his *La Philosophie Morale des Stoiques*. Du Vair is in the activist tradition of Cicero and Marcus Aurelius, while Lipsius follows Seneca and Boethius in advocating withdrawal from the world to facilitate the rational practice of virtue. Activist Neostoicism was also represented in Shakespeare's time, as I noted earlier, by Calvinists, such as Mornay, Hall, and La Primaudaye, who linked self-knowledge, knowledge of the divine, and duty to one's fellows. The concept of moral stewardship, generally regarded as a Calvinist notion with scriptural roots, could find support in the writings of the ancient Stoics, such as Epictetus, whose ideas in this regard are dramatized by Marston and Chapman. The emphasis on discipline and a sense of responsibility for the moral welfare of the community that gave Stoicism virtually the status of a state religion in ancient Rome also recommended it to Calvin and his followers. The point is relevant to a discussion of *Hamlet* because the prince himself progresses in the course of the play from a yearning to assume a passive Stoic stance to an activism that combines Stoic and Calvinist elements.

Shakespeare's treatments of Stoicism in other plays reveal both of these strains of the philosophy as potentially conducive to moral confusion. In *Julius Caesar,* he seems to be targeting Stoic activism, mainly, as I suggested earlier, the assumption, later dramatized by Chapman in *The Revenge of Bussy D'Ambois*, that a good man uncorrupted by passion can reconcile any task he perceives to be necessary with a correct moral purpose. In *Troilus and Cressida,* he represents the other type of Stoicism in Agamemnon. Addressing his lieutenants in the Greek council of war (I. iii.), Agamemnon enjoins "persistive constancy" and urges them to accept their frustrations as "naught else / But the protractive trials of great Jove" (I. iii. 19–20). By urging Stoic acceptance, he glosses over the fact that he really doesn't understand why the siege has failed. It remains for Ulysses, a politician and a realist, to exercise his *virtù* and, having identified the problem, to formulate a plan. What the activist *virtus* of Brutus and the passive *virtus* of Agamemnon have in common is a reliance upon reason that proves to be not merely unreliable but totally deceptive. One recalls Montaigne's definition of reason as man's capacity to delude himself:

I alwaies call reason that apparance or shew of discourses which every man deviseth or forgeth in himselfe: that reason of whose condition there may be a hundred, one contrary to another, about one selfe same subject: it is an instrument of lead and wax, stretching, pliable, and that may be

fitted to all byases and squared to all measures: there remaines nothing
but the skill and sufficiency to know how to turne and winde the same.[5]

In an important recent article, Mark Matheson points out how Hamlet "passes beyond" a reliance on reason and relinquishes himself to
the direction of his conscience, a transition which, Matheson argues,
parallels that of contemporary Protestantism from the traditional
Christian-humanist ideology, recently restated by Hooker, to "a new
cultural paradigm, one in which a Protestant concept of conscience
supplants reason as the crucial human faculty."[6] In Matheson's view,
Stoicism and humanism are failing ideologies in the world of the play.

Matheson's argument is persuasive, but the play reflects as well
Protestant, specifically Calvinist, adaptations of Stoicism. Hamlet's
speeches in the final act express, to use Gordon Braden's words, "a
Stoicism Christianized by an unclassically thorough humility before a
greater power," a philosophical stance closer to Montaigne than Seneca.[7] Moreover, the skepticism as well as the fideism of Montaigne is
clearly reflected in the last scenes. This does not really contradict
Matheson's argument, or Braden's, because, as noted earlier, Montaigne and Calvin have much the same view of *recta ratio* and its
limitations.

The attitude of Hamlet toward Stoicism and its embodiment in the
sage is obviously ambivalent. On the one hand, he admires Horatio
and envies his freedom from destructive passion, his *apatheia*. On the
other, he is acutely aware of the limitations of Stoic rationalism. When
he tells Horatio that there are more things in heaven and earth than
are dreamt of in his philosophy, he is apparently referring to the
limitations of natural philosophy in general and Horatio's Stoic rationalism in particular. Horatio's reputation as a "scholar" had prompted
Bernardo and Marcellus to seek his verification of the apparition they
saw on the battlements. With the confidence of an academic natural
philosopher and a rationalist whose learning has not been tested beyond the confines of Wittenberg University, Horatio had "explained"
the Ghost as a figment of their "fantasy" before he even saw it. The
explanation is obviously inadequate but no more so than the numerous attempts by Shakespearean scholar-critics to "explain" the Ghost
in terms of ideas and commonplace notions that were current in
Shakespeare's time. Like the motives of Iago, the more it is explained
the more elusive it becomes. Hamlet's remark to Horatio alerts the
audience to the danger of relying on learning that is insufficiently
based on experience in a world that challenges Stoic faith in its underlying all-permeating reason.

In his "To be, or not to be" soliloquy, Hamlet in effect juxtaposes Stoic *virtus* and Machiavellian *virtù*.[8] Passively enduring the blows of fortune and actively committing one's energies to mastering her are alternative responses that appear to be very different from each other. What they have in common is an adherence to purpose, the moral purpose of the sage and the political or military purpose of the man of action. Identifying the latter with Machiavellian *virtù*, rather than activist *virtus*, may not be wholly justified by the text but is, nonetheless, tempting because Shakespeare sets up the same juxtaposition, though in a different manner, in *Troilus and Cressida,* a play written soon after *Hamlet,* which exhibits some close affinities.

As noted earlier, Agamemnon is a Stoic sage, and his address to his lieutenants in the Greek council of war scene is a distillation of the main ideas in Seneca's *De Constantia Sapientis.* As a way of glossing over his own ignorance of the reasons why the Greek siege has failed, Agamemnon urges his lieutentants to manifest Stoic *virtus.* After Nestor attempts to "apply" Agamemnon's words, Ulysses utters his great speech on degree and order, whereby he attempts to draw Agamemnon out of his Stoic retreat into an assertion of leadership. His speech appeals to commonly held beliefs in the moral necessity of reverence for degree, but its purpose is thoroughly pragmatic. The obvious reason why he wants Agamemnon's authority reestablished is that Agamemnon is willing to let Ulysses do most of his thinking for him. Yet, in fact, Ulysses exerts no control whatever over the major events of the play. In terms of achieving concrete ends, he is as ineffectual as his commander, and the "policy" he practices, as Thersites remarks, "grows into an ill opinion"(V. iv. 8–16). Indeed the development of *Troilus and Cressida* as a whole illustrates Hamlet's point in the first five lines of "To be, or not to be," that Stoic resignation and commitment to action are equally futile courses. To take arms against a sea of troubles is to beat back the tide with a broom, yet, paradoxically, one may indeed "end them" for oneself if one could, by opposing them, achieve self-annihilation.

The key phrase in the soliloquy is "nobler in the mind." Even as he juxtaposes being and not-being and two opposed modes of adhering to purpose, Hamlet is also in effect juxtaposing subjective and objective reality and giving primacy to the former. The real question is not one of whether, in fact, passive endurance is a nobler course than active commitment but how the mind perceives the alternatives. Paradoxically, though his subjective stance appears to reduce Stoic *virtus* and *virtù* to the same level of futility, it is, in fact, in harmony with what Gordon Braden has called "the logic of Stoic retreat."[9] The external world is utterly devalued against the reality of the inner world, the judging self, the realm of *autarceia,* yet curiously this devaluing does not lead to any sort of affirmation of self-sufficiency. It leads instead, as Hamlet's soliloquy reveals, to a longing for the ultimate retreat—annihilation. Hamlet had expressed the same longing in an earlier soliloquy: "O that this too too sullied flesh would melt / Thaw, and resolve itself into a dew!"(I. ii. 129–30). In that soliloquy, too, he expresses Christian scruples about suicide, but as "To be, or not to be" reveals, they are based mainly on the fear that suicide will not lead to annihilation, that the burden of consciousness will continue in the next world.

Classical Stoic philosophy has little to say about "The undiscover'd country." Marcus Aurelius leaves open the question of whether or not there is an afterlife.[10] The Stoic eschatology presented in *The Aeneid* by Anchises (VI. 718–48) seems to express a belief that the divine spark lives on and presumably, after "nothing is left but pure / Ethereal sentience and the spirit's essential flame," it is destined for reunion with the *Logos spermatikos.*[11] Seneca is inconsistent on the subject, but Braden seems to be right in attaching greater significance to those passages in which he in effect denies the soul's immortality than those in which he seems to affirm it.[12] Again, Hamlet's sense of the limitations of Stoic natural philosophy is apparent. Among the things not dreamt of in natural philosophy is the whole realm of Christian eschatology, but the fact that Hamlet refers to this too as a "dream" emphasizes the extent of his own uncertainty. His superiority to the sage in understanding is, like the unmatched wisdom of Socrates, based on his superior awareness of what he does not know.

"To be, or not to be" may be fruitfully compared with Hieronimo's *"Vindicta mihi"* soliloquy in *The Spanish Tragedy* (III. xiii. 1–44) on which it may have been at least partly modeled. Like Hamlet, Hieronimo considers alternative responses to his situation—Christian patience or Stoic resignation versus active commitment against a sea of troubles. Like Hamlet's soliloquy, his speech reveals his growing awareness of the inadequacy of the conventional views of experience represented by these alternatives. By the end of *The Spanish Tragedy* Hieronimo is made to see what Hamlet intuits at the outset of his tragedy, that there are more things in heaven and earth than are dreamed of in anyone's "philosophy." Hieronimo, like Hamlet, is able to consider the alternatives critically, but, unlike Hamlet, he finds one acceptable and resolves to act: "And death's the worst of resolution" (III. xiii. 9). Hamlet's reflections are finally inconclusive and "resolution" is "sicklied o'er with the pale cast of thought." Hearing the soliloquy, Donne might remark to Cornwallis that a skeptic's meditations are always inconclusive.

For all his uncertainty, Hamlet is preoccupied with eschatology, mainly damnation, throughout much of the play, and he seems to have an unwavering emotional conviction of the reality of hell. The visitation of his father's spirit, contradicting his view that "no traveller returns" from the world beyond, evokes the literally unspeakable horrors of a purgatory that sounds more like Dante's infernal pit. Remembering this, he finds a ready excuse to put off killing Claudius at prayer. When he forges the letter dooming Rosencrantz and Guildenstern, he, in effect, wills their damnation as well by adding the phrase, "not shriving-time allow'd." He apparently maintains a Catholic belief in salvation *in articulo mortis,* which, along with purgatory itself, was denied by Protestant moral theology.[13]

His fear of being damned himself appears not merely in his scruples about suicide but in the meditation on corruption he utters just before his first encounter with the Ghost. Beginning with a discourse on Danish drunkenness and how it adds a "swinish phrase" to the name of Dane, he parallels the soiling of a national reputation with that of individuals by some inborn flaw or "mole of nature." No matter how virtuous or gifted an individual may be, he is doomed to disgrace by "the stamp of one defect":

> Being nature's livery or Fortune's star,
> His virtues else, be they as pure as grace,
> As infinite as man may undergo,
> Shall in the general censure take corruption
> From that particular fault. The dram of evil
> Doth all the noble substance often dout
> To his own scandal.
>
> (I. iv. 32–38)

The explicit concern is public opinion, as it affects both nations and individuals, identifying them with a single flaw.[14] But as is typical with Hamlet, such a meditation prompts introspection, and as Olivier sensed, he seems to be thinking of how not merely reputation but moral character, his own in particular, may be affected by a single inborn defect. Bearing in mind his preoccupation with eschatology, it is tempting to find in "the general censure" an ambiguous reference to both public judgment and the General Judgment.

If we choose to see an eschatological reference in these lines, we may see as well the beginning of a tension between the unambiguously Catholic eschatology shortly to be revealed in the Ghost's speeches, which stress the importance of the sacraments to salvation, and what appears to be an eschatology more in harmony with that of Luther and Calvin. Without referring specifically to predestination,

Hamlet seems to be describing how some otherwise blameless individuals are damned, as well as disgraced, by a "vicious mole" that has been imposed on them by nature.

One should not, of course, make too much of a possible ambiguity, but it can't be denied that Hamlet feels victimized by providence:

> The time is out of joint. O cursed spite,
> That ever I was born to set it right.
>
> (I. v. 196–97)

> For this same lord
> I do repent; but heaven hath pleas'd it so,
> To punish me with this and this with me,
> That I must be their scourge and minister.
>
> (III. iv. 174–77)

The latter speech, uttered over the slain Polonius, can be read as a bitter acceptance of the damnable role of scourge that has been imposed on him. As conventionally conceived, the role of scourge and the role of minister are very different from each other and do not coexist in the same actor. A scourge is a damned instrument of divine justice whose fitness for a damnable role is due to a corruption for which providence is not to blame. A minister is a benevolent agent of divine justice who may complete the work begun by a scourge, but the two agents are very different in kind.[15] In seeing himself as one coerced into assuming both roles, Hamlet is clearly rejecting any Christian or Stoic notion of providence as benevolent design. It is perhaps his most profoundly skeptical moment in the play. In musing on the battlement, he had spoken of those who are victimized by nature, disgraced, and perhaps damned as a result of something "wherein they are not guilty." Now he describes himself as one victimized by heaven into assuming a role that will damn him.

Referring to eschatology in the world of the play, specifically what he sees as the "moral barbarism" of the premise that a good man unlucky enough to die without receiving the last sacraments must suffer hellish or purgatorial fires, Graham Bradshaw observes, "Divine justice would appear to have the morals of a fruit machine; but for much of the play this barbaric idea seems to function as a premise."[16] From a purely human standpoint, this would seem to be the case, even as it is clearly the case in The Spanish Tragedy. In that play, as I have argued, Kyd deliberately emphasizes the discrepancy between the orthodox Christian Stoic beliefs expressed by the living characters with regard to the process of divine justice and what is revealed in the judgment scenes that frame the main plot. The play begins and ends skeptically with eschatological revelations that in no way agree with or fulfill the orthodox Christian assumptions or expectations of the characters who live and die in the intervening acts. In *Hamlet,* too, divine justice seems to be at odds with human reason and morality. But Shakespeare's tragic design is more encompassing than is Kyd's. The tragic vision of *The Spanish Tragedy* is like that of *Job* without the theophany. *Hamlet* does not include a theophany as such, but it includes elements that must have been extremely suggestive to an audience consisting largely of Protestants attuned to religious discourse in which the mystery of divine justice was an awe-inspiring matter beyond the application, let alone comprehension, of such crude instruments as human reason and moral judgment.

In an essay cited earlier in this study, Paul R. Sellin begins his discussion of Reformation awe by focusing on *Everyman* as an expression of the medieval Catholic theology about to be displaced by the Reformation in the very countries in which the play was especially popular—Germany, the Low Countries, and England. As Sellin observes, "*Everyman* exhibits a great deal of sureness about how God relates to man. The benevolence of divine concern for all humankind is assumed, and the means by which man can ensure the certainty of enjoying grace are relatively precise, systematic, and reliable."[17] Everyman exercises all his faculties, including knowledge and free choice, in preparing himself for death. He receives the sacraments of Penance, the Eucharist, and Extreme Unction, the bountiful means provided by God Himself through His Church of obtaining grace.

In stark contrast to this dramatic representation of how God relates to man is the vision of the Reformers. For Luther , "God is a terrible and glorious, though to be sure an infinitely loving and bountiful, mystery whose omnipotence is eternal, incomprehensible, inscrutable, infallible, immense, awesome and above all hidden—*verè a Deus absconditus* (Isa. 45:15)."[18] In the matter of His justice, Luther acknowledges that the palpable injustice in the world is a challenge to faith and that reason will lead man to impious conclusions:

> Behold! God governs the external affairs of the world in such a way that, if you regard and follow the judgment of human reason, you are forced to say, either that there is no God, or that God is unjust; as the poet said: "I am often tempted to think there are no gods." See the great prosperity of the wicked, and by contrast the great adversity of the good. . . . Is it not, pray, universally held to be most unjust that bad men should prosper, and good men afflicted? Yet that is the way of the world.[19]

As noted in an earlier chapter, Luther condemned Skepticism, believing that conscience informed by the reading of Scripture would lead one to certainty in religious matters, but his extreme antirationalism, his utter contempt for reason as the malleable "whore of the devil," is essentially in harmony with Montaigne's Skeptical view of reason's unreliability. And Calvin, who adapts so much Stoicism into his moral philosophy, has no faith in *recta ratio* as a guide to righteousness. Like Luther, he takes Augustine's interpretations of Paul's teachings concerning the state of fallen man to deterministic extremes. While the natural faculties of fallen man—understanding, judgment, and will—have been corrupted, he possesses enough reason, a vestige of his prelapsarian state, to seek the truth. But unaided reason cannot overcome the debilitating effects of vanity and sin, and since the will is inseparable from reason, it too is in bondage to vanity and sin.[20] Like Luther, he stresses the inadequacy of human judgment applied to divine justice:

> First, therefore, this fact should occur to us: that our discourse is concerned with the justice not of a human court but of a heavenly tribunal, lest we measure by our own small measure the integrity of works needed to satisfy the divine judgment. Yet it is amazing with what great rashness and boldness this is commonly defined.[21]

When Hamlet sees himself as one victimized by heaven, he is following the judgment of his human reason to an impious conclusion. Only when he comes to realize the futility of applying his reason to apprehend the design of his fate will he be able to relinquish himself to the will of heaven. This realization comes about mainly as a result of his adventure at sea, during which he is preserved by a combination of rashness and what he sees as special providence, but that voyage is preceded by a meditation in which reason, as in *The Apology of Raymond Sebond,* completely discredits itself. Throughout the play, it has become progressively more apparent that introspection has led him not to the self-knowledge that should be the basis of virtuous activity but instead into a Montaignean *profond labyrinthe* in which he moves ever further from an understanding of his own motives and, therefore, ever further from commitment to action. He is paralyzed by self-awareness, and the Stoic commonplace that self-knowledge leads to virtuous activity is obviously thrown into question.

In his final soliloquy, shamed by the example of Fortinbras marching his troops to battle for a worthless piece of Polish territory, Hamlet castigates himself for his failure to act. His reason and his blood concur in urging him to revenge. Moreover, honor is at stake. What is remarkable about this speech is that it contains so many self-contradictions and yet is, as Graham Bradshaw remarks, "remarkably coherent."[22]

When the Norwegian captain tells Hamlet how worthless the prize is and yet how costly in potential casualties, Hamlet's initial response is amazement at the absurdity of such extravagant waste, yet he understands how such wars occur. They are the ulcerous results of extended peace and prosperity. They break out without any discernible cause, but the effects are, nonetheless, fatal. As Kittredge notes, he is restating an old theory that war is the natural exercise of the body politic, and without it the national character is subject to deterioration analogous to that which idleness and luxury cause in the human body.[23] Hamlet's restatement of this old theory does not, however, include any reference to the healthful effects of such exercise on the national character. As with the ulcer hidden within, the only discernible effect is that "the man dies." And what astonishes him is that such a terrible price will be paid for "this straw."

But having said this, he goes on to reflect upon how this piece of rash dreadful folly rebukes him personally for his inaction. Again he raises the great question, "What is a man . . . ?" He has no doubt that what sets man apart from beasts is the exercise of his godlike reason, and he rebukes himself for abusing his own reason to justify what he suspects is more cowardice than wisdom. But then he expresses his envy and admiration of Fortinbras, who has mindlessly committed himself and his army to mortal danger "even for an eggshell." According to the principle he has just stated, that man functions qua man when he exercises reason, Fortinbras is behaving in a subhuman fashion. But Hamlet is, nonetheless, compelled to admire this rash young adventurer because he is willing to risk everything for the sake of honor.

> Rightly to be great
> Is not to stir without great argument,
> But greatly to find quarrel in a straw
> When honour's at the stake.
>
> (IV. iv. 53–56)

Honor magnifies any cause, even a "straw." The idea that a great man will not stir without great cause goes back to the model of the great-spirited man in Aristotle's *Nichomachean Ethics,* as does the idea that honor compels action when it is threatened. But Hamlet is carrying this latter principle a step further to justify the kind of mindset represented by Hotspur or Troilus. Bradshaw relates this passage to the Trojan debate in *Troilus and Cressida,* specifically to Troilus's question, "What's aught but as 'tis valued?" and Hector's response that "value dwells not in particular will."[24] Indeed Hamlet articulates

Troilus's whole view of honor, including his assumption that the involvement of national honor guarantees that any quarrel is honorable. Cassandra's

> . . . brain-sick raptures
> Cannot distaste the goodness of a quarrel
> Which hath our several honors all engaged
> To make it gracious.
>
> (II. ii. 123–26)

While Hamlet can sympathize with such a commitment to honor, he still maintains a full rational awareness of its insanity. Hesitating to take hostile action unless there is adequate cause implies rational deliberation, but if honor is involved the trivial becomes great and reason is irrelevant. Again the cause of Fortinbras is referred to as a "straw." But while honor can magnify a "straw" and make it, to use Troilus's phrase, a theme of honor and renown, honor itself is completely without substance, "a fantasy and trick of fame." Inspired by this illusion, thousands will fall, and their example shames him. He is shamed by his inability to act according to either the imperative of reason or the irrational imperative of honor, even though his cause, unlike that of Fortinbras, is sanctioned by reason as well as honor that is no illusion. And the precise cause of his paralysis eludes him.

Of course, at this particular moment he is hardly in a position to act. Guarded by Rosencrantz and Guildenstern and the rest of his escort, he no longer possesses either strength or means. He has forgone the perfect opportunity to take revenge and the likelihood of his having another seems remote. His final bloodthirsty flourish is an expression of frustrated impotence, as meaningless as the ranting for which he condemned himself in his second soliloquy. Once again he has unpacked his heart with words to no end.

As many have noted, Shakespeare seems to have been reading Montaigne when he wrote this play. Florio's translation had not yet appeared, but he could have been reading it in manuscript or in the original, and Anthony Burgess may be right in suggesting that he was writing about "a Montaigne-like man."[25] *Hamlet* is full of Montaignean echoes. The soliloquy I have been discussing, for instance, seems to echo Montaigne's contradictory views of war. On the one hand, he can speak of soldiering as a "profession or exercise, both noble in execution (for *the strongest, most generous and prowdest of all vertues, is true valour*) and noble in it's cause."[26] On the other, he can scoff at the stupidity of seeking glory in war: "So many names, so many victories, and so many conquests buried in darke oblivion, makes the hope to perpetuate our names but ridiculous, by the surprising of ten Argo-lettiers, or of a small cottage, which is knowne but by his fall."[27] And Hamlet's progress toward the Christian-Stoic fideism he expresses in the last act parallels *The Apology of Raymond Sebond* in many respects. Like Montaigne, Hamlet discovers the futility of relying on reason, which, as this soliloquy demonstrates, cannot refute the irrational imperative of a mindless appetite for military glory and is incapable by itself of moving one to take action in a just cause. In his first bitter soliloquy he condemns his mother's behavior as less seemly than that of "a beast that wants discourse of reason." His assumption, restated in the last soliloquy, is that it is reason that sets man above the beasts. But by exalting Fortinbras he is clearly jettisoning that assumption and putting the so-called rational and the irrational on a level, much as Montaigne does in *The Apology* when he presents his disturbingly persuasive argument that, viewed empirically, man is neither morally nor intellectually superior to other beasts. It is a profoundly humbling moment for Hamlet but essential to his progress toward a Montaignean recognition of man's need for God, without whom man is morally no better, is indeed worse, than a beast.

Though Montaigne was a devout Catholic who used Skepticism to support fideism and a complete submission to the teaching authority of the Catholic Church, he was, as noted earlier, in fundamental agreement with Luther and Calvin regarding the limitations of human reason and man's need for grace. What *Hamlet* reveals, among other things, is how Skepticism may prepare one for faith, contrary to the assumptions of the Reformers. Which is not to say that the play contradicts basic Protestant doctrine concerning the necessity of total submission to the divine will and the mysterious nature of the relationship between God and man. For Hamlet, as for Job, skeptical questioning that undercuts conventional assumptions and canned wisdom finally refutes itself and prepares the way for faith and acceptance.

Matheson rightly emphasizes "the emergence of a specifically Protestant discourse and of God's predestinating will" in the final act.[28] When Horatio expresses some shock at the fate of Rosencrantz and Guildenstern, Hamlet dismisses them as "not near my conscience." Since they had already damned themselves by willfully serving evil, he feels no guilt in having merely accelerated their inevitable progress into hell. His next speech to Horatio again emphasizes that he is at peace with his conscience and is indeed being directed by it in purging the state of Denmark. To refuse its mandate would be damnable:

> Does it not, think thee, stand me now upon—
> He that hath kill'd my king and whor'd my mother,
> Popp'd in between th' election and my hopes,
> Thrown out his angle for my proper life
> And with such coz'nage—is't not perfect conscience
> To quit him with this arm? And is't not to be damn'd
> To let this canker of our nature come
> In further evil?
>
> (V. ii. 63–70)

Thus Hamlet reveals that he has relinquished himself to the direction of God's voice within him. The Calvinist implications are unmistakable. As William Perkins wrote a few years before the play was first presented, conscience

> is (as it were) a little God setting in the middle of mens hearts, arraigning them in this life as they shall be arraigned for their offences at the Tribunal seat of the euerliving God in the day of iudgement. Wherefore the temporarie iudgement that is given by the conscience is nothing els but a beginning, or a fore-runner of the last iudgement.[29]

This is not to say that Hamlet has undergone a conversion to Calvinism during his adventure at sea. What he has discovered is the futility of opposing the divinity that shapes our ends and a consequent willingness to relinquish himself to it. As Jenkins and others have noted, his speech to Horatio assuring him of special providence echoes both Matthew x. 29 and Calvin, who emphasized special providence.[30] It also echoes the Stoic beliefs of Horatio.

Horatio does not utter Stoic precepts, like Chapman's Clermont D'Ambois or Marston's Pandulpho, but his self-characterization as more an antique Roman than a Dane and Hamlet's encomium defining him as an embodiment of Stoic perfection make clear the attitudes and beliefs he represents. When Hamlet says "There's a divinity that shapes our ends," Horatio recognizes an expression of his own faith as a Christian Stoic and responds, "That is most certain." Considering the extent to which Stoicism had been baptized by Calvinist Reformers, it is hardly surprising to find both Calvinist and Stoic resonances in a speech expressing total submission to providential design. While Calvin, in effect, replaced the Stoic concepts of *recta ratio* and the divine spark with his doctrine of Divine Illumination from within by the Holy Spirit, his followers in England, such as Perkins, maintained a view of the moral faculty as a divine agency within man, and the writings of other Protestant authors, such as Mornay and La Primaudaye, suggest that they incorporated the concept of the divine spark and identified it with the part of conscience dictating general principles.[31] The context of Hamlet's expressions of faith in the direction of his conscience must have been especially meaningful to an audience aware of the potential conflict between believers in the sovereignty of conscience and absolutist monarchs. The Protestant view of conscience as God within man, which found classical support in the doctrine of the spark, was an important doctrinal basis for resistance to absolutism and indeed tyranny in any form, and the tensions that would lead to the outbreak of civil war in the next century were already evident in the 1590s. Appropriately, Hamlet is being prompted by his conscience as he opposes a usurping tyrant.

Hamlet's acquired faith in special providence enables him to assume briefly the role of Stoic sage that he had idealized in his encomium on Horatio. It is not the role of passive Stoic that he had considered as an alternative in "To be, or not to be," but that of an activist ready to encounter evil and overcome it with guidance from within. A yearning for retreat from the pressures of the world into a subjective realm of reality has been replaced by an inner direction to change his world. Significantly, it is Horatio, not Hamlet, who exhibits anxiety about the impending duel with Laertes. Hamlet is perfectly resigned, in a state of "readiness," to encounter what can only be another murderous trap set by the plotting Claudius. To accept the challenge is rashness bordering on the suicidal, and understandably he feels "a kind of gaingiving as would perhaps trouble a woman." But, like Chapman's Stoic heroes Clermont and the Guise, he dismisses his well-grounded misgiving. Like Chapman, Shakespeare subtly undercuts the Stoic ideal of fortitude by having it prompt a denial of "unmanly" fear.

A Neostoic watching the final scene of the play might, nonetheless, be heartened by the spectacle of a man sustained by faith in providence carrying out the duty that his sense of moral purpose prescribes and having his faith vindicated as Claudius is destroyed by his own machinations. What a Skeptic might point out to him, however, is that Hamlet's performance in the role of the sage is dramatically undercut by the scenes that frame it. Moreover, if the ends of divine justice are being served, why is it that the process of serving it has paved the way for the emergence of a ruler probably less fit than Claudius?

In the scene immediately preceding the last one, Hamlet surrenders completely to his passions, and though his behavior toward Laertes is something he rightly repents, his exhibition of overwhelming grief over the death of Ophelia is clearly calculated to win him the sympathy of the audience that has been diminished by her suffering and the account of her miserable death. He is still clearly incapable of the *apatheia* he admires in the ideal of the sage. Nor are we likely to think less of him when he again surrenders completely to his passions as he kills Claudius. While he himself expresses a Stoic view of passion as evil and corrupting, his own actions imply a very different view of passion on the part of the playwright. For one thing, passion is shown to be the only means whereby Hamlet is ever able to overcome his inability to fuse thought with action. As long as he has even a moment to collect himself and reflect, he will refrain from acting on his resolutions, as he had clearly shown when he refrained from killing Claudius at prayer. Passion is potentially corrupting, but Shakespeare, like Marston in *Sophonisba,* reveals that a blend of passion with Stoic virtue is possible and even desirable. Complete *apatheia* is for the passive perfectionist who retreats from the world and objective reality itself.

If we can accept Horatio's hopeful prayer and farewell to Hamlet as reliable prophecy, the prince is not destined to suffer the hellish fires that afflict his father in purgatory, even though he too has died without the last sacraments. We probably shouldn't make much of Shakespeare's summary dismissal of the eschatology that was so prominently referred to earlier in the play. But the fact that Fortinbras will be inheriting the throne of Denmark can hardly be seen as part of a tragic affirmation. The glimpses and reports we have had of this young Norwegian adventurer throw into question his fitness to rule, and we are left to wonder when his boundless ambition will prompt him to risk even more lives for some straw or eggshell. The profound skepticism and pessimism implicit in this triumph of a ruthless appetite for power combined with a mindless commitment to glory seem to anticipate the darkness of *Troilus and Cressida.*

> Then everything includes itself in power,
> Power into will, will into appetite;
> And appetite, an universal wolf,
> So doubly seconded with will and power,
> Must make perforce an universal prey,
> And last eat up himself.
>
> (*Troilus and Cressida,* I. iii. 119–24)

Donne, always fascinated by the paradoxical, might point out this apparent contradiction to Cornwallis, but at the same time, as the future author of the Holy Sonnets, he might confess that he has been moved, perhaps to envy, by the spectacle of a good man raised from the anguish of skeptical despair to hope and certainty as he submits himself to a design beyond his comprehension and prepares to encounter death. He might also confess to being moved by a kind of wonder and fear as he ponders the great questions raised in the play, particularly those touching the nature of man and his relationship to God, whose mysterious designs for man according to His dreadful hidden will beget terror and mock the criteria of human judgment.

Notes

CHAPTER 1. REASON'S SPARK AND SKEPTICAL DOUBT

1. Cf. *The Taming of the Shrew* (I.i.31): "Let's be no stoics, nor no stocks, I pray." Thomas James defends the Stoics against this old gibe in the preface to his translation of Guillaume Du Vair's *La Philosophie Morale des Stoiques* (1598): "Indeed the licentious looseness of our times cannot well brooke the strictnes of this sect. The Stoicks are as odious vnto some men, as they themselves are hated of others; they call the professors hereof in their gibing manner stockes, and not Stoicks, because of the affinitie of their names. And I pray why may not wee call them wisards as well as wise men by the same reason?" Guillaume Du Vair, *The Moral Philosophie of the Stoicks,* trans. Thomas James, ed. Rudolf Kirk (New Brunswick, N.J.: Rutgers University Press, 1951), 45.

2. See Henry W. Sams, "Anti-Stoicism in Seventeenth and Early Eighteenth Century England," *Studies in Philology* 41 (1944): 65–78; R. S. Crane, "Suggestions toward a Genealogy of the 'Man of Feeling,'" *ELH,* 1 (1934): 214–20. According to Rudolph Kirk, 1614 marks the end of the Stoic revival in England, which had begun in 1560. Justus Lipsius, *Two Bookes of Constancie,* Englished by Sir John Stradling, ed. Rudolph Kirk (New Brunswick, N.J.: Rutgers University Press, 1939), 21.

3. E.g., Martha Tuck Rozett, *The Doctrine of Election and the Emergence of Elizabethan Tragedy* (Princeton: Princeton University Press, 1984); John S. Wilks, *The Idea of Conscience in Renaissance Tragedy* (London: Routledge, 1990).

4. See J. W. Cunliffe, *The Influence of Seneca on Elizabethan Tragedy* (London: Macmillan, 1893); F. L. Lucas, *Seneca and Elizabethan Tragedy* (Cambridge: Cambridge University Press, 1922). Howard Baker argues that Cunliffe had exaggerated Seneca's influence and finds it less significant than nondramatic poetry and medieval metrical tragedy. *Induction to Tragedy* (Baton Rouge: Louisiana State University Press, 1939). See also R. G. Palmer, *Seneca's De Remediis Fortuitorum and the Elizabethans* (Chicago: Chicago University Press, 1953); Jean Jacquot, *Les Tragédies de Sénèque et le Théâtre de la Renaissance* (Paris: Editions du Centre National de la Recherche Scientifique, 1964); G. K. Hunter, "Seneca and the Elizabethans: A Case-Study in 'Influence,'" *Shakespeare Survey* 20 (1967): 17–26. Frederick Kiefer, "Seneca's Influence on Elizabethan Tragedy: An Annotated Bibliography," *Research Opportunities in Renaissance Drama,* 21 (1978): 17–34; Anna Lydia Motto and John R. Clark, "Senecan Tragedy: A Critique of Scholarly Trends," *Renaissance Drama,* NS VI (1973): 219–36; Catherine Belsey, "Senecan Vacillation and Elizabethan Deliberations: Influence or Confluence?" *Renaissance Drama,* NS VI (1973): 65–88.

5. T. S. Eliot, "Shakespeare and the Stoicism of Seneca," *Selected Essays,* new edition (New York: Harcourt Brace & World, 1964), 112.

6. Ibid., 120.

7. G. K. Hunter, intro. to John Marston, *Antonio's Revenge* (Lincoln: Nebraska University Press, 1965), xiii.

8. Thomas Newton, ed., *Seneca His Tenne Tragedies,* intro. by T. S. Eliot (Bloomington: Indiana University Press, 1964), 5.

9. Norman T. Pratt, *Seneca's Drama* (Chapel Hill: University of North Carolina Press, 1983), 77. In addition to some illuminating discussions of the tragedies as philosophical drama, Pratt provides a useful survey of the major contributions of earlier scholars, including a summary of Otto Regenbogen's seminal essay "Schmerz und Tod in den Tragödien Senecas" *Vorträge der Bibliothek Warburg* 7 (1927–28). "Regenbogen finds in the Senecan tragedy a new form, partly ethical, partly psychological, stamped by the reflections on suffering and death, freedom and tyranny, to which the Neronian epoch gave rise." Laidlaw, in Maurice Platnauer, *Fifty Years of Classical Scholarship* (Oxford University Press, 1954), 261–62. Quoted by Pratt, p. 77.

10. The first view was argued by Berthe Marti, "Seneca's Tragedies: A New Interpretation," *Transactions of the American Philological Association* 76 (1945): 216–45. The latter view is that of F. H. Sandbach, *The Stoics* (London: Allen and Unwin, 1975), 160–61.

11. Gordon Braden, *Renaissance Tragedy and the Senecan Tradition* (New Haven: Yale University Press, 1985), 69.

12. Ibid., 30.

13. Thomas Rosenmeyer, *Senecan Drama and Stoic Cosmology* (Berkely: University of California Press, 1989), xiii. Rosenmeyer is quoting C. John Herington, "Senecan Tragedy," *Arion* 5: 443.

14. Ibid., 87 and 142. In his *Manductio,* Lipsius, too, argues that the perfect sage is only an ideal that doesn't exist in the flesh, but he also says that the man in a state of progress toward Stoic wisdom does exist. See Jason L. Saunders, *Justus Lipsius the Philosophy of Renaissance Stoicism* (New York: The Liberal Arts Press, 1955), 67–71.

15. Ibid., 110.

16. Ibid., 43.

17. F. J. Levy, *The History of the Reign of King Henry VII* (New York: Bobbs-Merrill, 1972), 6.

18. Braden, *Renaissance Tragedy,* 45.

19. Ibid., 13.

20. Rosenmeyer, *Senecan Drama,* 123.

21. Karen Cunningham, "Renaissance Execution and Marlovian Elocution: The Drama of Death," *PMLA* 105 (1990): 213. See also T. McAlindon, *English Renaissance Tragedy* (Vancouver: University of British Columbia Press, 1986), chap. 1.

22. Ibid., 217–18.

23. Anthony Burgess, *Shakespeare* (New York: Knopf, 1970), 72. In a similar vein, Lynn White Jr. comments on the coexistence of savagely dark and creative impulses that is characteristic of the age: "By the late thirteenth century, however, elaborate and calculated sadism, as contrasted with hot-blooded massacre, was appearing. So also we find masochism, necrophilia, and many other symptoms of inner personal derangement emerging at the level of social acceptance. The age of the Renaissance, 1300 to 1650, was a time of human tragedy unparalleled in Europe, and perhaps elsewhere in world history. Someday we may hope to know more exactly how such tragedy was related to the simultaneous creativity of that epoch." "Death and the Devil" in *The Darker Vision of the Renaissance* ed. Robert S. Kinsman (Berkeley: University of California Press, 1974), 43–44. Cf. the bloody context of Tamburlaine's meditation on unattainable beauty in *Tamburlaine I* (V.ii. 96–110).

24. Philip A. Smith, "Bishop Hall, 'Our English Seneca,'" *PMLA* 63 (1948): 1191.

25. Lipsius, *Two Books of Constancie,* ed. Kirk, 21. Robert Hoopes questions Kirk's "hypothesis," but does not, I believe, refute it in his *Right Reason in the English Renaissance* (Cambridge, Mass.: Harvard University Press, 1962), 135.

26. According to Ford Lewis Battles and Andre Malan Hugo, this expression was first used by Dr. Fairbairn in his *The Place of Christianity in Modern Theology* (1893). There is the contrary view of E. Doumergue, among others, that Calvin shows himself to be "anti-Stoïcien philosophiquement et moralement." *Calvin's Commentary on Seneca's De Clementia* (Leiden: E. J. Brill, 1969), 41.

27. Seneca, *Moral Essays* trans. John W. Basore (London: Heinemann, 1963) I, 377.

28. Ibid., 375. Cf. *De Beneficiis* I. x. 3: "Vices do not wait expectantly in just one spot, but are always in movement and, being at variance with each other, are in constant turmoil, they rout and in turn are routed; but the verdict we are obliged to pronounce upon ourselves will always be the same: wicked we are, wicked we have been, and, I regret to add, always shall be." Trans. John W. Basore, *Seneca Moral Essays* (Cambridge, Mass.: Harvard, 1964), III, 33.

29. Battles and Hugo, *Calvin's Commentary,* 129.

30. See L. D. Reynolds, *The Medieval Tradition of Seneca's Letters* (Oxford: Oxford University Press, 1965), chap. 6.

31. Basore, *Moral Essays* I, 374, note.

32. Basore, *Moral Essays* I, 437.

33. Battles and Hugo, *Calvin's Commentary,* 359–61.

34. Noted by Battles and Hugo, *Calvin's Commentary,* 359.

35. One of Calvin's English followers, Thomas James, in the introduction to his translation of Du Vair's *Traité de la Philosophie morale des Stoïques,* defends the use of "words and sentences of the Heathen" with an appeal to his unimpeachable authority: "this libertie Master *Calvin* in his Commentarie vpon those places liberally granteth vs, and I suppose it cannot lawfully bee denyed: for gold and siluer and pretious iewels were euer used as ornaments in the old law to decke and garnish the Temple withall." Du Vair, *The Moral Philosophie of the Stoicks,* trans. Thomas James, ed. Kirk, 45. James was Bodley's librarian and the author of various anti-Catholic tracts. His Calvinist zeal prompted him to urge the investigation of all English libraries, public and private, to ferret out patristic writings tainted with popery by Roman Catholic editors. Unable to obtain Parliament's support for this project, he attempted to carry it out himself singlehandedly. (D.N.B.) No less zealous than James, Anthony Munday (1553–33), translator of Philippe de Mornay's *The True Knowledge of a Man's owne Selfe,* began his literary career with "the English Romayne Life," an exposé based on his experience spying on the English seminary in Rome. After Edmund Campion and his associates were captured in 1581, he wrote five tracts exposing "the horrible and unnatural treasons of the catholics," and his savage indictment "A Discoverie of Edmund Campion and his Confederates" was read aloud on the scaffold to the martyred victims on 30 May 1582. He was also employed by Richard Topcliffe, Elizabeth's leading priest-hunter, to whom he dedicated his *A Banquet of Daintie Conceits* (1588). (See Celeste Turner, *Anthony Munday, An Elizabethan Man of Letters,* Berkeley: University of California Press, 1928, and *D.N.B.*)

Sir Philip Sidney's ardent Calvinist Protestantism is generally recognized. Arthur Golding (1536?–1605?), who completed Sidney's translation of Mornay's *The Trewnesse of the Christian Religion,* was known for his strong Puritan predilections. In addition to translating Ovid's *Metamorphoses* and Seneca's *De Beneficiis,* he also translated works by Calvin and Beza. (*D.N.B.*)

Samson Lennard (d. 1633) accompanied Sidney to the Netherlands and was with him when he received his fatal wound at the battle of Zutphen in 1586. In addition to Mornay's *Mystery of Iniquitie* and Charron's *Of Wisdome,* Lennard translated Perrin's *Luther's Fore-runners,* or a *Cloud of Witnesses deposing for the Protestant Faith.* (*D.N.B.*)

Another English translator of Mornay was John Healey (d. 1610). In addition to *Lord of Plessis, his Teares,* Healey translated Joseph Hall's satire on the Roman Church, *Mundus Alter et Idem* (1609) and *Epictetus his Manuall* (1610) as well as the first translation into English of St. Augustine's *The Citie of God* (1610). He dedicated the translation of Epictetus to John Florio (1553?–1625), translator of Montaigne and son of a Florentine Protestant whose family fled to England shortly before Edward VI's reign to avoid religious persecution. The elder Florio was a preacher to a congregation of Italian Protestants in London until he fell into disgrace. (*D.N.B.*)

A significant exception to the rule that translating the Stoics and Neostoics went hand in hand with Protestantism in England was Thomas Lodge (1558?–1625), translator of Seneca's *Workes both Morrall and Naturall* (1614). In middle life, well before he completed his great translation, he became a Catholic. (*D.N.B.*)

And Lodge is certainly not the only Catholic who found Stoicism congenial, either in England or on the continent. On the continent, in fact, most of the Neostoic writers were Catholics, but it is interesting to consider that the works of two of the most influential, Pierre Charron and Montaigne, were placed on the *Index Librorum Prohibitorum.* One gathers that this was because of the element of skepticism that is so prominent in their works. Sir William Cornwallis (1579–1614), who had a Catholic background, might be termed the first Neostoic moralist in English, if we enlarge the term *Neostoic* to include those writers whose point of view and temperament were Stoic and who tended to support their ideas with reference to Stoic writers. His writings include *Discourses upon Seneca the tragedian* (1601), *Essays on certain Paradoxes* (1616) and *The Miraculous and Happy Union between England and Scotland* (1604). Actually, Joseph Hall is more deserving of the title. His *Heaven upon Earth* (1606), a commentary on Seneca's *De Tranquillitate,* is the first critical exposition of Stoicism in English focusing on the extent to which it could be adapted to the needs of Christians.

36. *A Woorke Concerning the trewnesse of the Christian Religion,* written in French: Against Atheists, Epicures, Paynims, Iewes, Mahumetists, and other Infidels by Philip of Mornay Lord of Plessis Marlie. Begunne to be translated into English by Sir Philip Sidney Knight, and at his request finished by Arthur Golding. (London: Thomas Cadman, 1587), BM. C. 122.d.17. All quotations are from this edition and references will be given in the text in parentheses.

37. Sidney's sister, the Countess of Pembroke, translated Mornay's *Discourse of Life and Death,* along with Robert Garnier's tragedy *Antonius,* and the two translations appeared in a single volume in 1592. An earlier translation, *The Defence of Death. Containing a moste excellent discourse of life and death* by "E.A." (Edward Aggas) had been published in 1577, only a year after it appeared in France (Lausanne, 1576). The Countess of Pembroke's translation was reprinted in 1600, 1606, and 1607. A translation into Latin by A. Freitagius (1585) was translated into English in 1699. In 1602, Anthony Munday's translation *The True Knowledge of Mans owne Selfe* was published. Another work very much in the Stoic vein, *P. Mornai Lachrimae* (Paris, 1606) was translated by John Healey as *Lord of Plessis His Teares* (1609).

Among his various theological works translated rapidly into English is a seven hundred-page volume entitled *The Mystery of Iniquitty, that is to say, the history of the Papacy* (1611), which was rendered into English by Samson Lennard just a year after it appeared in French.

38. *The French Academie* by Peter de la Primaudaye The Third Edition and newly translated into English by T.B. (London: Geor. Bishop, 1594), part 1, p. 11. British Museum 8406 ccc 17. All quotations are from this edition and references will be given in the text in parenthesis.

39. The term *Synteresis* first occurs, according to W. R. Inge, in St. Jerome's commentary on *Ezechiel*. After that it occurs in Aquinas and in the Christian mystics. *Christian Mysticism* (London: Chapman and Hall, 1899), 359–60). Among the schoolmen generally, it was spelled *"Synderesis."* These writers present various views of its nature and functions as a moral agency within man. Cf. Bonaventure, *Commentary on the Sentences*, 2, dist. 39, art. 1, q. 1; Albert the Great, *Summa de Creaturis* q. 71, art. 1.2; St. Thomas Aquinas, *Commentary on the Sentences*, dist. 24, q. 2, art. 3. For discussion of these passages, see Eric D'Arcy, *Conscience and Its Right to Freedom* (London: Sheed & Ward, 1961), 20–71.

40. Eduard Zeller, *The Stoics, Epicureans and Sceptics*, trans. Oswald J. Reichel (New York: Russell & Russell, 1962), 172. "The human soul is not only a part, as are all other living powers, of the universal power of life, but because it possesses reason, it has a special relationship to the Divine Being—a relationship that becomes closer in proportion as we allow greater play to the divine element in ourselves, i.e. to reason." 216–17.

41. *Ep.* 41. *The Stoic Philosophy of Seneca Essays and Letters*, trans. Moses Hadas (New York: Norton, 1958), 189. Cf. Epictetus, *Discourses* II. viii. 12: "But you are a being of primary importance; you are a fragment of God; you have within you a part of Him. Why, then, are you ignorant of your own kinship? Why do you not know the source from which you have sprung? Will you not bear in mind, whenever you eat, who you are that eat, and whom you are nourishing? Whenever you indulge in intercourse with women, who you are that do this?" trans. W. A. Oldfather, *Discourses* I (Cambridge, Mass.: Harvard University Press, 1961), 261. And Marcus Aurelius, *Meditations* V. 27: "Walk with the Gods! And he does walk with the Gods, who lets them see his soul invariably satisfied with its lot and carrying out the will of that 'genius,' a particle of himself, which Zeus has given to every man as his captain and guide—and this is none other than each man's intelligence and reason." trans. C. R. Haines, *The Communings with Himself of Marcus Aurelius* (Cambridge, Mass.: Harvard University Press, 1961), 123.

42. Inge, *Christian Mysticism*, 359–60. See also Wilks, *The Idea of Conscience in Renaissance Tragedy*, 10; Timothy C. Potts (trans.), *Conscience in Medieval Philosophy* (Cambridge: Cambridge University Press, 1980), 79–80. Noted by Wilks.

43. As my colleague Michael Rudick has pointed out to me, Protestant and Roman Catholic casuists agreed essentially regarding synteresis and the operation of the practical syllogism, and it may be that some of the Protestants were merely appropriating Thomist thought.

44. William Ames, *Of Conscience and the Cases Thereof* (London, 1643), bk. 1, 3–4.

45. Ames, *Of Conscience* bk. 1, p. 5.

46. Noted by Anthony Caputi, *John Marston, Satirist* (Ithaca: Cornell University Press), 59–60.

47. John Marston, *The Scourge of Villanie*, in *The Poems of John Marston* ed. Arnold Davenport (Liverpool: Liverpool University Press, 1961), 208–320.

48. For discussion of this genre, see Thomas N. Tentler, *Sin and Confession on the Eve of the Reformation* (Princeton: Princeton University Press, 1977), chap. 2.

49. William Perkins, *The Whole Treatise of the Cases of Conscience* (London, 1614), 27. British Museum copy.

50. Ibid.

51. Perkins, *A Discourse of Conscience* (London, 1632), 517.

52. Ibid., 27.

53. Ibid., 12.

54. Perkins, *Whole Treatise,* 27.

55. See G. Gooch, *English Democratic Ideas in the 17th Century* (New York: Harper & Row, 1959); also Lawrence Stone, *The Crisis of the Aristocracy 1558–1641* (Oxford: Oxford University Press, 1965).

56. See Rozett, *The Doctrine of Election,* 65–73. This turning inward is also a tendency of contemporary Catholicism, as evidenced in Ignatius Loyola's *Spiritual Exercises.* See Jeffrey Burton Russell, *Mephistopheles* (Ithaca: Cornell University Press, 1986), chap. 2.

57. See Krister Stendahl, "The Apostle Paul and the Introspective Conscience of the West," *Harvard Theological Review* 56 (1963), 199–215; Rudolf Bultmann, "Paul's Demythologizing and Ours," *The Writings of St. Paul* ed. Wayne A. Meeks (New York: Norton, 1972), 409–22.

58. Braden, *Renaissance Tragedy,* 70.

59. This linkage is not of course exclusively Protestant. See St. Teresa of Avila, *Moradas del castillo interior* and *Camino de perfeccion.*

60. Joseph Hall, *Heaven upon Earth and Characters of Vertues and Vices,* ed. Rudolph Kirk (New Brunswick, N.J.: Rutgers University Press, 1948), 160.

61. Ibid.

62. F. L. Huntley, *Bishop Joseph Hall 1574–1656: A Biographical and Critical Study* (Cambridge: Cambridge University Press, 1979), 52.

63. Ben Jonson, *Bartholomew Fair,* ed. Eugene Waith (New Haven: Yale University Press, 1963). All quotations are from this edition.

64. E.g., Epictetus, *Discourses,* I. xix.

65. *Ep.* 25.5; cf. 11.8 ff. Quoted by Braden, *Renaissance Tragedy,* 26.

66. See Geoffrey Aggeler, "'Good Pity' in *King Lear,*" *Neophilologus* 77 (April 1993): 321–31.

67. Hall, *Heaven upon Earth,* 60.

68. According to Charron, the nature of the soul itself is determined by its choices between the injunctions of the divine spark and those of the flesh, "for according vnto that part towards which it applieth it selfe, it is either spirituall and good, or carnall and euill." *Of Wisdome three bookes* . . . , trans. Samson Lennard (London: Blount, 1608), p. 11. British Museum copy.

69. Hall, *Heaven upon Earth,* 85.

70. Ibid., 38–39.

71. E.g., such works as Edward Reynolds, *A Treatise of the Passions and Faculties of the Soul;* Fulke Greville, *A Treatie of Humane Learning;* John Davies of Hereford, *Microcosmos.* Calvin himself actually discouraged inquiry into the working of the faculties. *Institutes* I, xv 6; II, ii, 3. Noted by William Haller, *The Rise of Puritanism* (New York: Harper Torchbooks, 1957), 85.

72. Charron, *Of Wisdom,* 168. Such attacks on the Scholastic tradition probably did little to prevent *De la Sagesse* from being placed on the *Index Librorum Prohibitorum* but probably increased its popularity in Protestant England, where Samson

Lennard's translation went through many editions: 1608, 1612, 1630, 1640, 1656, 1658, and 1670.

73. E.g., Epictetus, *Discourses,* I. xix.

74. *Discourses,* IV. x. 10–13.

75. Seneca, *Hercules Furens,* II. 922–24, trans. John Milton, *Tenure of Kings and Magistrates. Works* V (New York: Columbia University Press, 1932), 19.

76. John Milton, 9. Ibid., 19–20.

77. Noted by Christopher Hill, *Milton and the English Revolution* (New York: Viking, 1977), 168.

78. F. P. Wilson, *Elizabethan and Jacobean* (Oxford University Press, 1945), 88.

79. Joel Altman, *The Tudor Play of Mind: Rhetorical Inquiry and the Development of Elizabethan Drama* (Berkeley: University of California Press, 1978), 6. Quoted by Rozett, *The Doctrine of Election,* 38.

80. Rozett, *The Doctrine of Election,* 38.

81. As I noted earlier, however, the works of both of these writers were placed on the *Index Librorum Prohibitorum.*

82. Braden, *Renaissance Tragedy,* 94.

83. I am especially indebted to Richard H. Popkin, *The History of Scepticism from Erasmus to Spinoza* (Berkeley: University of California Press, 1979); Anthony Levi, *The French Moralists* (Oxford University Press, 1966); Don Cameron Allen, *Doubt's Boundless Sea* (Baltimore: Johns Hopkins University Press, 1964); Robert Hoopes, "Fideism and Skepticism during the Renaissance: Three Major Witnesses," *HLQ* 14 (1951) 319–47 (chap. 6 of his *Right Reason*); Rosalie Colie, *Paradoxia Epidemica* (Princeton University Press, 1966); Ernest A. Strathman, *Sir Walter Ralegh A Study in Elizabethan Skepticism* (New York: Columbia University Press, 1951); W .R. Elton, *King Lear and the Gods* (San Marino: Huntington Library, 1966).

84. Strathmann, *Sir Walter Ralegh,* 219.

85. In *I Corinthians 2 : 14, psychikos anthropos* is variously translated: "the natural man" (Geneva and King James), "an unspiritual person" (New Jerusalem), "the sensual man" (Challoner-Rheims). ψυχικὸς can mean either of the soul, mental as opposed to bodily, concerned with this life only, animal or natural, as opposed to spiritual. (Liddell and Scott). The context of the verse, which opposes *psychikos* to *pneumatikos,* is a condemnation of the intellectually arrogant rationalists who teach "man's wisdom" and regard "the things of the Spirit of God" as "foolishness." Paul may have had in mind the Stoic and Epicurean natural philosophers he debated in Athens who reportedly "mocked" him when he preached the resurrection of the dead (*Acts* 17: 18–33). Though *psychikos anthropos* seems to refer primarily to unspiritual man, as opposed to man illumined by the Spirit of God, it may also refer to the intellectually arrogant rationalist who will not accept truths inaccessible to reason. In this sense, *psychikos* could mean "mental." The Challoner-Rheims translators observe that the "rulers of the world," referred to in *I Cor. 2:6* can be "interpreted as intellectual and political leaders among men, or as devils. The two interpretations can be harmonized." *The New Testament A Revision of the Challoner-Rheims Version* (New York: Catholic Book Publishing Co., 1948), 214.

86. Allen, *Doubt's Boundless Sea,* 4. He uses Edmund and D'Amville as examples of "practical atheists" and sees the final scene of *The Atheist's Tragedy* as emblematic: "when the godless D'Amville, about to execute another, accidentally brains himself with the ax, he (Tourneur) has the atheist see in this ill-chance the command of God and the weakness 'of natural understanding.' Nature and the wisdom of men are subordinate to a 'power above.' In other words, the atheist must knock his brains out to understand the divine." p. 27. Allen's distinction between practical and

speculative atheists is paralleled to some extent by Strathmann's distinction between the Machiavellian hypocritical "inward" atheist and the "outward" atheist who openly professes his disbelief. *Sir Walter Ralegh,* 86–87. See also Elton's discussion of these two types. *King Lear and the Gods,* 53–57.

87. Ibid., 19–27. "The contemplative atheist is rare," observes Francis Bacon in his essay "Of Atheism." He goes on to remark that slander caused by differences in religious opinion creates the illusion that they are more numerous: "yet they seem to be more than they are, for that all that impugn a received religion or superstition are by the adverse part branded with the name of atheists." *Francis Bacon A Selection of his Works,* ed. Sidney Warhaft (London: Collier Macmillan, 1988), 87–88.

88. Michael Lord of Montaigne, "An Apologie of Raymond Sebond," *The Essayes* trans. John Florio (London: Oxford University Press, 1906), 2, 314–15.

89. Popkin, *The History of Scepticism,* 7.

90. Quoted by Jacques Maritain, *Three Reformers* (New York: Scribner's, 1954), 36; and by Hoopes, *Right Reason,* 103.

91. Quoted by Hoopes, *Right Reason,* 111.

92. Ibid.

93. Quoted by Popkin, *The History of Scepticism,* 9.

94. Hoopes, *Right Reason,* 121.

95. Screech notes that Montaigne was "doubtless under the influence of Pyrrho" when he had this medal struck in 1576. Michel de Montaigne, *An Apology for Raymond Sebond,* trans. M. A. Screech (London: Penguin, 1993), 100, n 238.

96. Caputi, *John Marston,* 58. Noted by Elton, *King Lear,* 47.

97. See John M. Robertson, *Montaigne and Shakespeare* (New York: Haskell House, 1968); F. O. Matthiessen, *Translation An Elizabethan Art* (Cambridge: Harvard University Press, 1931); George C. Taylor, *Shakespeare's Debt to Montaigne* (Cambridge: Harvard University Press, 1925, p. 38: "In *Lear* and in other plays after [Florio's translation in] 1603, the impression one gets of the forces of nature at play around us is vaster, more terrible, than before." Quoted by Elton, p. 47.

98. Michael Lord of Montaigne, *The Essayes,* vol. 1, trans. John Florio (London: Henry Frowde, 1904), 53.

99. *Essayes,* I, 277.

100. Allen, *Doubt's Boundless Sea,* 80.

101. Braden, *Renaissance Tragedy,* 95, 98.

102. *Essayes,* II, 11, 14, 21. Another Stoic he probably had in mind was Seneca: "At times we ought to reach the point even of intoxication, not drowning ourselves in drink, yet succumbing to it; for it washes away troubles, and stirs the mind from its very depths and heals its sorrow just as it does certain ills of the body; and the inventor of wine is not called the Releaser on account of the licence it gives to the tongue, but because it frees the mind from bondage to cares and emancipates it and gives it new life and makes it bolder in all that it attempts." *De Tranquillitate Animi* xvii, 9. trans. John W. Basore, *Seneca Moral Essays* III, 283.

103. *Essayes* II, 123.

104. "Of Drunkennesse," *Essayes* II, 21.

105. Montaigne, *Essayes,* III, 383.

106. Ibid., 334.

107. Seneca, *De Consolatione Ad Marciam,* xi. 3, trans. Basore, *Moral Essays* II, 32.

108. Screech notes, in connection with the conclusion of the *Apology:* "The concluding words of the treatise *On the E'i at Delphi* emphasize its connection with Montaigne's themes of self-knowledge and the abasement of Man: 'And meanwhile

it seems that this word *E'i* is somewhat opposed to the precept *Know Thyself* and also in some ways accordant and agreeable to it: the one is a kind of verbal astonishment and adoration before God, as being Eternal and Ever in Being, while the other is a warning and reminder to mortal Man of the weakness and debility of his nature." *An Apology for Raymond Sebond,* trans. M. A. Screech (London: Penguin, 1993), 189, n 482.

109. Montaigne, *The Essayes* II, 153. As Hoopes remarks, "Calvin himself could hardly have given voice to a more Calvinistic utterance." *Right Reason,* 118.

110. Ibid., 154–55.

111. Popkin, *History of Scepticism,* 46.

112. Montaigne, *Essayes* II, 169.

113. Strathmann, *Sir Walter Ralegh,* 87. He is quoting one of the opening lines of *The Atheist's Tragedy.*

114. Charles Darwin, *The Descent of Man,* chap. 21.

115. Montaigne, *Essayes* II, 367–68.

116. Colie, *Paradoxia Epidemica,* 399.

117. Sextus Empiricus, *Outlines of Pyrrhonism,* trans. R. G. Bury (Buffalo, N.Y.: Prometheus Books, 1990), 17.

118. Colie, 406.

119. See chap. 1, fn 72.

120. Sextus Empiricus groups them with Aristotle and the Epicureans as "dogmatists" at the beginning of his *Outline.*

121. M. Pierre Le Charron, *De La Sagesse Livres Trois* (Bovrdeavs: Simon Millanges, 1601), British Museum copy, 1.

122. See especially his discussion of "misericorde": "Il y a double misericorde, l'une forte, bonne, & verteuse, qui est en Dieu & aux Saincts, qui est par volonté & par effect secourir aux affligés sans s'affliger soi-mesmes, sans rié raualler de la iustice & dignité; l'autre est une sotte & feminine pitié passionnée, qui vient de mollesse & foiblesse d'ame, de laquelle a esté parlé aux passions ci dessus." *De la Sagesse,* 730.

123. Sir William Cornwallis, the Younger, *Essayes* ed. Don Cameron Allen (Baltimore: Johns Hopkins, 1946), Essay 41, "Of Sorrow," 163.

CHAPTER 2. ENGLISH SENECA

1. Aristotle, *Poetics,* 1448a.

2. "For the young person is not able to judge what is allegory and what is not; but he will keep in his mind indelible and unchangeable whatever opinions he receives at that age." *Republic* II (378 C), trans. W. H. D. Rouse, *Great Dialogues of Plato* (New York: Mentor, 1956), 176.

3. For discussion of the skepticism in the *Oresteia,* see Philip Vellacott, "Has Good Prevailed?" *Harvard Studies in Classical Philology* 81 (1977): 197–22.

4. Philip Vellacott, *Ironic Drama a Study of Euripides' Method and Meaning* (Cambridge University Press, 1975), 22.

5. H. D. F. Kitto, *Greek Tragedy* (London: Methuen, 1973), 133–135.

6. Stanley Cavell, *Disowning Knowledge in Six Plays of Shakespeare* (Cambridge, 1991), 5.

7. Rosenmeyer, *Senecan Drama,* 189–90.

8. Jonathan Dollimore, *Radical Tragedy,* 2d ed., (London: Harvester Wheatsheaf, 1989), 29.

9. Lily Bess Campbell, "Theories of Revenge in Renaissance England," *Modern Philology* 28 (1931), 281.

10. Fredson Bowers, *Elizabethan Revenge Tragedy* (Princeton: Princeton University Press, 1940); Eleanor Prosser, *Hamlet and Revenge* (Stanford: Stanford University Press, 1971); Charles A. and Elaine S. Hallett, *The Revenger's Madness: A Study of Revenge Tragedy Motifs* (Lincoln: University of Nebraska Press, 1980).

11. Philip J. Ayres, "Degrees of Heresy: Justified Revenge and Elizabethan Narratives," *Studies in Philology* 69 (1972): 465.

12. John Sibly, "The Duty of Revenge in Tudor and Stuart Drama," *Review of English Literature* 8 (1967): 51.

13. Harry Keyishian, "Shakespeare and the Revenge Traditions," paper read at the World Shakespeare Congress, Tokyo, 18 August 1991. I am indebted to Professor Keyishian for his summary of the arguments against the "Campbellist position."

14. As Curtis B. Watson does in his *Shakespeare and the Renaissance Concept of Honour* (Princeton, 1960).

15. *Beyond Good and Evil*, 260.

16. William Ames, *Of Conscience and the Cases Thereof* (London, 1643) book 5, 114–17.

17. Martin Luther, *Lectures on Romans*, trans. Wilhelm Pauck, Library of Christian Classics XV (Philadelphia, 1961), 354–55.

18. Richard Hooker, *Of the Laws of Ecclesiastical Polity* VII. xvii. 2. *Works*, 2 vols. (Oxford University Press, 1865).

19. Aristotle, *The Nichomachean Ethics*, III. 7, trans. Sir David Ross (Oxford, 1961).

20. Ibid., 1. 5.

21. Ibid., 4. 3.

22. *Republic*, bk 1. 2e.

23. *Ethics*, IV. 5.

24. *Rhetoric* bk 1, chapter 9. 1367a. Quoted by Harry Keyishian, "Shakespeare and the Revenge Traditions." Commenting on the line καὶ τὸ τοὺσ ἐξθρουσ τιμωρεῖσθαι μᾶδδον, Edward M. Cope renders it "and the heavier vengeance on, punishment of, one's enemies" (μᾶλλοω may be either to punish them in a higher degree, the more the better: or as contrasted with καταλλάπεσθαι "rather than the reverse") and "refusing to be reconciled, come to terms with them." The reason being, that "retaliatory" or "reciprocal justice" requires this, and therefore, it is right, and of course laudable: and also because "not to be beaten" (an unyielding resolution) is a sign of a "manly character." Cope observes that this was "a constant article of the popular morality," and he cites for comparison passages in Xenophon, Euripides, and Cicero's *De Officiis*. *The Rhetoric of Aristotle with a Commentary* (New York: Arno Press, 1973), 169–70.

25. See note 42, below.

26. Vellacott, *Ironic Drama*, 225; Braden, *Renaissance Tragedy*, 10.

27. Edgar Wind has pointed out how Seneca contributed to the ennobling of anger during the Renaissance. "Yet under the influence of Seneca's *De Ira*, although the medieval classification continued, a 'noble rage' was separated off from the common vice and defended as a virtue by Florentine humanists, in particular by Bruni, Politian, and Landino. By a similar transmutation the vice of sloth, the horrid *acedia*, was distilled into noble melancholy; for although *acedia* remained a deadly sin, an Aristotelian refinement of the affliction became the privilege of inspired men." *Pagan Mysteries of the Renaissance* (New Haven: Yale University Press, 1958), 69–70.

Quoted by Walter Kaiser, *Praisers of Folly* (Cambridge: Harvard University Press, 1963), 54.

28. Vellacott, *Ironic Drama,* 226.

29. E.g., G. B. Harrison in the introduction to the play in his edition of the *Complete Works.*

30. Jeremy Taylor, *Ductor Dubitantium,* book 3. 2. Rule 6. ed. Reginald Heber, London, 1883, vol. 10 of *The Whole Works,* 132–44.

31. Francis Bacon, "Of Revenge."

32. Taylor, *Ductor Dubitantium,* X, 134.

33. Francis Bacon, "Of Revenge," *Francis Bacon a Selection of His Works,* ed. Sidney Warhaft (New York: Macmillan, 1982), 55–56.

34. Ames, *Of Conscience,* 115–16.

35. Ibid., 115.

36. Seneca, *De Constantia Sapientis* 7. 2. *Seneca Moral Essays,* I, trans. John W. Basore (London: Heinemann, 1963), 71–73.

37. Ibid., IX. 1–2.

38. Ibid.

39. Seneca, *De Ira,* I. III. 3. *Seneca Moral Essays* I, trans. J. W. Basore (London: Heinemann, 1963), 113–15.

40. Ibid., 1. 6. 3.

41. Ibid., I. VI. 1.

42. Martha C. Nussbaum, *The Therapy of Desire Theory and Practice in Hellenistic Ethics* (Princeton: Princeton University Press, 1994), 426.

43. Epictetus, *Discourses,* I. XVIII. 5–9. *Epictetus,* trans. W. A. Oldfather, I (London: Heinemann, 1961), 123.

44. "Rufus. From Epictetus on friendship," fragment, trans. Oldfather, *Epictetus* II, 445–47.

45. *Discourses,* IV. V. 11–13, trans. Oldfather, *Epictetus* II, 335. Cf. Marcus Aurelius, *Meditations,* VI. 6; Cicero, *De Officiis,* I. xxv. 88–89.

46. Braden, *Renaissance Tragedy,* 221.

47. For discussion of conventional views of these roles, see Fredson Bowers, "Hamlet as Minister and Scourge," *PMLA* LXX (1955), 740–49.

48. James M. Redfield, *Nature and Culture in the Iliad The Tragedy of Hector,* (Chicago: University of Chicago Press, 1975), 131.

49. All quotations are from Thomas Kyd, *The First Part of Hieronimo and the Spanish Tragedy,* ed. Andrew S. Cairncross (Lincoln: University of Nebraska Press, 1967).

50. For comparison of these three descents into the Underworld see Howard Baker, *Induction to Tragedy.*

51. Concerning this scene in the *Iliad,* Redfield remarks: "Men and cities are the counters in a game played between the gods. The game can become absorbing, but it is never really worth a quarrel. The gods can always repair their differences by allowing the destruction of another ephemeral human thing. . . . Nietzsche wrote, in *The Birth of Tragedy,* 'The gods justified human life by living it themselves—the only satisfactory theodicy ever invented.' Perhaps; but one could also say that the Homeric gods, by living human life *forever,* reduce our lives to insignificance or remind us that its significance is something privately shared among ourselves." (*Nature and Culture in the Iliad,* 132).

52. See Vellacott, *Ironic Drama,* chap. 2.

53. Ernst de Chickera, "Divine Justice and Private Revenge in *The Spanish Tragedy,*" *Modern Language Review* 57 (1962): 228.

54. Ibid.

55. Scott McMillin, "The Figure of Silence in *The Spanish Tragedy*," *ELH* 39 (1972): 28.

56. McMillin, 28–36, and Jonas Barish,"*The Spanish Tragedy,* or The Pleasures and Perils of Rhetoric," in *Elizabethan Theatre,* ed. John Russell Brown and Bernard Harris, *Stratford-Upon-Avon Studies* 9 (New York: St. Martin's Press, 1967), 58–85.

57. See Herbert R. Coursen, "The Unity of *The Spanish Tragedy*," *SP* 65 (1968): 768–82; William Empson, "The Spanish Tragedy," in *Elizabethan Drama: Modern Essays in Criticism,* ed. R. J. Kaufmann (New York: Oxford University Press, 1961); and Cairncross's introduction to his edition *The First Part of Hieronimo and The Spanish Tragedy.*

58. Edwards notes that an English Knight Marshal was "A Law officer whose authority was exercised in the English royal household, in hearing and determining all pleas of the crown, and suits between those of the king's house and others within the verge (sc. within a radius of twelve miles), and in punishing transgressions committed within his area." (Note to I. i. 25 in Edwards's edition of the play.)

59. In the words of Edwin Sandys, "Such as are magistrates, to whom the deciding of causes and punishing offenses is committed, should be chosen out of all the people, the best and fittest men for their wisdom and courage, their religion and hearty affection to the truth, and for the hatred which they bear to covetousness. For this is no office for a fool; and he that loveth not the truth will shew pariality: he that loveth not the truth will justify the wicked, and condemn the innocent." ("Owe Nothing to Any Man," a sermon made at York [1585] in *Sermons,* Parker Society, vol. 42 (Cambridge University Press, 1842), 201.

60. Baker, *Induction to Tragedy,* 214.

61. See Ronald Broude, "Time, Truth, and Right in *The Spanish Tragedy*." *SP* 68 (1971): 130–45. In the opinion of de Chickera, Hieronimo's speeches of grief are "so ambiguous that at first sight they appear to refer to private revenge. But Isabella's reply, implying neither rebuke nor reproach, points out their true significance." ("Divine Justice," 228–29).

62. Henry Bullinger, "Of the Second Precept of the Second Table, Which is in Order the Sixth of the Ten Commandments, Thou Shalt Not Kill: and of the Magistrate" (1549), in *The Decades of Henry Bullinger Minister of the Church of Zurich,* trans. H. I., ed. for the Parker Society by Rev. Thos. Harding (Cambridge: Cambridge University Press, 1849), VII. 347: "Now touching the office of a good judge, the first point thereof is that he repel no man, but hear every one, the small, the great, the citizen, the stranger, the known and unknown. And he must hear the parties willingly, diligently, and attentively. Herein there is admitted no sluggishness of the judge, nor a mind busied about other matters. Judgement before the matter be decided is utterly excluded, because it carrieth away the mind of the judge before the matter is known. The thing itself crieth out, that the matter must first be heard and well understood, before the magistrate proceed to judgement."

63. De Chickera, "Divine Justice," 230.

64. Fredson Bowers, *Elizabethan Revenge Tragedy* (Princeton: Princeton University Press, 1966), 78.

65. Empson, "The Spanish Tragedy," 76.

66. See Kitto, *Greek Tragedy,* 134–35. In his discussion of Sophocles' *Electra,* Kitto suggests that while δίκη in Aeschylean tragedy is "a moral and social word, 'retributive justice' in *Agamemnon,* mellowing into 'justice' as things improve," it and its opposite, ἀδικία, have in Sophocles the "amoral sense" that they have in the writings of the Ionian philosophers.

67. S. F. Johnson attaches a great deal of importance to this reference in connection with Hieronimo's playlet in four languages and various scriptural analogues ("*The Spanish Tragedy*, or Babylon Revisited," in *Essays on Shakespeare and Elizabethan Drama in Honor of Hardin Craig*, ed. Richard Hosley (Columbia: University of Missouri Press, 1962), 28–29.

68. M. D. Faber and Colin Skinner, "*The Spanish Tragedy*: Act 4," *Philological Quarterly* 49 (1970), 444–59.

69. Johnson, "Babylon Revisited," 36.

70. G. K. Hunter, "Ironies of Justice in *The Spanish Tragedy*," *Renaissance Drama* 8 (1965): 104.

71. Philip Edwards, introduction to his edition of *The Spanish Tragedy* (Cambridge, Mass: Harvard University Press, 1959), liii.

72. Norman Rabkin discusses the complexity of Shakespeare's histories in *Shakespeare and the Problem of Meaning* (Chicago: University of Chicago Press, 1981).

73. For discussion of a comparable vindication of illusion in Marlowe's *Tamburlaine*, see Geoffrey Aggeler, "Marlowe and the Development of Tragical Satire," *English Studies* 58 (1977): 209–21.

CHAPTER 3. JOHN MARSTON'S SPARKLING STEEL

1. Alvin Kernan, *The Cankered Muse: Satire of the English Renaissance* (New Haven: Yale University Press, 1959), 123–26.

2. Caputi, *John Marston, Satirist*, 52–79. In his edition of Marston's poems, Arnold Davenport reveals a strong Calvinist bent, along with what he sees as inconsistencies in Marston's philosophical positions. *The Poems of John Marston*, (Liverpool English Texts and Studies, 1961). Philip J. Finkelpearl argues against Caputi's view that Marston was a Neostoic in his *John Marston of the Middle Temple* (Cambridge, Mass.: Harvard University Press, 1969), 110. Apparently, like Caputi and Kernan, he believes that Calvinism and Neostoicism were incompatible.

3. See chapter 1 of the present study.

4. Paul R. Sellin, "The Hidden God, Reformation Awe in Renaissance English Literature," *The Darker Vision of the Renaissance*, 173. Sellin adds: "Much more Genevan in their expression than, say, the Augsburg Confession or the Formula of Concord, the Forty-Two Articles [of the Edwardine formulary of 1553] provided the basis of Queen Elizabeth's religious settlement, and accordingly the Thirty-Nine Articles (1563 and 1571) still remain an admirable expression of moderate Calvinist orthodoxy touching matters of grace, sin, and predestination."

5. C. S. Lewis, *English Literature in the Sixteenth Century* (New York: Oxford University Press, 1954), 43. He discusses this point at some length.

6. To this day, one may observe the headless and otherwise mutilated statues and read the inscriptions attributing the damage to the cathedral's having been "*purgé*" in 1562.

7. See John Marston, *The Dutch Courtesan*, ed. M. L. Wine (Lincoln: Nebraska University Press, 1965), note to II. iii. 6–9, p. 43.

8. E.g., Philip Stubbes, *The Anatomie of Abuses* (1583).

9. E.g., in *The Malcontent*, II. v. 112–22; IV. iii. 91–92, Ed. M. L. Wine.

10. T. S. Eliot, "John Marston," *Essays on Elizabethan Drama* (New York: Harvest, 1960), 174.

11. Samuel Schoenbaum, "The Precarious Balance of John Marston," in *Elizabethan Drama Modern Essays in Criticism,* ed. R. J. Kaufmann (New York: Oxford, 1961), 127.

12. Theodore Spencer, "Reason and Passion in Marston's *The Dutch Courtezan,*" in *Shakespeare's Contemporaries,* ed. Max Bluestone and Norman Rabkin, (Englewood Cliffs: Prentice Hall, 1961), 204. More recently, A. D. Cousins has argued that "Marston [in his verse satires] proposes a view of human nature which implies the need to revalue Christian Humanism's great orthodoxy concerning the peculiar excellence of man." He finds this view profoundly pessimistic, a representation of man as dominated by a soul-destroying master impulse: "This impulse to corruption literally makes man 'base muddy scum,' just moving matter with no spiritual faculty." A. D. Cousins, "The Protean Nature of Man in Marston's Verse Satires," *JEGP* 79 (1980): 517–29.

13. Plutarch, *Stoic. Absurd. Poet.* 3. 105. 8a, quoted by Rosenmeyer, *Senecan Drama,* 56.

14. Caputi, *John Marston,* 61.

15. *John Marston's The Wonder of Women or The Tragedy of Sophonisba,* A Critical Edition, ed. William Kemp (New York: Garland, 1979), 108.

16. *Antonio's Revenge,* IV. ii. 69, ed. G. K. Hunter (Lincoln: Nebraska, 1965). All quotations will be from this edition.

17. Finkelpearl, *John Marston of the Inner Temple,* 199.

18. I would cite in particular Gustav Cross, "Marston, Montaigne, and Morality: *The Dutch Courtezan Reconsidered,*" *ELH* 27 (1960), 30–43; M. L. Wine has provided an appendix to his edition of this play with quoted passages from Florio's Montaigne that Marston borrows or echoes. John Marston, *The Dutch Courtesan,* ed. M. L. Wine (Lincoln: University of Nebraska Press, 1965), 112–20.

19. R. A. Foakes, "John Marston's Fantastical Plays: *Antonio and Mellida* and *Antonio's Revenge,*" *Philological Quarterly* 41 (1962): 229–39.

20. Richard Levin, "The New *New Inn* and the Proliferation of Good Bad Drama," *Essays in Criticism* 22 (1972): 41–47; "The Proof of the Parody," *Essays in Criticism* 24 (1974): 312–17. Levin expands his argument in *New Readings vs. Old Plays* (Chicago: University of Chicago Press, 1979). In support of Levin's view is T. F. Wharton, "Old Marston or New Marston: The *Antonio* Plays," *Essays in Criticism* 25 (1975): 357–69.

21. Elizabeth M. Yearling, "'Mount Tufty Tamburlaine': Marston and Linguistic Excess," *Studies in English Literature* 20 (1980): 269.

22. G. K. Hunter, "English Folly and Italian Vice: The Moral Landscape of John Marston," in *Jacobean Theatre,* Stratford-upon-Avon Studies, vol. 1, ed. John Russell Brown & Bernard Harris (New York: St. Martin's), 88.

23. Ibid., 89.

24. John Marston, *Antonio and Mellida,* ed. G. K. Hunter (Lincoln: University of Nebraska Press, 1965), Induction 104–13. All quotations are from this edition.

25. William Babula, "The Avenger and the Satirist: John Marston's Malevole," in *Elizabethan Theatre VI,* ed. G. B. Hibbard (Hamden, Conn.: Archon, 1977), 51.

26. See Hunter's illuminating discussion of Marston's source in "English Folly and Italian Vice," 95–96.

27. Braden, *Renaissance Tragedy and the Senecan Tradition,* 30.

28. Hardin Craig, "The Shackling of Accidents: A Study of Elizabethan Tragedy," in *Elizabethan Drama,* ed. Ralph J. Kaufmann (New York: Oxford, 1961), 33.

29. Rosenmeyer, *Senecan Drama,* 88–89.

30. Ibid.

31. Hunter, "English Folly and Italian Vice," 89.

32. Seneca, *Thyestes,* ll. 451–53 in *Tragedies,* trans. Frank J. Miller (London: Heinemann, 1968) II, 129.

33. See Hunter's discussion of this in the introduction to his edition of *Antonio and Mellida,* xiv.

34. See discussion of this passage in chapter 1 of this study.

35. Especially III. ii. 58–62:

> For every man that Bolingbroke hath press'd
> To lift shrewd steel against our golden crown,
> God for his Richard hath in heavenly pay
> A glorious angel. Then, if angels fight,
> Weak men must fall; for heaven still guards the right.

36. Caputi, *John Marston, Satirist,* 149.

37. Michael Higgins, "The Convention of the Stoic Hero as handled by Marston," *Modern Language Review* 39 (1944): 343.

38. Caputi, *John Marston,* 149.

39. Cyrus Hoy, *The Hyacinth Room* (New York: Knopf, 1964), 216.

40. E.g., the execution of Dr. Roderigo Lopez. "On the scaffold he stated, according to Camden, that 'he loved the queen as well as he loved Jesus Christ, which [CAMDEN continues], from a man of the Jewish profession, moved no small laughter in the standers-by'(*Annals,* 676) He was afterwards hanged and quartered (STOW, *Chronicle,* 1631, p. 768)." *DNB* 12, p. 134.

41. Hunter, "English Folly and Italian Vice," 100.

42. See Gustav Cross's discussion "Marston, Montaigne, and Morality: *The Dutch Courtezan* Reconsidered," for discussion of the play as a critique of Stoicism.

43. E.g., Fredson Bowers, *Elizabethan Revenge Tragedy* (Princeton: Princeton University Press, 1959).

44. Elaborated by Epictetus, *Discourses,* book 1 xix.

45. See Stephen Greenblatt, *Renaissance Self-Fashioning,* chapter 5.

46. Seneca, *Moral Essays* I, trans. J. W. Basore (London: Heinemann, 1963), 107.

47. Ibid., 115.

48. Hoy, *The Hyacinth Room,* 216.

49. Fredson Bowers believes that the play must be understood in terms of "Senecan morality," but by "Senecan morality" he clearly means the morality of the avengers in Seneca's tragedies: "Of far more importance than the large number of Senecan quotations and echoes in the mouths of the characters is this imposition of the Roman callousness on the conventional English ethical view of the limits to which a revenger could go and the methods he should pursue. No other matter in the play illustrates so well the direct influence of Seneca on Marston. By every English tenet, Antonio is a cruel bloodthirsty villain who has over-stepped the bounds of revenge. Yet by Marston's Senecan morality Antonio is a dutiful son sacrificing the blood of the murderer's kindred to appease the ghost of his slain father, and he remains a hero to the end." *Elizabethan Revenge Tragedy,* 124.

50. See R. H. Barrow, *Plutarch and his Times* (Bloomington: Indiana University Press., 1967), 102–8.

51. Plutarch, "On Stoic Self-Contradictions," trans. Harold Cherniss, *Plutarch's Moralia,* 17 vols. (London: Heinemann, 1976), 13, 415–17.

52. John Marston, *The Malcontent,* ed. M. L. Wine (Lincoln: University of Nebraska Press, 1964). All quotations are from this edition.

53. Plutarch, "On the Delays of the Divine Vengeance," trans. Phillip DeLacey and Benedict Einarsen, *Moralia,* 7. 195–197.

54. Ibid., 207–27.

55. Caputi believes that Marston uses the term *synderesis* to designate a Neo-Stoic concept of a vestige of divinity in man in the form of a spark and that he derived it from the Christian mystics. "This spark was described by the mystics as the 'apex of the soul,' the 'natural will toward God,' or 'the remnant of the sinless state before the fall.'" (*John Marston, Satirist,* 59–60). Obviously Marston was aware of the Stoic concept of the spark of divinity in man; however, the contexts in which he uses synderesis in *The Scourge* indicate that he is referring to that part of the conscience that inclines the understanding toward basic moral principles. I am in agreement on this point with Arnold Davenport (*The Poems of John Marston,* 347). Marston's use of the term is the same as Aquinas's, and his spelling points to a Scholastic source. I am not, however, suggesting that he found the term in Aquinas, but he certainly need not have gone to the "Christian mystics," whom Caputi does not identify, to have found discussions of it. He could have found discussions of synteresis in any of the numerous contemporary Calvinist works of devotional literature. For discussion of these, see Wilks, *The Idea of Conscience,* 34–43.

56. Ames, *Of Conscience and the Cases Thereof,* I., 43.

57. Ames, *Of Conscience,* 43: "A *troubled Conscience,* is that which *accuseth* in such a manner, that it suffereth not the Conscience to be at rest. It bringeth with it an *astonishing feare,* and oppressing *griefe.* It is called in the Scripture, *sadnesse,* a *casting downe, affliction,* or *disquieting* of the minde, a *broken spirit, Prov.* 18. 14. A *troubled Conscience* is sometimes *honestly good* and sometimes *sinnefully evil. Honestly good* it is, when it *accuseth justly.*"

58. Epictetus illustrates the point in one of his fragments: "What man among us does not admire the saying of Lycurgus the Lacedaemonian? For when he had been blinded in one eye by one of his fellow-citizens, and the people had turned over the young man to him, to take whatever vengeance upon the culprit he might desire, this he refrained from doing, and brought him up and made a good man of him, and presented him in the theatre. And when the Lacedaemonians expressed their surprise, he said, "This man when I received him at your hands was insolent and violent; I am returning him to you a reasonable and public-spirited person." "Rufus. From Epictetus on Friendship," fragment, trans. Oldfather, *Epictetus* II, 335.

59. Caputi, *John Marston,* 75–76.

60. Jeremy Taylor, *Ductor Dubitantium,* book 1, I, Rule I, ed. Reginald Heber (London, 1883): "Our mind being thus furnished with a holy rule, and conducted by a divine guide is called conscience; and is the same thing which in scripture is sometimes called, 'the heart', there being in the Hebrew tongue no proper word for conscience . . ."

61. As Gordon Braden observes, "Renaissance culture is an expanding timocracy. The company that Stoicism keeps in the Renaissance is part of this expansiveness. *Virtus* in its fight against *fortuna* grades naturally, almost inevitably, into *virtù:* inner resource translating itself back into public action at a new pitch of self-confidence." *Renaissance Tragedy,* 80. See also Neal Wood's valuable article "Some Common Aspects of the Thought of Seneca and Machiavelli," *Renaissance Quarterly* 21 (1968), 11–23.

62. George L. Geckle, *John Marston's Drama* (Cranbury, N.J.: Associated University Presses, 1980), 108.

63. Ibid., 119.

64. See Wood, "Seneca and Machiavelli," for a useful summary.

65. Babula, "The Avenger and the Satirist," 56. Cf. Finkelpearl, *John Marston,* chapter 11.

66. Niccolò Machiavelli, *The Prince* and *The Discourses,* trans. Luigi Ricci and E. R. P. Vincent (New York: Modern Library, 1950), 92.

67. Ibid., 94.

68. Ibid., 20–21.

69. Cf. Machiavelli's discussion of how Remirro de Orco was used by Francesco Sforza, Duke of Milan, in *The Prince,* chapter 7.

70. Marlowe's attitude toward providentialism, it should be noted, is very different from that of either Shakespeare or Marston. As Dena Goldberg convincingly argues, Marlowe demonstrates both in the *Tamburlaine* plays and *Dido* "that the belief in special providence—in a personalized god, Christian or otherwise, who looks after individuals or groups—is absurd. History, as retold by Marlowe, proves that gods don't work that way." "Whose God's on First? Special Providence in the Plays of Christopher Marlowe," *ELH* 60 (1993): 569–87.

71. Caputi, *John Marston,* 75.

72. Seneca, *De Ira,* I. VI. 3.

73. Cyril Tourneur, *The Atheist's Tragedy,* ed. Irving Ribner (Cambridge, Mass.: Harvard University Press, 1964).

74. *John Marston's The Wonder of Women or The Tragedy of Sophonisba,* ed. William Kemp (New York: Garland, 1979), epilogus 5–7, p. 118. All quotations are from this edition.

75. Caputi, *John Marston,* 241.

76. Marston, *The Wonder of Women,* ed. Kemp, 21.

77. Finkelpearl, *John Marston of the Inner Temple,* 201.

78. Montaigne, *Essayes,* III, Chap. 5, "Upon Some Verses of Virgil," trans. Florio, (New York: Dutton, 1938), 74.

79. Ibid., 73.

80. Kemp, *The Wonder of Women,* 13–14.

81. Noted by Kemp, *The Wonder of Women,* 12.

82. Ibid., 24.

83. Thucydides, *History,* V. 84–116.

84. Cf. Boethius, *Consolation of Philosophy,* V. v.

85. See Sams, "Anti-Stoicism in Seventeenth and Early Eighteenth-Century England."

86. John Donne, *Biathanatos,* ed. Michael Rudick and M. Pabst Battin (New York and London, 1982), introduction.

87. Montaigne, *Essayes,* II. iii., 25–27.

88. Rowland Wymer, *Suicide and Despair in the Jacobean Drama* (New York: St. Martin's Press, 1986), 143.

89. Augustine, *The City of God,* trans. Marcus Dods (New York: Modern Library, 1950), I. 19.

CHAPTER 4. THE DIALECTIC OF VIRTUE IN CHAPMAN'S *BUSSY* PLAYS

1. T. M. Parrott, ed., *The Plays and Poems of George Chapman* (New York: Russell and Russell, 1961), 546; Michael Higgins, "The Development of the 'Senecal Man': Chapman's *Bussy D'Ambois* and some Precursors," *Review of English Studies*

23 (1947): 24–33; Herschel Baker, *The Image of Man* (New York: Harper, 1961), 302–4.

2. E.g., Ennis Rees, *The Tragedies of George Chapman: Renaissance Ethics in Action* (Cambridge, Mass.: Harvard University Press, 1954).

3. Millar MacLure, *George Chapman: A Critical Study* (Toronto: Toronto University Press, 1966), 111.

4. A. R. Braunmuller, *Natural Fictions George Chapman's Major Tragedies* (Newark: University of Delaware Press, 1992), 51.

5. As Bussy describes them in ll. 8–11, they are caricatures of Aristotle's great-spirited man. Cf. *Nichomachean Ethics*, IV. 3.

6. For a summation of the Stoic doctrine of virtue and moral goodness, see Cicero, *De Officiis*, I. iv—xxx.

7. *Epistle xxv*. Quoted by Wood, "Seneca and Machiavelli," 17. Wood notes that "When discussing *virtus*, he (Seneca) refers to the moral journey of man through life." Ibid., 15.

8. Peter Bement, *George Chapman: Action and Contemplation in his Tragedies* (Salzburg: Salzburg Studies in English Literature, 1974), 111.

9. Alan Bergson calls attention to the "loss or absence of self-awareness endemic to the ironic-tragic hero" in the tragedies of Chapman and Marston. In sharp contrast to Shakespearean tragedy wherein the protagonist agonizes toward "a new and mysterious knowledge" of himself and his situation in the universe, the "dramatic evolutions" of Marston's Antonio and Chapman's Bussy are "essentially ironic not merely because their nearsighted self-assurance remains uncorrected by the kind of self-knowledge that Lear so agonizingly attains, but even more because their actions lead them increasingly to betray whatever fixity of character they once possessed." "The Ironic Tragedies of Marston and Chapman: Notes on Jacobean Tragic Form," *JEGP* LXIX (1970): 614.

10. Quoted by MacLure, *George Chapman*, 74.

11. Ibid., 75.

12. *The Tears of Peace*, l. 374.

13. Bement, *George Chapman*, 117.

14. Elias Schwartz, "Seneca, Homer and Chapman's *Bussy D'Ambois*," *JEGP* 56 (1957): 175.

15. Bement, *George Chapman*, 118.

16. Ibid., 121.

17. Or the Sophist Thrasymachos in Plato's *Republic* (338c–39a) arguing that "justice," i.e., morality, is the interest of the stronger party. For a Marxist reading of Chapman's whole dramatic canon, see Leonard Goldstein, *George Chapman: Aspects of Decadence in Early Seventeenth-Century Drama* (Salzburg: Salzburg Studies No. 31, 1975), 2 vols.

18. Richard S. Ide, *Possessed with Greatness: The Heroic Tragedies of Chapman and Shakespeare* (London: Scolar Press, 1980), 216.

19. Elton, *King Lear and the Gods*, 125–29.

20. Ibid., 127.

21. Cf. Joseph Hall, *Heaven upon Earth*: "The power of nature is a good plea for those that acknowledge nothing above nature. . . . Wherefore serves Religion, but to subdue or governe nature: We are so much Christians, as wee can rule our selves, the rest is but forme and speculation." See above, chap. 1, note 68. In Ford's *'Tis Pity She's a Whore*, Giovanni makes a similar equation, even as he denies it: "'tis not, I know, / My lust, but 'tis my fate that leads me on." (I. ii. 153–54).

22. Gunilla Florby, *The Painful Passage to Virtue* Lund Studies in English 61 (1982), 107.

23. Ibid., 138.

24. Ibid., 98.

25. R. H. Perkinson, "Nature and the Tragic Hero in Chapman's Bussy Plays," *Modern Language Quarterly* 3 (1942): 269.

26. Indeed, Epicureans and Skeptics were commonly attacked together in treatises directed against atheism. E.g., Mornay's *A Woorke Concerning the trewnesse of the Christian Religion, written in French: Against Atheists, Epicures, Paynims, Iewes, and other Infidels.* See above, chap. 1, Elton notes that "While in England unrestrained public expression of the Epicurean view of providence had to wait until later in the seventeenth century, promulgation of such ideas, as in Italy and France, occurred during the England of Shakespeare's time and earlier." *King Lear and the gods,* 17. Regarding the replacement of providence by Fortune, he observes: "In place of providence, the blind and fickle Fortuna, with her counterpoise, *virtù*, was reemphasized in, for example, the historical *scienza nuova* of Machiavelli; for him, as later for Napoleon, providence seemed on the side of the strongest battalion." Ibid., 10–11.

27. Jonathan Dollimore sees it as "one of the most direct repudiations of teleology, providence and natural law to be found anywhere in Jacobean tragedy." *Radical Tragedy,* 186.

28. Discussed by Florby, *The Painful Passage to Virtue,* 91–93.

29. In the 1607 quarto of the play, this is the final speech. The recension that is the 1641 quarto continues the scene with an attempt by the Friar to reconcile Montsurry with the repentant Tamyra and Montsurry's forgiveness of her and their decision to live apart. The question of which text has the greater authority has been much discussed. See Berta Sturman, "The 1641 Edition of Chapman's *Bussy D'Ambois,*" *HLQ* 14 (1950–51): 171–201; Peter Ure, "Chapman's 'Tragedy of Bussy D'Ambois': Problems of the Revised Quarto," *MLR* 48 (1953): 257–69. Albert H. Tricomi, "The Revised *Bussy D'Ambois* and *The Revenge of Bussy D'Ambois:* Joint Performance in Thematic Counterpoint," *English Language Notes* 9 (1972): 253–62; Florby, *The Painful Passage,* 150–57.

30. Eugene Waith, *The Herculean Hero in Marlowe, Chapman, Shakespeare and Dryden* (London: Chatto and Windus, 1962), 11, 22, 26.

31. Homer, *The Odyssey,* trans. E. V. Rieu (Baltimore: Penguin, 1967), 316.

32. Florby, *The Painful Passage,* 108.

33. Jean Jacquot, *George Chapman: Sa vie, sa poésie, son théâtre, sa pensée* (Paris: Les Belles Lettres, 1951), 231.

34. Seneca, *Hercules Oetaeus* 1744–49 in *Tragedies,* trans. Frank Justus Miller (London: Heinemann, 1968), 323.

35. *Revelation,* VIII. 8–11, Coverdale (1538). Quoted by Florby, 109.

36. Rosenmeyer, *Senecan Drama,* 149.

37. Bergson, "The Ironic Tragedies of Marston and Chapman," 614. See also Geoffrey Aggeler, "Marlowe and the Development of Tragical Satire," *English Studies* 58 (1977): 209–20.

38. Travis Bogard, *The Tragic Satire of John Webster* (Berkeley: University of California Press, 1955), 96.

39. Gustave Flaubert, Correspondence: "I believe in the eternity of only one thing, that of Illusion, which is the real truth."

40. E.g., Albert C. Baugh, *A Literary History of England,* 2d ed. (London: Macmillan, 1967), 558.

41. MacLure, *George Chapman,* 126.

42. Florby, *The Painful Passage,* 21.

43. Ibid., 259.

44. As Peter Ure expresses it, *"The Revenge of Bussy D'Ambois* raises acutely a problem that haunts every investigation into Chapman's merits as a dramatist. How far did Chapman succeed in reconciling his obligations as a writer for the public playhouse with his interests in political morality and the relations between greatness and goodness"? ("Chapman as Translator and Tragic Playwright," in *Guide to English Literature* II, Baltimore: Penguin, 1963), 326. Most Chapman critics seem to share Janet Spens's feeling that in this play at least he did not succeed very far. Spens cites *The Revenge* as evidence that Chapman's "genius was undramatic: it was merely his material needs which drove him to the form. . . . He uses the formula of the Revenge Play, and by thrusting his ideal man into the part of hero he breaks the form to pieces: his death has no relation to the vengeance at all." ("Chapman's Ethical Thought," *Essays and Studies* 11 (1925): 150. MacLure concurs with the judgment that Chapman's ethical ideals have been yoked uncomfortably with the conventions of the Revenge Play. He notes that "except for one important moment, placed, like a different and 'outward' crisis . . . in the centre of the play the revenge theme is virtually withdrawn, while the audience is invited to concentrate for three acts upon the virtues of the hero." (*George Chapman,* 127–28). Cf. Charlotte Spivack, *George Chapman* (New York: Twayne, 1967), 139; John W. Wieler, *George Chapman—The Effect of Stoicism Upon His Tragedies* (New York: King's Crown Press, 1949), 80–82; Hardin Craig, "Ethics in the Jacobean Drama: The Case of Chapman," *Essays in Dramatic Literature: The Parrott Presentation Volume,* ed. Hardin Craig (Princeton, 1935), 25–46.

45. MacLure, *George Chapman,* 125.

46. An observation that has been made by many commentators. Ennis Rees argues that Chapman's tragedies "fall into two categories roughly analogous to the *Iliad* and the *Odyssey.*" In the analogy he draws, "Bussy and Byron correspond to Achilles, a character about whom Chapman was never able to feel quite comfortable." (*The Tragedies of George Chapman,* 30–31). Eugene Waith quarrels with the sharp ethical distinction Rees makes on the basis of this analogy, asserting that "This distinction, though grounded in Chapman's stated opinions, greatly oversimplifies Chapman's attitude towards Achilles and Ulysses, and towards the two kinds of heroes in his own tragedies." (*The Herculean Hero,* 105–8). I agree with Waith.

47. As Waith points out, in the classical Stoic point of view, "the physical strength of Hercules is identified with moral strength as in the allegorical interpretations of the labours or in the story of Hercules at the crossroads. Hercules becomes the supreme example of greatness of soul, of steadfastness, of scorn of fate and circumstance, of self-sacrifice, and of aspiration for the highest." Ibid., 30–31. Waith discusses Seneca's attitude toward Hercules as shown both in his tragedies and his moral essays, but he does not discuss Epictetus's remarks, which are, I believe, more relevant to Chapman. In his moral essays, Seneca praises Hercules as an unselfish benefactor and mocks Alexander and other selfish conquerors for aspiring to put themselves on a level with him (*De Beneficiis,* I. xiii. 2; VII. iii. 1; *De Tranquillitate Animi,* XVI.4). Seneca does not, however, seem to have quite the same admiration for the wisdom of Hercules that we find in Epictetus. He finds Cato "a truer exemplar of the wise man" than either Hercules or Odysseus (*De Constantia Sapientis,* I. 1). Cicero, like Seneca, praises Hercules for unselfish service to mankind and for preferring an active, useful life to one of pleasurable seclusion (*De Officiis,* III. v. 25). He also cites him as an example of an extraordinary being who could choose the path of virtue without

being influenced by other human beings (*De Officiis*, I. xxxii. 118). Spens considers *De Officiis* an important source of Chapman's ethical ideals ("Chapman's Ethical Thought," 147–48).

48. E.g., Coluccio Salutati (*De Laboribus Herculis*), Natalis Comes (*Mythologiae*), Vincenzo Cartari (*Imagini dei Dei Antichi*), Cesare Ripa (*Iconologia*), Marsilio Ficino (*Platonic Theology*), Pico della Mirandola (*Oration on the Dignity of Man*), Cristoforo Landino (*De vita activa et contemplativa*), Thomas Cooper (*Thesaurus Linguae Latinae et Britannicae*), George Sandys (*Ovid's Metamorphosis*). For discussions of the didactic uses of the figure of Hercules in these and other works, see Dewitt T. Starnes and Ernest Talbert, *Classical Myth and Legend in Renaissance Dictionaries* (Chapel Hill: University of North Carolina Press, 1955); Jean Seznec, *The Survival of the Pagan Gods,* trans. Barbara F. Sessions (New York: Pantheon Books, 1953); Douglas Bush, *Mythology and the Renaissance Tradition* (New York: Norton, 1963); Waith, *The Herculean Hero,* 39–59.

49. See Waith, *The Herculean Hero,* 16–38.

50. Epictetus, *Discourses,* vol. 2, III. xxiv. 12., trans. W. A. Oldfather (London: Heinemann, 1966), 189.

51. Ibid., III. xxvi. 33–38.

52. Ibid., II. xvi. 41; I. xii. 3.

53. Ibid., IV. x. 10–13. It should be noted that a similar degree of supra-conventional autonomy is alloted the man of preeminent virtue by Aristotle in the third book of the *Politics:* "But if there is one man so superlatively excellent (or several but not enough to make the whole complement of a city) that the goodness and ability of all the rest are simply not to be compared with his (or theirs), such men we take not to be part of the state but to transcend it. To judge them worthy of mere equality with the rest would be to do them an injustice, so far superior are they in virtue and political capacity. We may reasonably regard such a one as a god among men. In that case clearly legislation, the aim of which we have been discussing, is not relevant, since legislation must refer to equals in birth and capacity; and there is no law that can govern these exceptional men. They are themselves law and anyone who tried to legislate for them would be snubbed for his pains." Trans. T. A. Sinclair (Baltimore: Penguin, 1966), 132. Charles W. Kennedy feels that this passage may have influenced Chapman ("Political Theory in the Plays of George Chapman," *Essays in Dramatic Literature: The Parrott Presentation Volume,* 77–79.) See also Michael Higgins, "Chapman's 'Senecal Man' A Study in Jacobean Psychology," *Review of English Studies* 21 (1945): 183–91; Edwin Muir, "'Royal Man': Notes on the Tragedies of George Chapman," *Shakespeare's Contemporaries,* ed. Max Bluestone and Norman Rabkin, (Prentice Hall, 1961), 230–38.

54. Rees, *Tragedies of George Chapman,* 119.

55. All quotations are from George Chapman, *The Revenge of Bussy D'Ambois A Tragedie,* ed. Robert J. Lordi, in *The Plays of George Chapman The Tragedies with Sir Gyles Goosecappe,* ed. Allan Holaday (Cambridge: D. S. Brewer, 1987).

56. *Discourses,* I. xxviii. 11–20. Noted by Parrott, *The Plays of George Chapman* II, 581.

57. Rees suggests that this defense is one way Chapman makes Clermont "a truly dramatic character" by showing that he is capable of rationalizing an ethical problem for the sake of friendship (*The Tragedies of George Chapman,* 105). But if this is Chapman's intention, then why does he have Clermont reproach the Guise so severely for his involvement in another plot "For propogation of the Catholique cause" (V. i. 60)? This rebuke and the severe self-reproach he expresses earlier for "inconstancy" to his principles (III. i. 8–25) indicate that he is too scrupulous and

sensitive ethically to rationalize anyone's actions. Florby suggests that "the passage is a more or less private declaration of allegiance to the Catholic Howards" (*The Painful Passage,* 245). Chapman dedicated *The Revenge* to Sir Thomas Howard, and his poem *Andromeda Liberata* celebrates the marriage of Sir Thomas Howard's sister, Frances Howard, to Robert Carr, Earl of Somerset.

58. Perkinson, "Nature and the Tragic Hero," 274.

59. *Discourses,* IV. x. 1–3.

60. Eliot, "Shakespeare and the Stoicism of Seneca," 112.

61. Justus Lipsius is representative of this type of Stoicism during the Renaissance and expresses it in his *De Constantia.* See Bement, *George Chapman,* 183–86.

62. Florby, *The Painful Passage,* 259.

63. Parrott, *The Plays of George Chapman,* II., 275.

64. Perkinson, "Nature and the Tragic Hero," 275–76.

65. Bement, *George Chapman,* 203–5.

66. Ibid., 204.

67. Rees, *The Tragedies of George Chapman,* 120.

68. See Fredson Bowers, "Hamlet as Minister and Scourge," *PMLA* 70 (1955): 40–49.

69. *Discourses,* I. xix.

70. Florby, *The Painful Passage,* 256–57.

71. Ibid.

72. *Discourses,* III. xxiv. 12.

73. *Discourses,* I. ix. 16.

74. Montaigne, *Essayes,* II, 21.

75. See Marvin L. Vawter, "Division 'tween Our Souls": Shakespeare's Stoic Brutus," *Shakespeare Studies* 7 (1974): 173–95). Vawter's essay is a perceptive reading of *Julius Caesar,* but he oversimplifies Cicero's view of Stoicism, disregarding what he says about it in *De Officiis.*

76. *The Revenge* was presented at a coterie theater, the Whitefriars, by the Children of the Queen's Revels. For discussion of the types of plays offered the select audiences of the Whitefriars and other private theaters, see chaps. 2–3, Alfred Harbage, *Shakespeare and the Rival Traditions* (New York: Macmillan, 1952).

77. Henry Hitch Adams, "Cyril Tourneur on Revenge," *JEGP* 48 (1949): 72–87.

78. Clifford Leech, "*The Atheist's Tragedy* as a Dramatic Comment on Chapman's *Bussy* Plays," *JEGP* (52): 526.

79. Ibid., 528.

80. Ibid., 529.

CHAPTER 5. NOBLER IN THE MIND: THE DIALECTIC IN *HAMLET*

1. Harold Jenkins, ed., *Hamlet,* New Arden edition (London: Methuen Press, 1982). All citations are from this edition.

2. Robert Miola, *Shakespeare and Classical Tragedy The Influence of Seneca* (Oxford University Press, 1992), 59.

3. Seneca, *De Constantia Sapientis,* II. 2.

4. This contradicts somewhat his early work, the *Politiques,* which is concerned with the theory of man and society and the concept of government. See Levi, *The French Moralists,* 55. See also Bement's excellent discussion of Lipsius and Du Vair as representative of the two types of Renaissance Neostoicism, *George Chapman,* 183–86.

5. Montaigne, "An Apologie of Raymond Sebond," *Essayes*, trans. Florio, II, 314–15. Cited in chapter 1 above.

6. Mark Matheson, "*Hamlet* and 'A Matter Tender and Dangerous,'" *Shakespeare Quarterly* XLVI (1995): 383–97.

7. Braden, *Renaissance Tragedy and the Senecan Tradition*, 221–22.

8. For discussion of what these concepts have in common, see above chapter 3, n. 61.

9. Braden, *Renaissance Tragedy*, 23.

10. *Communings with Himself*, XII. 5.

11.   *donec longa dies, perfecto temporis orbe,*
        concretam exemit labem, purumque reliquit,
        aetherium sensum atque aurai simplicis ignem,
        has omnes, ubi mille rotam volvere per annos

trans. II. 747–48 C. Day Lewis, *The Aeneid of Virgil* (New York: Doubleday, 1953), 151. Cf. Diogenes Laertius, *Lives of the Eminent Philosophers*, VII. 148–49.

12. Braden, *Renaissance Tragedy*, 23–24, 228, note 27.

13. For discussion of the purgatorial context in the play and Protestant doctrine regarding purgatory, see Matheson, *"Hamlet* and 'A Matter Tender and Dangerous,'" 384–85.

14. Harold Jenkins believes that the meaning is confined to this specific reference: "What the single fault corrupts is not, as so widely assumed, the man's character, but the opinion that is formed of it, his reputation, or 'image.'" Note to I. iv. 35 in his edition.

15. See Bowers, "Hamlet as Minister and Scourge," 740–49.

16. Graham Bradshaw, *Shakespeare's Scepticism* (New York: St. Martin's Press, 1987), 121.

17. Sellin, "The Hidden God," 150.

18. Ibid., 154.

19. Martin Luther, "The Bondage of the Will," in *Martin Luther Selections from his Writings*, ed. John Dillenberger (New York: Anchor, 1961), 201.

20. See chapter 1, notes 90 and 91.

21. John Calvin, *Institutes* book 3, chap. 12, 1, ed. John T. McNeill (Philadelphia: Westminster Press, 1960).

22. Bradshaw, *Shakespeare's Scepticism,* 10.

23. *Hamlet*, ed. G. L. Kittredge (New York: Ginn, 1939), note to IV. iv. 27.

24. Bradshaw, *Shakespeare's Scepticism,* 5–10.

25. Burgess, *Shakespeare,* 119.

26. Montaigne, *Essays,* III. xiii. 361, "On Experience," trans. Florio.

27. Ibid., "Of the Institution and Education of Children," I. xxv, 179–80. M. A. Screech renders it, "So many names, so many victories and conquests lying buried in oblivion, make it ridiculous to hope that we shall immortalize our names by rounding up ten armed brigands or by storming some hen-house or other known only by its capture." *The Complete Essays* (New York: Penguin, 1987), 177.

28. Matheson, "'A Matter Tender and Dangerous,'" 390.

29. William Perkins, *A Discourse of Conscience* (London, 1596), 27. British Museum copy. See above, chapter 1.

30. Jenkins, note to V. ii. 215–16, refers to Calvin, *Institutes,* I, esp. xvi. 1, xvii. 6.

31. See chapter 1.

Bibliography

PRIMARY DRAMATIC WORKS

Chapman, George, *Bussy D'Ambois.* Edited by Robert J. Lordi. Lincoln: Nebraska University Press, 1964.

———. *The Revenge of Bussy D'Ambois.* Edited by Robert J. Lordi. In *The Plays of George Chapman, The Tragedies with Sir Gyles Goosecappe.* Edited by Allan Holladay. Cambridge: D. S. Brewer, 1987.

Jonson, Ben. *Bartholomew Fair* Edited by Eugene Waith. New Haven: Yale University Press, 1963.

Kyd, Thomas. *The First Part of Hieronimo and The Spanish Tragedy.* Edited by Andrew S. Cairncross (Lincoln: University of Nebraska Press, 1967).

Marston, John. *Antonio and Mellida.* Edited by G. K. Hunter. Lincoln: University of Nebraska Press, 1965.

———. *Antonio's Revenge.* Edited by G. K. Hunter. Lincoln: University of Nebraska Press, 1965.

———. *The Malcontent.* Edited by M. L. Wine. Lincoln: University of Nebraska Press, 1964.

———. *The Dutch Courtesan.* Edited by M. L. Wine. Lincoln: University of Nebraska, 1965.

———. *The Wonder of Women or The Tragedy of Sophonisba,* a critical edition. Edited by William Kemp. New York: Garland, 1979.

———. *The Poems.* Edited by Arnold Davenport. Liverpool: Liverpool University Press, 1961.

Seneca. *Seneca His Tenne Tragedies.* Edited by Thomas Newton, introduced by T. S. Eliot. Bloomington: Indiana University Press, 1964.

Seneca, *Tragedies.* Translated by Frank Justus Miller, 2 vols. London: Heinemann, 1958.

Shakespeare, William. *Hamlet.* New Arden edition Harold Jenkins. London: Methuen Press, 1982.

———. *The Riverside Shakespeare.* Edited by G. Blakemore Evans. Boston: Houghton Mifflin, 1974.

Tourneur, Cyril. *The Atheist's Tragedy.* Edited by Irving Ribner. Cambridge, Mass.: Harvard University Press, 1964.

PRIMARY WORKS CONCERNED WITH ETHICS AND PHILOSOPHY

Ames, William. *Of Conscience and the Cases Thereof.* London, 1643.

Aquinas, Thomas. *Aquinas Ethicus.* Translated by Joseph Rickaby, 2 vols. London: Chapman and Hall, 1892.

185

Antoninus, Marcus Aurelius. *The Communings with Himself Together with His Speeches and Sayings.* Translated by C. R. Haines. London: Heinemann, 1961.

Aristotle, *The Nichomachean Ethics.* Translated by Sir David Ross. London: Oxford, 1961.

———. *The Politics.* Translated by T. A. Sinclair. Baltimore: Penguin, 1966.

———. *Poetics.* Translated by Kenneth A. Telford. Chicago: Henry Regnery, 1961.

———. *Rhetoric.* Translated by Edward M. Cope. New York: Arno Press, 1973.

Augustine. *The City of God.* Translated by Marcus Dods. New York: Modern Library, 1950.

Bacon, Francis. *Essays.* In *Francis Bacon a Selection of his Works.* Edited by Sidney Warhaft. London: Macmillian, 1982.

———. *The History of the Reign of King Henry VII,* Edited by F. J. Levy. New York: Bobbs-Merrill, 1972.

Boethius, *Tractates Consolation.* Translated by H. E. Stewart and E. K. Rand (Cambridge, Mass.: Harvard University Press, 1956.

Bullinger, Henry. "Of the Second Precept of the Second Table and of the Magistrate." [1549] In *Decades of Henry Bullinger.* Translated by H. I., Parker Society Vol. VII, 342–53. Cambridge: Cambridge University Press, 1849.

Calvin, John. *Commentary on Seneca's De Clementia.* Edited by Ford Lewis Battles and Andre Malan Hugo. Leiden: E. J. Brill, 1969.

———. *Institutes of the Christian Religion.* Edited by John T. McNeill. Philadelphia: Westminster Press, 1960.

Charron, Pierre. *De La Sagesse Livres Trois.* Bovrdeavs: Simon Millanges, 1601.

———. *Of Wisdom three bookes.* Translated by Samson Lennard. London: Blount, 1608.

Cicero. *De Officiis.* Translated by Walter Miller. London: Heinemann, 1961.

———. *De Finibus Bonorum et Malorum.* Translated by H. Rackham. Cambridge, Mass.: Harvard University Press, 1951.

Cornwallis, Sir William. *Essayes.* Edited by Don Cameron Allen. Baltimore: Johns Hopkins University Press, 1946.

DuVair, Guillaume. *The Moral Philosophie of the Stoicks.* Translated by Thomas James, edited by Rudolf Kirk. New Brunswick, N.J.: Rutgers University Press, 1951.

Empiricus. Sextus. *Outlines of Pyrrhonism.* Translated by R. G. Bury. Buffalo, N.Y.: Prometheus Books, 1990.

Epictetus, *The Discourses, Encheiridion, Fragments.* Translated by W. A. Oldfather, 2 vols. London: Heinemann, 1961.

Hall, Joseph. *Heaven upon Earth and Characters of Vertues and Vices.* New Brunswick, N.J.: Rutgers University Press, 1948.

Hooker, Richard. *Of the Laws of Ecclesiastical Polity.* Edited by Georges Edelen, vol. I of *The Folger Library Edition of the Works.* Edited by W. Speed Hill. Cambridge, Mass.: Harvard University Press, 1977.

La Primaudaye, Peter de. *The French Academie.* Translated by T. B. London: Geor. Bishop, 1594.

Lipsius, Justus. *Two Books of Constancie.* Edited by Rudolf Kirk. New Brunswick, N.J.: Rutgers University Press, 1939.

Luther, Martin. *Lectures on Romans*. Translated by Wilhelm Pauck. Philadelphia: Library of Christian Classics XV, 1961.

———. "The Bondage of the Will," *Martin Luther Selections from His writings*. Edited by John Dillenberger, 166–203. New York: Anchor, 1961.

Milton, John. *The Tenure of Kings and Magistrates*. In *Works* V. New York: Columbia University Press, 1932.

Montaigne, Michael de. *The Essayes*. Translated by John Florio, 3 vols. London: Henry Frowde, 1904.

———. *The Complete Essays*. Translated by M. A. Screech. New York: Penguin, 1987.

Mornay, Philippe de. *A Woorke Concerning the Trewnesse of the Christian Religion*. Translated by Sir Philip Sidney and Arthur Golding. London: Thomas Cadman, 1587.

———. *Discourse of Life and Death*. Translated by the Countess of Pembroke. London, 1592.

———. *The True Knowledge of Mans owne Selfe*. Translated by Anthony Munday. London, 1602.

———. *Lord of Plessis his Teares*. Translated by John Healey. London, 1609.

Perkins, William. *A Discourse of Conscience*. London, 1596.

———. *The Whole Treatise of the Cases of Conscience*. London, 1614.

Plutarch, *Moralia*. Translated by Harold Cherniss, 17 vols. London: Heinemann, 1976.

———. *Moralia*. Translated by Philemond Holland (1603). Edited by E. H. Blakeney. New York: Dutton, 1911.

Sandys, Edwin. "Owe Nothing to Any Man." Sermon made at York [1585] in *Sermons,* Parker Society, vol. 42. Cambridge University Press, 1842, 195–206.

Seneca, *Moral Essays*. Translated by J. W. Basore. 3 vols. London: Heinemann, 1963.

———. *Epistulae Morales*. Translated by Richard M. Gummere. London: Heinemann, 1970.

———. *The Stoic Philosophy of Seneca*. Translated by Moses Hadas. New York: Norton, 1958.

Taylor, Jeremy. *Ductor Dubitantium* in *The Whole Works*. Edited by Reginald Heber. London, 1883.

Secondary Sources

Books

Allen, Don Cameron. *Doubt's Boundless Sea*. Baltimore: Johns Hopkins, 1964.

Altman, Joel B. *The Tudor Play of Mind*. Berkeley: University of California Press, 1978.

Baker, Howard. *Induction to Tragedy*. Baton Rouge: LSU. Press, 1939.

Baugh, Albert C., ed. by *A Literary History of England*, 2d ed. Reprint, London: Macmillan, 1967.

Bement, Peter. *George Chapman: Action and Contemplation in His Tragedies.* Salzburg Studies in English Literature: Jacobean Drama Studies, No. 8, Salzburg, 1974.

Bogard, Travis. *The Tragic Satire of John Webster.* Berkeley: University of California Press, 1955.

Bowers, Fredson. *Elizabethan Revenge Tragedy.* Princeton University Press, 1959.

Braden, Gordon. *Renaissance Tragedy and the Senecan Tradition.* New Haven: Yale University Press, 1985.

Bradshaw, Graham. *Shakespeare's Scepticism.* New York: St. Martin's Press, 1987.

Braunmuller, A. R. *Natural Fictions: George Chapman's Major Tragedies.* Newark: University of Delaware Press, 1992.

Burgess, Anthony. *Shakespeare.* New York: Knopf, 1970.

Bush, Douglas. *Mythology and the Renaissance Tradition.* New York: Norton, 1963.

Caputi, Anthony. *John Marston, Satirist.* Ithaca: Cornell University Press, 1961.

Cavell, Stanley. *Disowning Knowledge in Six Plays of Shakespeare.* Cambridge University Press, 1991.

Charron, Jean Daniel. *The "Wisdom" of Pierre Charron An Original and Orthodox Code of Morality.* Chapel Hill: University of North Carolina Press, 1960.

Colie, Rosalie. *Paradoxia Epidemica.* Princeton: Princeton University Press, 1966.

Cunliffe, J. W. *The Influence of Seneca on Elizabethan Tragedy.* London: Macmillan, 1893.

D'Arcy, Eric. *Conscience and Its Right to Freedom.* London: Sheed & Ward, 1961.

Dollimore, Jonathan. *Radical Tragedy.* London: Harvester Wheatsheaf, 1989.

Elton, W. R. *King Lear and the Gods.* San Marino: Huntington Library, 1966.

Finkelpearl, Philip J. *John Marston of the Middle Temple.* Cambridge, Mass.: Harvard University Press, 1969.

Florby, Gunilla. *The Painful Passage to Virtue.* Lund Studies in English 61: CWK Gleerup, 1982.

Gooch, G. *English Democratic Ideas in the 17th Century.* New York: Harper & Row, 1959.

Greenblatt, Stephen. *Renaissance Self-Fashioning from More to Shakespeare.* Chicago: University of Chicago Press, 1980.

Hoopes, Robert. *Right Reason in the Renaissance.* Cambridge, Mass.: Harvard University Press, 1962.

Hoy, Cyrus. *The Hyacinth Room.* New York: Knopf, 1964.

Ide, Richard S. *Possessed with Greatness: The Heroic Tragedies of Chapman and Shakespeare.* London: Scolar Press, 1980.

Inge, W. R. *Christian Mysticism* London: Chapman and Hall, 1899.

Jacquot, Jean. *Les Tragédies de Sénèque et le Théâtre de la Renaissance.* Paris: Editions du Centre National de la Recherche Scientifique, 1964.

―――. *George Chapman: Sa vie, sa poésie, son théâtre, sa pensée.* Paris: Les Belles Lettres, 1951.

Kaiser, Walter. *Praisers of Folly.* Cambridge, Mass..: Harvard University Press, 1963.

Kernan, Alvin. *The Cankered Muse: Satire of the English Renaissance.* New Haven: Yale University Press, 1959.

Kitto, H. D. F. *Greek Tragedy.* London: Methuen, 1973.

Levi, Anthony. *The French Moralists: The Theory of the Passions 1585 to 1649.* Oxford University Press, 1964.

Lewis, C. S. *English Literature in the Sixteenth Century.* Oxford University Press, 1954.

Lucas, F. L. *Seneca and Elizabethan Tragedy.* Cambridge University Press, 1922.

MacLure, Millar. *George Chapman: A Critical Study.* Toronto: University of Toronto Press, 1966.

Miola, Robert. *Shakespeare and Classical Tragedy: The Influence of Seneca.* Oxford University Press, 1992.

Nussbaum, Martha C. *The Therapy of Desire Theory and Practice in Hellenistic Ethics.* Princeton: Princeton University Press, 1994.

Palmer, R. G. *Seneca's Remediis Fortuitorum and the Elizabethans.* Chicago: University of Chicago Press, 1953.

Parrott, T. M. ed. *The Plays and Poems of George Chapman.* New York: Russell and Russell, 1961.

Pratt, Norman T. *Seneca's Drama.* Chapel Hill: University of North Carolina Press, 1983.

Redfield, James M. *Nature and Culture in the Iliad The Tragedy of Hector.* Chicago: University of Chicago Press, 1975.

Rees, Ennis. *The Tragedies of George Chapman: Renaissance Ethics in Action.* Cambridge, Mass.: Harvard University Press, 1954.

Reynolds, L. D. *The Medieval Tradition of Seneca's Letters.* Oxford University Press, 1965.

Rosenmeyer, Thomas. *Senecan Drama and Stoic Cosmology.* Berkeley: University Of California, 1989.

Rozett, Martha Tuck. *The Doctrine of Election and the Emergence of Elizabethan Tragedy.* Princeton: Princeton University Press, 1984.

Starnes, Dewitt T., and Ernest Talbert. *Classical Myth and Legend in Renaissance Dictionaries.* Chapel Hill: University of North Carolina Press, 1955.

Stone, Lawrence, *The Crisis of the Aristocracy 1558–1641.* Oxford: Oxford University Press, 1965.

Turner, Celeste. *Anthony Munday, An Elizabethan Man of Letters.* Berkeley: University of California Press, 1928.

Vellacott, Philip. *Ironic Drama A Study of Euripides' Method and Meaning.* Cambridge: Cambridge University Press, 1975.

Wilks, John S. *The Idea of Conscience in Renaissance Tragedy.* London: Routledge, 1990.

Wymer, Rowland. *Suicide and Despair in the Jacobean Drama.* New York: St. Martin's Press, 1986.

Zeller, Eduard. *The Stoics, Epicureans and Sceptics.* Translated by Oswald J. Reichel. New York: Russell & Russell, 1962.

Articles and Essays

Adams, Henry Hitch. "Cyril Tourneur on Revenge." *JEGP* 48 (1949): 72–87.

Aggeler, Geoffrey. "'Good Pity' in *King Lear:* The Progress of Edgar," *Neophilologus* 77 (1993): 321–31.

————. "Marlowe and the Development of Tragical Satire," *English Studies* 58 (1977): 209–21.

Ayres, Philip J. "Degrees of Heresy: Justified Revenge and Elizabethan Narratives," *Studies in Philology* 72 (1972): 445–68.

Babula, William. "The Avenger and the Satirist: John Marston's Malevole," *Elizabethan Theatre* VI. Edited by G. B. Hibbard (Hamden, Conn.: Archon, 1977): 48–58.

Barish, Jonas. "*The Spanish Tragedy*, or The Pleasures and Perils of Rhetoric," *Elizabethan Theatre.* Edited by John Russell Brown and Bernard Harris, Stratford-Upon-Avon Studies 9. New York: St. Martin's Press, 1967.

Belsey, Catherine. "Senecan Vacillation and Elizabethan Deliberations: Influence or Confluence?" *Renaissance Drama* NS 6 (1973): 65–88.

Bergson, Alan. "Dramatic Style as Parody in Marston's *Antonio and Mellida.*" *SEL* 11 (1971): 307–25.

————. "The Ironic Tragedies of Marston and Chapman: Notes on Jacobean Tragic Form," *JEGP* 69 (1970): 613–30.

Bowers, Fredson. "Hamlet as Minister and Scourge."*PMLA* 70 (1955): 740–49.

Broude, Ronald. "Time, Truth, and Right in *The Spanish Tragedy.*" *Studies in Philology* 68 (1971): 130–45.

Campbell, Lily B. "Theories of Revenge in Renaissance England," *Modern Philology* 28 (1930–31): 281–96.

Coursen, Herbert R. "The Unity of *The Spanish Tragedy.*" *Studies in Philology* 65 (1968): 768–82.

Cousins, A. D. "The Protean Nature of Man in Marston's Verse Satires." *JEGP* 79 (1980): 517–29.

Craig, Hardin. "The Shackling of Accidents: A Study of Elizabethan Tragedy." In *Elizabethan Drama.* Edited by Ralph J. Kaufmann. New York: Oxford University Press, 1961.

————. "Ethics in the Jacobean Drama: The Case of Chapman," *Essays in Dramatic Literature: The Parrott Presentation Volume.* Edited by Hardin Craig. Princeton University Press, 1935.

Crane, R. S. "Suggestions toward a Genealogy of the "Man of Feeling.'" *ELH* 1 (1934): 214–20.

Cross, Gustav. "Marston, Montaigne, and Morality: *The Dutch Courtezan* Reconsidered." *ELH* 27 (1960): 30–43.

Cunningham, Karen. "Renaissance Execution and Marlovian Elocution: The Drama of Death." *PMLA* 105 (1990): 209–22.

De Chickera, Ernst. "Divine Justice and Private Revenge in *The Spanish Tragedy.*" *Modern Language Review* 57 (1962): 228–32.

Edwards, Philip. Introduction to his edition of *The Spanish Tragedy.* Cambridge, Mass.: Harvard University Press, 1959.

Eliot, T. S. "Shakespeare and the Stoicism of Seneca." *Selected Essays.* New Edition, New York: Harcourt Brace, 1964.

————. "John Marston." *Essays on Elizabethan Drama.* New York: Harcourt Brace, 1960.

Empson, William. "The Spanish Tragedy." in *Elizabethan Drama: Modern Essays in Criticism.* Edited by R. J. Kaufmann. New York: Oxford University Press, 1961.

Foakes, R. A. "On Marston, *The Malcontent* and *The Revenger's Tragedy.*" *The Elizabethan Theater* VI, Edited by G. R. Hibbard. Archon, 1978.

——. "John Marston's Fantastical Plays: *Antonio and Mellida* and *Antonio's Revenge.*" *Philological Quarterly* 41 (1962): 229–39.

Goldberg, Dena. "Whose God's on First? Special Providence in the Plays of Christopher Marlowe." *ELH* 60 (1993): 569–87.

Higgins, Michael. "Chapman's 'Senecal Man' A Study in Jacobean Psychology." *Review of English Studies* 21 (1945): 183–91.

Hunter, G. K. "English Folly and Italian Vice The Moral Landscape of John Marston." *Jacobean Theatre* Stratford-upon-Avon Studies, vol. 1. Edited by J. R. Brown and Bernard Harris. New York: St. Martin's, 1965.

——. "Ironies of Justice in *The Spanish Tragedy.*" *Renaissance Drama* 8 (1965): 89–104.

——. "Seneca and the Elizabethans: A Case-Study in 'Influence.'" *Shakespeare Survey* 20 (1978): 17–26.

Johnson, S. F. "*The Spanish Tragedy* or Babylon Revisited." In *Essays on Shakespeare and Elizabethan Drama in Honor of Hardin Craig.* Edited by Richard Hosley. Columbia: University of Missouri Press, 1962.

Kennedy, Charles W. "Political Theory in the Plays of George Chapman." In *Essays in Dramatic Literature: The Parrott Presentation Volume.* New York: Columbia University Press.

Kiefer, Frederick. "Seneca's Influence on Elizabethan Tragedy: An Annotated Bibliography." *Research Opportunities in Renaissance Drama* 21 (1978): 17–34.

Leech, Clifford. "*The Atheist's Tragedy* as a Dramatic Comment on Chapman's *Bussy* Plays." *JEGP* 52 (1953): 526–30.

Levin, Richard. "The New *New Inn* and the Proliferation of Good Bad Drama." *Essays in Criticism* 22 (1972): 41–47.

——. "The Proof of the Parody," *Essays in Criticism* 24 (1974): 312–17.

Matheson, Mark. "*Hamlet* and 'A Matter Tender and Dangerous.'" *Shakespeare Quarterly* 46 (1995): 383–97.

McMillin, Scott. "The Figure of Silence in *The Spanish Tragedy.*" *ELH* 39 (1972): 25–38.

Motto, Anna Lydia, and John R. Clark. "Senecan Tragedy: A Critique of Scholarly Trends." *Renaissance Drama* NS 6 (1973): 219–36.

Perkinson, R. H. "Nature and the Tragic Hero in Chapman's *Bussy* Plays." *Modern Language Quarterly* 3 (1942): 263–85.

Regenbogen, Otto. "Schmerz und Tod in den Tragödien Senecas." *Vorträge der Bibliothek Warburg* 7 (1927–28): 25–73.

Sams, Henry W. "Anti-Stoicism in Seventeenth and Early Eighteenth-Century England." *Studies in Philology* 41 (1944): 65–78.

Sellin, Paul R. "The Hidden God: Reformation Awe in Renaissance English Literature." *The Darker Vision of the Renaissance Beyond the Fields of Reason.* Edited by Robert S. Kinsman. Los Angeles: University of California Press 1974.

Sibly, John. "The Duty of Revenge in Tudor and Stuart Drama." *Review of English Literature* 8 (1967): 46–58.

Smith, Philip A. "Bishop Hall, 'Our English Seneca.'" *PMLA* 58 (1948): 1191–1204.

Spencer, Theodore. "Reason and Passion in Marston's *The Dutch Courtezan.*" In *Shakespeare's Contemporaries.* Edited by Max Bluestone and Norman Rabkin. Englewood Cliffs: Prentice-Hall, 1961.

Spens, Janet. "Chapman's Ethical Thought." *Essays and Studies* 11 (1925): 145–69.

Sturman, Berta. "The 1641 Edition of Chapman's *Bussy D'Ambois.*" *Huntington Library Quarterly* 14 (1950–51): 171–201.

Ure, Peter. "Chapman as Translator and Tragic Playwright." In *Guide to English Literature,* vol. 2 Baltimore: Penguin, 1963.

———. "Chapman's *Tragedy of Bussy D'Ambois:* Problems of the Revised Quarto." *Modern Language Review* 48 (1953): 257–69.

Vawter, Marvin L. "Division 'tween Our Souls': Shakespeare's Stoic Brutus." *Shakespeare Studies* 7 (1974): 173–95.

Vellacott, Philip."Has good Prevailed?" *Harvard Studies in Classical Philology* 81 (1977): 197–122.

Wharton, T. F. "Old Marston or New Marston: The *Antonio* Plays." *Essays in Criticism* 25 (1975): 357–69.

White, Lynn. "Death and the Devil." in *The Darker Vision of the Renaissance.* Edited by Robert S. Kinsman. Berkeley: University of California Press, 1974.

Yearling, Elizabeth M. "'Mount Tufty Tamburlaine': Marston and Linguistic Excess." *SEL* 20 (1980): 259–69.

Index

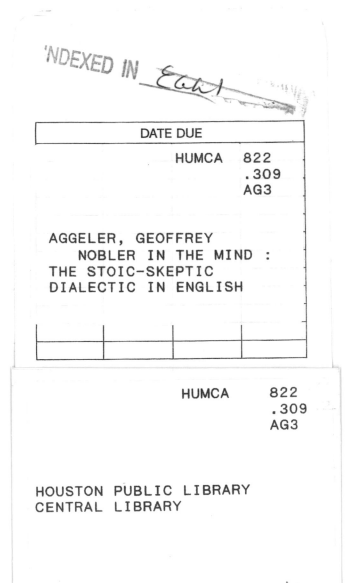